The Book of Guy Hawkes Day And its BONFIRE NIGHT

Justice For Men,

A Celebration FIT for God, Vol.1b

Conrad Jay Bladey

©Hutman Prodctions, 2020

The Book of Guy Fawkes Day And its Bonfire Night

Justice For Men, A Celebration for God, Vol.1b, Conrad Jay Bladey

ISBN: 978-1-7320830-7-3

Cover image left:execution of Plotters, George Cruikshank, In: William Harrison Ainsworth Guy Fawkes or The gunpowder Treason An Historical Romance, 1841-right:Bonfire, Playing Cards,1679

©Hutman Productions, 2020

Robert Keyes gentleman / Guydo Faux gentleman, Trevellian ms.1606,[Guy Fawkes] Earliest known portrait.

Contents

Contents 3

Introduction 7

    Account, Robert Cecil, Lord Salisbury, 1605, (Ed.: Philip Sidney,1905 8

    An Answere To Certaine Scandalous Papers, Scattered abroad under colour Of a Catholicke Admonition. Qui facit vivere, docet orare , Robert Cecil, 1606. 14

    The Weekely Newes Numb.9, Jeffrey Chorlton, Munday 31 January 1606 27

    The Araignement and Execution of the Late Traytors, with a relation of the other traytors, which were executed at Worcester, the 27 of January last past. Jeffrey Chorlton, 1606 31

    Account of the Miracle of Garnet's Straw, Trial of the Conspirators, 1606. 38

    Investigations noted in the Calendar of State Papers Domestic: James I, Parliament, 1603-1610. 44

Constructing Celebration 102

    Psalm 66 102

    From the Story of King Asa of Judah 103

    Psalm 33 103

    Proverbs 33 103

    Psalm 94 103

    Proverbs 15 104

    Frontispeece "Discovered" from Novembris Monstrum, A.B.C.D.E., 1641 105

    Paradise Lost, John Milton, 1667 106

    Video Rideo- I See and Laugh to Scorn 106

    Psalm 37 108

"The Double Deliverance of England from the Spanish armada and Gunpowder Plot," Samuel Ward, 1621 111

Volpone; Or, The Foxe. Ben Jonson January 1606- February 1607 112

Making the Commemoration Official 116

Gunpowder Plot- A learned and religious Speech. - 116

Noah's Thanksgiving 117

Robert Bowyer,"Book I, Stanford MS," 1606-1607. 118

Here begins the Official Annual Commemoration of the Great Deliverance. 120

Thanksgiving Act, James I, 1605 121

The Sermon Preached at Paules Crosse, the tenth day of November, Being the next Sunday after the Discoverie of this late Horrible Treason, William Barlow(e), November 10, 1605. 125

William Barlow 140

Some thoughts about this sermon 141

Lancelot Andrewes 158

Some Thoughts About this Sermon And Lancelot Andrewes' other Gunpowder Treason Sermons 159

Sermons by Lancelot Andrewes on the Gunpowder Treason: Excerpts Prescribing Means and Nature of Celebration and Thanksgiving 161

William Leigh Preaches 187

William Leigh 1550-1639 189

Thomas Dekker Published on December 9, 1605 189

Introductory Riddle from :THE DOUBLE PP.,Thomas Dekker, 1605. 189

O Lord How Joyful Is The King –For the Fifth of November, Thomas Weelkes, c.1605 190

Gun-Powder Plot: Or, A Brief Account of that bloudy and subtle design laid against the King, his Lords and Commons in Parliament, and of a Happy Deliverance by Divine Power, 1605 191

A Forme of True Repentance, fit for Traytors to Sing and use now, and at all times while life is in them: made in part by one of Babingtons Conspiracy. And may be sung to the tune of the 25. Psal. John Rhodes, minister of Enborne: From A Briefe Summe, 1606 193

A Real Blast 196
Comes William 200
    Proclimation Two Additional Prayers to be Added to the Fifth of November Litany, William and Mary, October 30, 1689.............................201
    Protestant Day,1885, Douglas B. W. Sladen, 1885 204
The Evolution of the Celebration..206
Conclusion..207
    Remember, Remember the Fifth of November...207
    Apendix I Cast of Characters...209
The Plotters...209
    Robert Catesby:...209
The Popes and Priests 218
Priests...218
Citizens 221
Popes..221
    The Government Officials 223
    Charles I..225
   225
    Elizabeth of Bohemia...226
    Thomas James Knyvet, 1st Baron Knyvet (or Knevytt, Knyvett, Knevett, Knevitt), 1558 – 27 July 1622. 229
    Sir William Wade (or Waad, or Wadd), 1546 – 21 October 1623 230
    Apendix II Chronology of The Gunpowder Plot..231
    Appendix III , Places Relating to the Rebellion in the Midlands 236
    Apendix IV Architecture 238
    Apendix V, Two important accounts from outside of the Political Establishment...241
    Apendix VI, Early Analytical Sources 241
    Apendix VII Guy Fawkes did not say: "A dangerous disease requires a desperate remedy."..242
    Appendix VIII Harrison Ainsworth's Confusing Psuedo History................243

Appendix VIV The Official End of Celebration 243

Appendix X Discovery of the Plot results in Oath of Allegiance 245

The Gunpowder Prepares the Colonists at Jamestown 1607 245

Appendix XI The Celebration of the Deliverance in the American Colonies
.... 246

Fifth of November Roystering in Plymouth 1624 246

Childrens Hour. Ellen Welby, 1897

Introduction

In this volume we present more stories. We have stories about what happened. We learn what the kings representatives to God, the theologians think should be done about it and what we are to do. They are experts in what is known of the dark folkloric landscape-the "world unseen."

We witness the construction of the first artifacts of celebration fit for god and see the terrorists tried and executed. These are the first reactions. Remember, no one story is better than another but that all were products of the celebrants of the time. Once they were created they began to play an active, causal role in the unfolding of celebration, its disclosure of the " dark folkloric landscape" and were carried through time in the luggage of countless celebrants. Do not argue with them! Let them speak to you and set the rules.

Account, Robert Cecil, Lord Salisbury, 1605, (Ed.: Philip Sidney, 1905

LORD SALISBURY'S ACCOUNT OF THE PLOT

ROBERT CECIL, Earl of Salisbury, Secretary, of State, has left behind him an account of the Plot, which may certainly claim to be the earliest historical record of the great event, for the manuscript is dated only four days later than the fatal fifth of November. This account is contained in a letter sent by him to Sir Charles Cornwallis, the British Ambassador in Spain.[1] I reproduce below the whole of the despatch, which is of great interest and historical importance—

'It hath pleased Almighty God out of his singular goodness to bring to light the most cruel and detestable Conspiracy against the person of his Majesty and the whole state of this Realm that ever was conceived by the heart of man, at any time or in any place whatsoever. By the practice there was intended not only the extirpation of the King's Majesty and his royal issue, but the whole subversion and downfall of

---

1 Cornwallis was our Ambassador from 1605 till 1609. In 1614. he was imprisoned in the Tower. He died in December, 1629. A man of straightforward character, he was badly treated by King James.

---

this Estate; the plot being to take away at one instant the King, Queen, Prince, Council, Nobility, Clergy, Judges, and the principal gentlemen of the Realm, as they should have been altogether assembled in the Parliament-House in Westminster, the 5th of November, being Tuesday. The means how to have compassed so great an act, was not to be performed by strength of men, or outward violence, but by a secret conveyance of a great quantity of gunpowder in a vault under the Upper House of Parliament, and so to have blown up all out of a clap, if God out of his mercy and just revenge against so great an abomination had not destined it to be discovered, though very miraculously, even some 12 hours before the matter should have been put into execution. The person that was the principal undertaker of it is one Johnson, a Yorkshire man, and servant to one Thomas Percy, a Gentleman Pensioner to his Majesty, and a near [1] kinsman to the Earl of Northumberland.

This Percy had about a year and a half ago hired a part of Vyniard House in the Old Palace, from whence he had access into this vault to lay his wood and coal; and, as it seemeth now, had taken this place on purpose to work some mischief in a fit time. He is a Papist by profession, and so is his man Johnson,[2] a desperate fellow, who of late years he took into his service. Into this vault Johnson had at sundry times very privately conveyed a great quantity of powder, and therewith

1 This he was not, and the false statement illustrates Salisbury's unscrupulous methods of incriminating the innocent Northumberland.

2 Guy Faukes

filled two hogsheads, and some 32 small barrels; all which he had cunningly covered with great store of billets and faggots; and on Monday, at night, as he was busy to prepare his things for execution, was apprehended in the place itself,[1] with a false lantern, booted and spurred. There was likewise found some small quantity of fine powder for to make a train, and a piece of match, with a tinder-box to have fired the train when he should have seen time, and so to have saved himself from the blow, by some half an hour's respite that the match should have burned. Being taken and examined, he resolutely confessed the attempt, and his intention to put it into execution (as is said before) that very day and hour when his Majesty should make his oration in the Upper House. For any complices in this horrible act, he denieth to accuse any; alleging, that he had received the Sacrament a little before of a Priest, and taken an oath never to reveal any; but confesseth that he hath been lately beyond the seas, both in the Low Countries and France, and there had conference with divers English priests; but denieth to have made them acquainted with this purpose.

Guy Fawkes Lantern, Ashmolean Museum, Oxford, Postcard c. 1950.

It remaineth that I add something, for your better understanding, how this matter came to be discovered. About 8 days before the Parliament should have begun, the Lord Mounteagle received a letter about six o'clock at night (which was delivered to his footman in the dark

1 This does not tally with other accounts, which say that he was captured outside the building.

to give him) without name or date, and in a hand disguised; whereof I send you a copy, the rather to make you perceive to what a strait I was driven. As soon as he imparted the same unto me, how to govern myself, considering the contents and phrase of that letter I knew not; for when I observed the generality of the advertisment and the style, I could not well distinguish whether it were frenzy or sport; for from any serious ground I could hardly be induced to believe that that proceeded, for many Reasons; 1st., because no wise man could think my Lord[1] to be so weak as to take any alarm to absent himself from Parliament upon such a loose advertisement: secondly, I considered, that if any such thing were really intended, that it was very improbable that only one nobleman should be warned and no more. Nevertheless, being loath to trust my own judgment alone, and being always inclined to do too much in such a case as that is, I imparted the letter to the Earl of Suffolk, Lord Chamberlain, to the end I might receive his opinion,[2] whereupon perusing the words of the letter, and observing the writing (that the blow should come without knowledge who hurt them), we both conceived that it could not be more

1 Lord Mounteagle.

2 Cecil's story that the receipt of the letter took him entirely by surprise, and that its contents proved an enigma to him, is very cleverly told, but is a concoction not to be believed. He omits the fact that, although the letter was received late at night, he lost not a minute in placing it before his colleagues, who were all (suspiciously) close at hand when Mounteagle arrived post haste from Hoxton.

proper than the time of Parliament, nor by any other way like to be attempted than with powder, whilst the King was sitting in that Assembly; of which the Lord Chamberlain conceived more probability, because there was a great vault under the said chamber, which was never used for any thing but for some wood and coal, belonging to the Keeper of the Old Palace. In which consideration, after we had imparted the same to the Lord Admiral, the Earl of Worcester, the Earl of Northampton, and some others, we all thought fit to impart it to the King, until some 3 or 4 days before the Sessions. At which time we shewed his Majesty the letter, rather as a thing we could not conceal because it was of such a nature, than anything persuading him to give further credit unto it until the place had been visited.

'Whereupon his Majesty, who hath a natural habit to contemn all false fears,[1] and a judgment so strong as never to doubt anything which is not well warranted by Reason, concurred thus far with us, that seeing such a matter was possible, that should be done which might prevent all danger or nothing at all. Hereupon it was moved, that till the night before his coming, nothing should be to interrupt any purpose of theirs that had any such devilish practice, but rather to suffer them to go on till the end of the day.[2] And so, Monday, in the afternoon, the Lord Chamberlain, whose office is to see all places of assembly put

1 This the King most certainly had not. He was ever suspicious, and prone to take unnecessary alarm.

2 This stratagem resulted in the capture of the plotters, for it deceived them into thinking that their particular plan had not been discovered, acd encouraged them to persevere to the end.

in readiness when the King's person should come, taking with him the Lord Mounteagle, went to see all the places in the Parliament House, and took also a slight occasion to peruse the vault; where, finding only piles of billets and faggots heaped up, his Lordship still inquiring only who owned the same wood, observing the proportion to be somewhat more than the housekeeper was likely to lay in for his own use: And when answer was made that it belonged to one Mr. Percy, his Lordship straight conceived some suspicion in regard of his person; and the Lord Mounteagle taking some notice, that there was great profession between Percy and him, from which some inference might be made that it was the warning of a friend, my Lord Chamberlain resolved absolutely to proceed in a search, though no other materials were visible. And being returned to the Court, about 5 a clock took me up to the King and told him, that though he was hard of belief that any such thing was thought, yet in such a case as this, whatsoever was not done to put all out of doubt was as good as nothing. Whereupon it was resolved by his Majesty, that this matter should be so carried as no man should be scandalized by it, nor any alarm taken for any such purpose. For the better effecting whereof, the Lord Treasurer, the Lord Admiral, the Earl of Worcester, and we two agreed, that Sir Thomas Knyvet, should under a pretext for stolen and embezzled goods both in that place and other houses thereabouts, remove all that wood, and so to see the plain ground under it.

'Sir Thomas Knyvet going thither about midnight unlooked for into the vault, found that fellow Johnson newly come out of the vault, and without asking him more questions stayed him; and having no sooner removed the wood he perceived the barrels, and so bound the catiff fast; who made no difficulty to acknowledge the act, nor to confess clearly, that the morrow following it should have been effected. And thus have you a true narration from the beginning of this, which hath been spent in examinations of Johnson, who carrieth himself without any fear or perturbation, protesting his constant resolution to have performed it that day whatsoever had come of it; principally for the institution of the Roman religion, next out of hope to have dissolved this Government, and afterwards to have framed such a State as might have served the appetite of him and his complices. And in all this action he is no more dismayed, nay scarce any more troubled, than if he were taken for a poor robbery upon the highway. For notwithstanding he confesseth all things of himself, and denieth not to have some partners in this particular practice, (as well appeareth by the flying of divers Gentlemen upon his apprehension known to be notorious Recusants), yet could no threatening of torture draw from him any other language than this, that he is ready to die, and rather wisheth ten thousand deaths, than willingly to accuse his master or any other; until by often reiterating examinations, we pretending to him that his master was apprehended, he hath come to plain confession, that his master kept the key of that cellar whilst he was abroad; had been in it since the powder was laid there, and inclusive confessed him a principal actor in the same.

In the meantime, we have also found out, (though he denied it long) that on Saturday night the third of November, he[1] came post out of the north; that his man rid to meet him by the way; that he dined at Sions[3] with the Earl of Northumberland on Monday; that as soon as the Lord Chamberlain had been in the vault that evening, this fellow went to his master about six of the clock at night, and had no sooner spoken with him but he fled immediately, apprehending straight that to be discovered, which at that time was held rather unworthy belief, though not unworthy the after trial. In which I must need do my Lord Chamberlain his right, that he could take no satisfaction until he might search that matter to the bottom; wherein I must confess I was much less forward; not but that I had sufficient advertisement, that most of those that now are fled (being all notorious Recusants) with many other of that kind, had a practice in hand for some stir this Parliament; but I never dreamed it should have been in such nature, because I never read nor heard the like in any State to be attempted ingross by any conspiration, without some distinction of persons, [2] I do now send you some proclamations, and withal think good to advertize you, that those persons named in them, being most of them gentlemen spent in their fortunes, all inward with Percy and fit for all alterations, have gathered themselves to a head of some four score or 100 horse, with purpose (as we conceive) to pass over

1 Thomas Percy.

2 Faukcs.

3 Sion House, Islcworth.

Seas; whereupon it hath been though meet in policy of State (all circumstances considered) to commit the Earl of Northumberland to the Archbishop of Canterbury, there to be honourably used, until things be more quiet: Whereof if you shall any judgment made, as if his Majesty or his Council could harbour a thought of such a savage practice to be lodged in such a Nobleman's breast, you shall do well to suppress it as a malicious discourse and invention, this being only done to satisfy the world,-that nothing be undone which belongs to policy of State, when the whole Monarchy was proscribed in dissolution; and being no more than himself discreetly approved as necessary, when he received the sentence of the Council for his restraint.

'It is also fit that some martial men should presently repair down to those countries where the " Robin Hoods" are assembled, to encourage the good and to terrify the bad. In which service the Earl of Devonshire is used, and commission going forth for him as General; although I am easily persuaded, that this faggot will be burned to ashes before he shall be 20 miles on his way. Of all which particulars I thought fit to acquaint you, that you may be able to give satisfaction to the State[1] wherein you are; and so I commit you to God.

Your assured loving friend, '(Signed) SALSBURY.

'From the Court at Whitehall.

1 Spain.

'POSTSCRIPT.

'Although all ports and passages are stopped for some time as well as for Ambassadors as others, yet I have thought good to advertize you hereof with the speediest, the rather because his Majesty would have you take occasion to advertize the King his brother [1] of this miraculous escape.

2 POSTSCRIPT.

'Since the writing of this letter, we have assured news that those traitors are overthrown by the Sheriff of Worcestershire, after they had betaken themselves for their safety in a retreat to the house of Stephen Lyttleton in Staffordshire. The house was fired by the Sheriff; at the issuing forth Catesby was slain; Percy sore hurt, Grant and Winter burned in their faces with gunpowder; the rest are either taken or slain; Rookewood or Digby are taken.'

It is much to be deplored that this letter to Cornwallis has not met with closer attention at the hands of historians, for to those able to read, as it were, between the lines, the contents reveal some important facts about the discovery of the Plot.

For example, this letter completely contradicts the old story that the Government knew nothing of a Plot till the arrival of Mounteagle's letter, for Lord Salisbury distinctly says, 'I had sufficient advertisement that most of those that

---

[1] The King of Spain.

---

now are fled (being all notorious Recusants) with many other of that kind, had a practice in hand for some stir this Parliament.' As to the writer's excuse that he was less forward in causing a strict inquiry to be made than the Lord Chamberlain, it is easy to see that Lord Salisbury's object was not to show his hand too much, but to let others obtain some credit for discovering what was already known to him. That Lord Salisbury was well posted up in the facts, and felt quite secure as to the result of his preparations, is evident from the account he renders as to how he determined not to inform the King until the last moment. His astuteness in making no open move thus deceived Catesby, and culminated in the ruin of the unsuspecting conspirators.

Salisbury's language in regard to Percy ends, if further contradiction were necessary, the absurd theory propounded by a Jesuit author that the Government did not wish Percy to be taken alive because he *I* knew too much.' Lord Salisbury's anxiety, on the contrary, to capture Percy alive is obvious. He evidently hoped that under examination, and probably after torture, Percy would be compelled to incriminate his patron, Lord Northumberland. How little the Government knew of Faukes, well posted up though they were as to the antecedents of the other plotters, can be gathered from the circumstance that Salisbury terms him 'Johnson' throughout the letter.

-Sidney, Philip, A History of the Gunpowder Plot, 1905, p.191.

An Answere To Certaine Scandalous Papers, Scattered abroad under colour Of a Catholicke Admonition. Qui facit vivere, docet orare , Robert Cecil, 1606.

Cecil Answers Critics in 1606 – An Amplification of the Official Paradigm

An

Answere

To Certaine

Scandalous Papers,

Scattered abroad under colour

Of a Catholicke Admonition.

Qui facit vivere, docet orare

Imprinted at London by Robert Barker,

Printer to the Kings most

Excellent Majestie

Anno 1606

Having lately resolved to recall my thoughts from the earthly theatre, where they sate and beheld the variable motions of men, with those cares and cogitations which are the proper compilations of publicke ministers, hoping thereby to bee made partaker of their contentments, which borrow from publicke action, to give to private Contemplation; I perswaded my self, that I could never make choice of a better subject for my meditation, then of the late Treatise Intitled: *His Majesties Speech in the Late Session of Parliament, together with a Discourse of the maner of the discoverie of this late intended Treason.* Wherein, so many true and lively images of Gods great favour and providence, are represented: *(every line discovering where* Apelles *hand hath beene)* As all that observe the natural description of this Tree of Treason, and *in Ramo And in Radice*, may truly say, there needs no *Elisha* in our dayes, to tell the King of Israel, what the *Aramites* doe in their privatest Councels. In this Princely and religious worke, his Majestie (like to those kings of whome *Seneca* speaketh, that doe more good by Example then by laws) hath increased our obligation, by leaving under his owne hand, such a plaine and perfect record of his owne true thankefulnes to Almighty God, for his so great and miraculous graces; as neither the present Time, nor ages to come can ever be so ingrate, as not to retaine the same in perpetual memorie. A duety required by God of all his creatures, *Non ad premium, sed ad honorem.* For as amongst all the excellent faculties of the minde (next to the understanding.) Remembrance hath the precedencie, for *necessitie and use*: So in the accounts of all those services we owe to God, (who desireth rather, wee should remember what he hath been to us, then curiously to affect what he is in himselfe,) Remembrance is the first, and the first commanded. In this facultie we excel the beasts, and imitate the Angels: For they being present beholde at once, Gods Goodnesse and Love, in the mirrour of his deitie; and wee upon earth, (in the Table of his Workes) have a present and full view of that which God is, by that which hee doeth. So as, although we cannot see him in himself, yet we doe particularly see him in his means, especially in those great works of deliverances and defences, which he provideth for whole Nations and people, against publicke and private practices. And therefore if wee shall grow forgetful, or thinke it sufficient for a day or a yeere to pay him our Tributes of humble thankefulnesse, when the Heathen themselves doe continually offer unto their false gods, their Cynamon and frankincense, Then shall our error be no lesse, then that of Israel, whose prayse and prayers ended almost as soone as they had passed the Red Sea.

But now while I was in this most serious and silent Meditation, (sometimes ravished with the infiniteness of God's Mercie and Justice, who restraineth the power of the wicked, as hee did the Viper from the hands of *Paul*; sometimes comforted in calculating my dayes of happiness, to live under a King, blessed in himself, blessed in his Olive branches, beloved of men for his integritie and wisedome, and pleasing to God for his zealous endeavours, to cleanse the Vessels of his Kingdome from the Dregs and Lees of the Romish grape;) Even then (I say) when my heart was not a little cheared, to observe so much as the least note of my Name, in his Register, for one that had beene of any use in this so fortunate a Discoverie, (much like to the poore day labourer, who taketh contentment many yeeres after, when hee passeth by that glorious Architecture, to the building whereof he can remember to have carried some few stickes or stones;) Even then, was I most bitterly calumniated, with many contumelious Papers and Pasquils, dispersed abroad in divers parts of the citie, without any Author, and yet so continually coming upon me, one after another (like the messengers of *Job*) as I could neither devise to whom to turne mee to make my answer, nor yet imagine by what hard destiny I had drawne upon me their furie, thus to single me out for a subject of so much bitternesse, in the dayes of so great joy and gladnesse: Yea even in the time when I was perswaded, that they which had divided themselves for conscience sake from all Communion with us in our religious offices, would yet have tuned their harps, to have joyned with us in cheerful Songs for this our happy deliverance.

Resting long in this debate with myself, whether I should now begin a warfare of words, that had so long put on an habite of suffering, especially against any of those, with whom disputes are endlesse; because their ende is clamor, without desire to receive satisfaction; after I had taken secret and faithfull consell, from the love and duetie, which liveth always in me towards my soveraigne, and entred into serious consideration, how easily the errors of publike ministers, may reflect upon the best deserving princes; having also heard from forraine parts, how farre my name was there proscribed for a man of blood; I thought it fit in regarde to the place I hold, to take some occasion to expresse my selfe in some cleare tearmes; lest any of those clouds which are unjustly cast upon mee, might darken the brightnesse of his royall minde, which hath beene always watered with the mildest deawe of Mercie and Moderation.

And therefore although I know, that *Stylus prudentiae est silentium*, and doe remember well the caution prescribed by *Salomon*, in the apprehension off scattered calumnies, wherein the follyes of men like clouds of tempest are inraged, when they lacke occasion to powre foorth showers of malice, on the heads of Persons in place of government: Yet finding my selfe in such an absolute possession over my owne soule in patience, as it is not in the power of any calumniator to disturbe the peace of a quiet minde; I though it meete to breake silence, and to the intent my answere might be the better conceived, to set downe first the copie of one of their original writings whereof the tenour followeth.

To the Earle of Salisbury

My Lord, Whereas the late unapprovable & most wicked designe, for the destroying of his Majestie, the Prince, and Nobilite, with many others of worth and qualitie (attempted through the undertaking spirits of some more fierie & turbulent, than zealous & dispassionate Catholicks) hath made the generall state of our Catholicke cause so scandalous in the eye of such, whose corrupted judgments are not able to fanne away and sever the fault of the professor from the profession it selfe; as that who is now found to be of that Religion, is perswaded, at least in minde, to allow (though God knoweth as much abbhoring as any Puritane *whatsoever) the said former most inhumane, and barbarous project: And whereas some of his Majesties Councill, but especially your L.* [Lordship] *as being Knowen to bee, (as the* Philosopher *termeth it) a primus motor in such uncharitable proceedings, are determined (as it is feared) by taking advantage of so foule a scandall, to roote out all memory of* Catholicke *Religion, either by sudden banishment, Massacre, imprisonment, or some such unsupportable vexations, and pressures; and perhaps by decreeing in this next Parliament, some more cruell and horrible Lawes against Catholicks, than already are made: In regard of these premises, there are some good men who through their earnest desire for continuing the* Catholicke *Religion, and for saving many soules, both of this present, and of all future posteritie; are resolved to prevent so great a mischiefe, though with a full assurance aforehand of the losse of their dearest lives.*

You are therefore hereby to be admonished, that at this present there are five, which have generally undertaken your death, and have vowed the performance thereof, by taking already the blessed Sacrament, *if you continue your dayly plotting of so tragicall Stratagems against Recusants* [those who refused to attend the Protestant church]. *It is so ordered, that no one of these five knoweth who the other foure be, for the better preventing the discovery of the rest, if so any one by attempting and not performing, should be apprehended. It is also already agreed, who shall first attempt it by shotte, and so who in order shall follow. In accomplishing of it, there is expected no other than assurance of death. Yet it will willingly bee embraced for the preventing of those generall Calamities, which by this your transcendent Authoritie, and grace with his Majestie are threatened unto us all. And indeed the difficulties herein are more easily to be disgested, since tow of the intended Attemptors, are in that weake state of body, that they cannot live above three or foure monthes. The other three are so distressed in themselves and their friends; as that their present griefes (for being only Recusants) doe much dull all apprehension of death. None is to bee blamed (in the true censuring of matters) for the undertaking hereof: For we protest before GOD, wee knowe no other meanes left us in the world, since it is manifest that you serve but as a match, to give fire unto his Majestie (to whome the worst that wee wish, is that hee may be as great a Saint in Heaven, as hee is a King on Earth), for intending all mischiefes against the poore distressed* Catholickes. *Thus giving your Lordship this charitable admonition, the which may perhaps bee necessary hereafter, for some others your Inferiours (at least in grace and favour) if so they runne on their former inhumane and unchristian rage against us, I cease, putting you in minde, that where once true and spirituall Resolution is, there notwithstanding all dangers whatsoever, the weake may take sufficient revenge of the great.*

Your L. well admonishing friends, &c
A. B. C. &c.

Postscript.
It may be your Lordship will take this but as some forged Letter of some Puritanes, thereby to incense you more against Recusants. But wee protest upon our salvation it is not so, neither can any thing in humane likelyhood prevent the effecting thereof, but the change of your course towards Recusants.

This being now one of their charges *verbatim*, because it is not my meaning to wander further, then the paths of their own uncharitable passions do lead me; I will only direct my answere to the several parts thereof; though the same as they lie, divert me from any other good or regular method.

For the first part therefore, wherein this writer in the *Name of the Catholikes* protesteth against the fact as an unapprovable and most wicked desseigne; I must shortly say, that whosover shall read the *Panegyricall* oration of *Sextus Quintus*, made upon the murder of *Henry* the third the French king, shall well perceive that sinne to bee preferred before the act of *Judith* to *Holofernes*, by which Gods people were delivered, and may also observe in divers other cases, how generally our adversaries are inclined, to make an ill interpretation onely of those thinges, which faile in execution (for otherwise *foelix scelus virtus vocatur*) to which may be added that which is vulgarly knowen, what number of Authors are illustrated in Rome , which strongly mainteine the doctrine of deposing kings. Neverthelesse, because I have ever loved to measure others by my selfe, and always wished that by some cleare and constant course, the state of Christendome might be freed from all pernicious instruments, which seeke not to plant peace, but to worke confusion; I have bin a longtime sorie, that those which imploy so many seditious spirits, dayly to instruct the unlearned Catholickes in those mysteries of deposing Princes, have not, by some publike and definitive sentence orthodoxall (in which it is supposed the Pope can not erre) made some such cleare explication of their assumed power over Sovereaigne Princes, as not onely those which acknowledge his superiority, might be secured from feares and jealousies of continuall treasonous and bloody assacinates against their persons, but those Kings also which doe not approve his

Papal jurisdiction, and yet would faine reserve a charitable opinion of their subjects, might know how farre to repose themselves in their fidelitie, in civil obedience, howsoever they see them divided from them in point of conscience. For whoever shall attribute most to the force of Excommunication, shall never finde it (if I mistake it not) further powerfull either by the original institution, or in the succeeding practice for many yeeres after Christ, then onely to deprive men from spirituall graces, and shut them as it were out of the dores of heaven, without so grosse an usurpation, as to remove them out of the earth, or to destroy their being in Nature. Insomuch as the writ it selfe *de excommunicato capiendo*, and other such like courses, which are variable in sundry governments, have rather issued from the goodness of such Christian kings, as were desirous to worke the better obedience to the rules of the Church, then from any power of Excommunication in his owne nature, all censures of the Church having left life untouched, *siue fuerat Ethnicus siue Publicanus*: Many of the heathen themselves having taught this for a rule, *Bonos imperatores voto expetere oportet, quoscunq tolerare*. And therefore I cannot but marvaile the more at some dark and cautelous writings published of late upon this accident, and avowed under the name of one of their Prime men, wherein he hath bestowed many thundering words, against those which shall attempt against Princes by private authoritie, and yet reserveth thereby a tacite lawfulnesse thereof, in case it be directed by publicke warrant. A matter no lesse discrediting the sinceritie pretended in this particular, then that most strange and grosse doctrine of *Equivocation*, which is so highly extolled in the Church of *Rome*, though it teare in sunder all the bondes of humane conversation. For who so shall please to reade one place of the holy Father Saint *Augustine* (of whose Bookes by this occasion I have turned over some fewe leaves) shall finde, that when the *Priscillian* Hereticks in all their examinations before the Rulers of that time, did seeke to dissemble their heresie, by using those answeres of *Equivocation*, wherewith the Papists now maintaine it lawfull to deny all trueth under a mentall reservation, and wresting the words of S. *Paul*, who requireth every man to speake the trueth to his neighbor, inferred, as if they might speake falsely to all others. This reverend Father soundly and clearely refuted that irreligious principle, with this short sentence; *Corde creditor ad Iustitiam, ore fit confessio ad salutem;* Otherwise (saith hee) *Peter, who professed Christ in heart, and denyed him in words, would never have redeemed his denyall with so many teares. This were to take away the Crowne off Martyrdome and to make all the holy Martyrs fooles; who, making a conscience to dissemble with Heathen Magistrates, sealed with their blood the inward thoughts of their hearts and confessions of their mouthes. Neither should any man professe this opinion, but hee that seeketh to subvert all Lawes and dueties of Civil societie, breaking out into this Expostulation,* O fonts lachrymarum, *Where are ye to be found, O ye fountains of teares? How shall we hide our selves from the displeased face of Trueth?*

For the second part, where you pretend *an apprehension of so many massacres and pressures to come against Catholickes, or some more horrible Lawe to bee decreed in Parliament, then is already allowed,* and therein taxe *me as one that am like to prove a fierie Instrument,* Give me leave to tell you, that those are false pretences, which some lewd Impostor hath used as false glasses to multiply your feares.

These poore Calumniations are like to *Adams* figge leaves, unable to cover your shame. For as hee sought a covering, *non quia nudus sed quia lapsus*; So is it your fault, not your feare, that maketh you cast those unjust Imputations upon your Prince and State, *Sed pereuntibus mille figura.*

These men that rule your consciences, have first dazzled your eyes with fearefull, but false objects, thereby hoping to engage you more deeply in their pernicious attempts.

They have fought with *Nero* to set Rome on fire, and after to lay the blame on Christians.

Thus hath your credulitie bene overtaken with vaine shadowes, whereas the children of Wisedome are of slow belief.

If therefore you had measured those things by the rules of Time, and had entred into a true comparison of things past, with things present; you must needs have concluded better of things to come. For if you behold the precedent Reignes of the two late sister Queenes of different Religion, you shall finde more blood in five or sixe yeeres of the first, then in five and fourtie yeeres of the second.

Examine likewise, whether you have seene since this Kings time, any the least prints of bloody steps. Hath he added new seuerities to the Lawes of the former Time, which he found established? Or hath he not in some things qualified them? And in other forborne to execute them, even upon those persons which publish with sound of trumpet the sentence of divorce betwixt his subject and his sovereigntie? Let me appeale to your owne consciences (which in every man holdeth place of Judge and Witnesse) whether upon the present fury of this fiery treason, which inflamed so many against the generalitie of the Papists (according to the nature of suddaine peril, which hardly admits of just distinctions) there hath beene any one acte of blood or crueltie committed, though all men know, that the greatest violences that could have been used in such cases, under colour of publicke safetie, would have been interpreted to be the true effects of care and providence. *Nam crudelitas si a vindicta, iustitia est si a periculo, prudentia.*

Nay rather behold the excellent temper of his Majesties mind, who doubting what the humour of sudden apprehension might produce at such a time, no sooner had performed his owne publicke duety of Praise and Thanksgiving to God, but hee pronounced in open Parliament how farre he was from the condemnation of the general for particulars. All which being laid together, I doubt not, but those which are not in the desperate consumption of sinne, will freely acknowledge his Majestie to be a Prince of Peace and Mercy, that delighteth not in the noyse of Chaines and fetters, but rather with *Theodosius* deferreth Execution, and wisheth *Se potuisse potius mortuos a morte revocare.*

And now for the imaginary Power, which it pleaseth you to ascribe unto us of his Majesties Concel, in which number, as a plotter against Romish Catholiques, you make me to be one of the *Quorum*, I should take it always for an Honor and happinesse, for me to receive not onely injury, but persecution it selfe in so Noble a Societie, where persons of so great Honour and Judgement are Actors; who know full well, that Counsailors of Kings doe stand for thousands or hundreds, onely as it pleaseth them to place them; and that all their greatnesse groweth merely from humble endeavours, no further meritorious then as they are valued by a gracious acceptance. Neverthelesse, seeing I am made by you a divided Member from the Body, and graced with so hard an Epithete as *Boutefeu*, and that you are content to borrow my Name to scandalize the State you live in; I must freely say to you without bitternesse, That howsoever it may serve your turne for a while, to make me the marke of your malice; yet those that rightly judge of the spirit in which this writer speaketh, will hardly imagine, that this Faction followeth any other Body, then the Body of Authoritie. It is not the Head alone, nor any other particular members that these men shoot at, but at the Church and Common-wealth; which like *Hippocrates* twines have long both wept and laughed together. These are the things which the Enemies of this time doe studie to subvert, and not any poore greatnesse of mine, who am onely great in the eyes of Envy. Nay rather they are angry with *Aristotle*, who bids wise Princes keepe downe Faction, which is ever humble till it get the Key of Power. They are grieved, or rather heart-broken, to behold such an Unitie of State and Councell, as dares bid the world doe, as she would be done unto. These are knowen so well to bee the true causes of their Despaire and Discontentment, as they shall ground a faith upon very weake Principles, if they imagine, that open vowes of my destruction (a matter of so small consequence) can make them free from imputation of contriving higher Practices.

But now for that which commeth in the third place, which is their protestation, that *for the avoiding new mischief to come, it is intended by good men upon a spiritual Resolution, to take my life, and that there are five persons upon the secret, but all bound up by the Sacrament, where of two are so weake and so sickely, as they can hardly forfeit two or three months of life.* To these I can onely say, that having their feete so nigh the grave, their ghostly father deserves small thankes, that will send them thither in bloody coffins. For they doe neither carrie the markes of Rome Heathen, nor of Rome Christian, for under Heathen Emperours, the victories were scorned, which were barbarously gotten, *mixtis veneno fontibus*: And when Rome was pure and primitive, yous hall finde the Armes of the Church were Teares and Prayers. But now their Oracles are so farre degenerate from the former puritie of that ancient Church, as they make murder *spirituall Resolution*, and openly threaten the lives of Kings that are Gods breathing Images, when the Prophet *David* trembled to violate the skirt of King *Sauls* garment.

All which considered, I doubt not but those recusants which doe discover such pernicious spirits, will out of the light of this fire perfectly discerne the darkenesse and danger of that Religion, whereof the faith is lapped up in such an ignorant and implicite obedience, and so much the rather, because it hath fallen out soften, that the scruples of Conscience and seeds of Treason, have growen up as close together, as the huske and Corne in one eare. And therefore I should thinke that those men, which carie the unlearned Papists, like Hawkes hooded, into those dangerous positions, may justly challenge any that shall seeke to rob them of the deserved Titles of *Boutefeux* and fiery matches. For these are they that have made their Church a Court, their religion a vassal to ambition, and are so hot upon earthly Honours, as they cannot distinguish *Inter summa et praecipitia*. These are they that enjoyne men to eate their God, upon the bargaine of blood, where those whom they deprave doe know, that whatsoever God doth affect in goodness, he doth effect by good meanes. And howsoever they terme our Sacraments as bare and naked signes, we may justly say that wee have never hitherto brought them into the combination of murder, or into the house of crying sinnes. As for that sort of them which pretend to bee so full of present griefe, through the distresse of themselves and their friends (for being onely Recusants) as it dulleth all apprehension of death: Those that lacke charitie, will judge this dulnesse to be, *Plus tristitiae quam poenitentiae*, more for sorrow than the project hath failed, then that it was conceived. As for the Plotters and stratagems whereof they complain, If those which use lawfull meanes to prevent conspiracies, must bee esteemed Plotters, and subjects fit for proscription, howe shall his Magestie escape their coensure, that was Gods chosen minister upon Earth for this particular discoverie? Or to what ende doe Princes admit of Councellors care or Secretaries Vigilancie, (whose Offices are to stand Sentinell over the life of Kings, and safetie of States) if their endevours to countermine the secret mynes of Treason, be thus exposed to misconstruction? Or if by stratagems those Lawes are meant, by which all branches of Treason are punished; why doe they forget that those ordinances are derived from the wisdome of Parliaments, two hundred yeeres before my cradle?

Besides, if any thinke it in the power of fewe, much lesse of anyone, to be able to extort determinations of extremitie, or procure new Lawes in Parliament by selfe humour, those neither understand the course of Law-making, nor the wisdom, gravitie, or nature of Lawmakers in this State, where Kings themselves, from whom (as from the Center) all the lives and executions of Lawes take their beginning, are pleased freely to admit their Subjects negatives, with good and gracious acceptation.

And now for myself, with whom you would condition to leave Plotting, as you tearme it, against Recusants: First, discretion telleth me, that as the Husbandman, which casteth his eye over-curiously upon winds and clouds, doeth neither sow nor reape in season, so, that servant, whose faith and zeale in the service of Kings, becometh awfull of enemies either for their power or envy, is neither worthy of favour nor protection. For when I consider the Prince I serve, that hee hath not taken up wisedome of Government upon credit, but carrieth still the *Jethro* of order in his owne bosome, disposing the meane causes, to those that are fit to rule over hundreds, and over fifties, reserving still the greatest to the greatness of him selfe, like a King such in the experience of many yeeres Raigne, over a free and valiant people, both by nature, seat, and education: I freely professe both before mine owne and all other Nations, that although I participate not with the follies of that Flie, who though her selfe to raise the dust, because she sate on the Chariot wheele, Yet am I so farre from disavowing my honest ambition of my Masters favour, as I am desirous that the world should hold me, not so much his creature, by the undeserved Honours I hold from his Grace and Power, as by my desire to bee in the shadowe of his minde, and to frame my judgements, knowledge and affections according to his, towards whose Royall Person I shall glory more to bee always found an honest and humble Subject, then I should so command absolutely in any other calling. For the rest which may concerne mee in my Religion (howsoever darkened with this middle vaile of sinne and frailtie) it is built upon the sacred grounds of Hope and Faith, in the precious blood of my Redeemer, without presuming upon any particular merits. And whereas they alledge, that men resolved to die, are masters over other mens lives; My answere is, they have no more power then the least Spider, who by permission can doe as much. And if the dayes of my life were in their hands, as they might peradventure take from me some moneths of joys: So am I assured that they should take mee from yeeres of sorrowes. But these poore threats amaze no hopes of mine, I am none of those that believe with the men of the olde world, that the Mountaines shake, when the Moules doe cast. And farre I hope, it shall be from mee, who know so well in whose Holy Booke my dayes are numbered, once to entertaine a thought to purchase a spanne of time, at so deare a rate, as for the feare of any mortall power, in my poore Talent, *Aut Deo, aut Patriae, aut Patri patriae deesse.* For who doubteth that the Magistrates who converse with varietie of spirits, must not sometimes undergo tempests? All our actions are upon the open stage, and can be no more hidden then the Sunne. If we deserve ill, we shall heare ill, Or if the present time doe flatter us, yet when our glasses are runne, (which can not be long) that glory which maketh worthy men live for ever, dyeth with us, and our posteritie shal be the heirs of our dishonor. And therefore *suadeat loquentis vita non oratio*. Besides, that errour which in all mortall things hath her power, strength and declination; hath now her foundations discovererd and her Towers taken, so as it is to bee suspected, shee will play so long with the temporall Soveraigntie of Kings, as it shall bee the glorious worke of Kings to breake downe her walles and strongest defences: And therefore ill becoming servants to slacke their pace, for feare of malice, but rather to rest assured, that unto such as faithfully bestow their time in the service of God, the evening and the night shall come upon them naturally one after another: Their faith shall ascend before them, and their good fame shall remaine after them.

To conclude, seeing God hath pleased to deliver us from so many unspeakeable miseries and afflictions ready to have fallen upon us, like the visitation of *Jerusalem*, whereof the Prophet speaketh; When their candle hath his clearest light, and when they sleepe in the armes of peace, loe then shall be the time of their visitation: And seeing this should have happened unto us in the dayes of a just and gracious king, when every man rejoiced under his Vine and under his figge Tree: Let us both for the honour of our Nation, and the good of our soules, be mindfull to inform our selves so perfectly of all our dueties both divine and humane, as wee may not become (through our owne grosse ignorance) the authors of our own confusion. Let no man set so high a price on that false reputation of keeping oathes to private friends, as for their sake to forfeit faith and loyaltie to Prince and countrey. Will you finde true friends, saith *Seneca*? Search them *inter recta official*, and there shall you finde them. So saith the Canon Law, *Non est appellanda fides, quae ad peccatum inuitat*. Tully in his bookes of Offices disputing the case *inter Patrem et Patriam*, If thy father (saith he) intend a Treason to his Countrey and State, and tell thee of it, thou must first diswade, aftere threaten, and after accuse. For this is a Rule approved; *In promissorio pro re iniusta, iurans illicitum, obligatur ad contraium*. And therefore seeing God hath saved us so miraculously from this confusion whereof the minde of man (which within a moment searcheth from East to the West) can no way finde the bottome; Let us make it appeare into the world, by the difference of our constant measure of thankefulnesse, that we esteeme not this an ordinary acte of Gods providence, nor a thing to be imputed to any fault or fayling in their plots or projects, but a miraculous effect of the trancendent power, farre beyond the course and compasse of all his ordinary proceedings. Who although hee seeme for a time to give way, as though he regarded not how men come to their ends and purposes,(letting them grow like poisonfull herbes,) yet at length when they are ripest, hee will cut them off, and when they are fullest of their venomous qualitie, pull them up for other mens medicine, having made the Scorpion to carry the oyle about him, which cureth the wounds he giveth. To which let us adde this further Faith, that as the place where this prodigious Massacre should have bene committed, is the same place where the ancient Religion of the primitive Church, shooke off the bonds and fetters of the Romane corruption under which it had long continued in servitude: So whiles the same Faith shall be Religiously and constantly professed, that it shall never be in the power of mortall man, to shake the least corner stone of that blessed and sure foundation.

Thus have I given my pen her libertie to runne her stage, thereby to free my minde travelling (as a woman with childe) with more waighty cogitations then I could containe in silence, or express in order; hoping my intentions shall receive a favourable censure, seeing they are bounded with honest and humble limittes. If it be saide that I have taken too slight an occasion to answere a slander that lacks an Authour, I desire to be thus rightly conceived, that no man would have sooner contemned those Shewells or dead papers, which move with the winde, then I should, if so many advertisements from abroad, and confessions at home (concurring with this calumnie) did not in Justice challendge at my hands some speedy course to preserve my poore reputation from these cruell aspersions. In which consideration, although my desires to weare out many dayes, are drawen within as small a circle as my feares, and both my spirit and Judgement, farre from such a dejection or weakenesse, as to endvour, or expect a remoove of fixed resolutions, by force of Arguments or protestations; Yet when I remember with *Seneca*, that even the great and fairest Kingdomes, whose Lawes abound in bloody lines, doe loose so much of their beautie, as they become no lesse deformed, then the basest Shambles, and when I know that our greatest Judge, and Saviour of the World, who alloweth voyces to all kinds of sinnes, hath made the voyce of blood to speake so lowd, as it pearceth Heaven it selfe, I doe presume so well of all indifferent and equal judgements, as my defence in this degree, shall never bee held for a needlesse curiositie; *Quia Inauditi, tanquam innocentes pereunt*; Especially seeing mine owne conscience telleth me so plainely, that as Clemencie is the truest keeper of Kingdoms, So Cruelties are of al others the falsest Guards. If it be said, I have bene too sharpe in censuring the Romish Catholiques in generall, because I have been injured by some Infested spirits of that Profession, I doe protesse ingenuously, 1 that I am not perswaded that such a Malice as this, which hath no Paralell, can ever fall into those hearts that hold any seeds of conscience, or that these fine pretended good-men, which are combined in this resolution, have any sense of any Religion at all, but rather that they are some dispersed remnant of that impious Consort, whose eyes and hearts are dayly wounded, to behold so many faire Mornings, to follow after so blacke a Day, as had prepared miserie even for the childe unborne.

And when I doe remember upon the death of the late Queene of happy memory with what obedience and applause, both professions did concurre to his Majesties succession, and now observe how little assistance was given to these late savadge Papists, who had gathered together some few rotten branches, fallen from such decayed and withered Trees as Christ had cursed in the Gospel, hoping therewith to have set a Fire, and made a combustion in the State: Although my prayers shall never cease, that wee may see the happy dayes, when onely one Uniformitie of true Religion is willingly imbraced in this Monarchie, Yet I shall ever (according to the Law of God) make so great difference in my Conscience between seeing sinnes, and sinnes of Ignorance, as I shall thinke it Just by the Lawes of men, *Solum necis artifices arte perire sua.*

And now for answere to your Postscript, wherein you seek so much to divert me from suspecting those whome you call Puritanes to be Authors of this Slander; I have onely this to say, That you should never have needed to put yourselfe to so much paines for that perswasion, seeing neither the regular Protestant, nor those that are unconformable to the present Discipline of the Church, can ever be justly charged to have mixed their private differences with any Thoughts, much lesse with any Actes of bloody Massacres. *Et hic baculum fixi.*

Further replyes expect not therefore at my hands. I will henceforth rest in peace in the House of mine own Conscience, where if I doe good deedes, no matter who sees them; if bad, (knowing them my selfe) no matter from whom I hide them: for they are of record before a Judge, from whose presence I cannot flee. If all the world applaud me, and hee accuse me, their praise is vaine. *Falli potest fama, conscientia nunquam.* If this may not suffice, but that you will still threaten and exclaime, I must heare with patience, and say with *Tacitus*, You have learned to curse, and I to contemne:

Tu linguae, ego aurium sum Dominus.

Cecil, Robert, An Answere To Certaine Scandalous Papers, Scattered abroad under colour Of a Catholicke Admonition. *Qui facit vivere, docet orare.* Imprinted at London by Robert Barker, Printer to the Kings most Excellent Majestie, 1606.

The Weekely Newes Numb.9, Jeffrey Chorlton,

Munday 31 January 1606

London: Printed for Jeffrey Chorlton, and are to be Sold at his Shop, at the great North Door of St. Paul's 1606-

A Brief Discourse upon their Arraignment and Execution of the eight traytors- Digby, the two Winters, Graunt, Rookewood, Keyes, Bates, and Johnson, alias Guy Fawkes, four of which were executed in St. Paul's Churchyard, in London, upon Thursday, the 27th last, the other four in the Old Palace Yard, in Westminster, over against the Parliament house, and with a relation of the other traytors which were executed at Worcester.

Execution of the Conspirators in the Gunpowder Plot in Old Palace Yard Westminster, in 1606. 1795, Nicolas Visschere after Nicolas (Claes) Jansz

Not to aggravate the sorrow of the living in the shame of the dead, but to dissuade the idolatrously blind from seeking their own destruction, the following account is written of the carrage of the eight papists herein named, of their little show of sorrow, their usage in prison, and their obstinacy to their end. First for their offence--it is so odious in the ears of all human creatures that it could hardly be believed that so many monsters in nature should carry the shapes of men--murder! Oh! it is the crying sin of the world, and such an intended murder as, had it taken effect, would have made a world to cry; and, therefore, the horror thereof must needs be hateful to the whole world to hear of it. My intent is chiefly to make report of the manner of their Execution: for after their apprehension in the country they were brought up to London upon the appearance of their foul treason before his Majesties most honourable Council, they were, by their commandment, committed to his Majesty's Tower of London, where they wanted nothing that, in the mercy of a Christian Prince, was thought fit, and indeed too good for so unchristian offenders.

After the traytors went from the Tower by water, and came to Westminster, before they came into the hall they made some half-hour stay or more in the Star Chamber, wether being brought and remaining till the Court was all ready to hear them. It was strange to note their carriage even in their very countenances--some hanging down the head as if their hearts were full of doggedness, and others forcing a stern look as if they would "fear death with a frown," never seeming to pray--unless it were by the dozen upon their beads--and taking tobacco as if that hanging were no trouble to them; craving mercy of neither God nor the King for their offenses, and making their conscience, as it were, as wide of the mind, and to the very Gates of Hell to be the cause of their Hellish Courses to make a work meritorious.

Coming into the Hall, and upon the scaffold at the bar, they all pleaded "not guilty," but they were all found "Guilty."

Digby--without craving mercy or favour of either God or the King--made only five requests: That his wife might have her jointure; his children the lands entailed by his father; his sisters their legacies in his hands unpaid; his debts paid; and for his death, to be beheaded and not hanged.

Robert Winter, in like manner, thinking himself already half a saint for his whole villainy, said little to any purpose, but only made a request to the King for Mercy towards his brother in regard of his offence, as he said, "Through his only persuasion." His brother said little, but, with a guilty conscience, swallowed up a concealed grief with little show of sorrow for that time.

Graunt, stubborn in his idolatry, seemed nothing penitent for his villainy, asked little mercy; but as it were, careless of grace, received the doom of his desert.

Rookewood, out of a studied speech, would fain made his idolatry and bringing up an excuse for the foul deed, but he had his judgment with the rest of the traytors. Now, after their condemnation and judgment they were sent to the Tower of London, and when the day of execution arrived they were drawn upon sledges and hurdles into Saint Paul's Churchyard, four of them, --namely, Everard Digby, the elder Winter, Graunt and Bates.

First went up Digby, a man of goodly personage and manly aspect, but with vain and superstitious crossing of himself he betook himself to his Latin prayers, mumbling to himself, refraining to have the prayers of any but the Roman Catholicks, went up the ladder, and, with the help of the hangman, made an end to his wicked days in this world.

After him Winter went up the scaffold, and staid not long for his execution. Then came Graunt, who followed him, showing how so bloody a religion can make such bloody consciences. Then came Bates, and when he was hanged the Executioners prepared to Draw and Quarter them; and when this was done the business of the day was ended.

Franz Hogenberg, 1605 Conspirators being drawn through the streets to their execution

The next day being Friday, were drawn from the Tower to the Old Palace Yard in Westminster Thomas Winter, Rookewood, Keyes, and Fawkes. Winter went first up the scaffold, and he died a true Catholic, with a very pale face and dead colour, he went up the ladder, and; after a swing or two with the halter, to the quartering block was drawn, and there quickly despatched. Next came Rookewood, who protested to die in his idolatry a Romish Catholick, went up the ladder, hanging till he was almost dead, then was drawn to the block, where he gave up his last gasp.

Then came Keyes, who was so sturdy a villain that he would not wait the hangman's turn, but turned himself off with such a leap that he broke the halter with the swing; but after his fall he was drawn to the block, and there his bowels withdrawn, and he was divided into four parts.

Last of all came the great Devil of all, Guy Fawkes, alias Johnson, who should have put fire to the powder. His body being weak with the torture and sickness he was scarce able to go up the ladder, yet, with much ado, by the help of the hangman, went high enough to break his neck by the fall. He made no speech, but with his crosses and idle ceremonies made his end upon the gallows and the block, to the great joy of all beholders that the land was ended of so wicked a villainy.

The Araignement and Execution of the Late Traytors, with a relation of the other traytors, which were executed at Worcester, the 27 of January last past.

Jeffrey Chorlton, 1606

To All faithful and obedient subjects

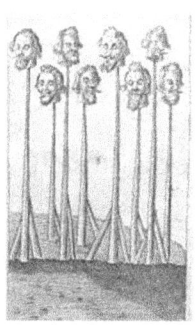

Heads of the Conspirators, Franz Hogenberg, 1605

Gentle Reader, the horrible and abhominable Treason of the Traytours lately executed, with many others, some already executed at Worcester, and others their confederates, whome God of his mercie at his good pleasure bring to light, and give the due punishment of their deserts. This treason I say, so horrible and detestable in the sight both of God and man, for which their bewitched hearts, not having that true repentance, that in true Christians may be required : I have set thee downe a briefe discourse touching the Arraignment of these that were here in London and Westminster, upon just condemnation executed upon Thursday and Friday being the 30. and 31. dayes of Januarie last past, to the joy of all true subjects, that living under so blessed and gratious a King, may rejoyce to see the cutting off, of all such accursed traytors, as entend the death of his Majestie, and subversion of the whole kingdome: and so beseeching God to roote out all such wicked weedes as may be hurtful in so good a ground as this our land, which I hope dooth containe a world of loving Subjects unto his Majestie, and their Countrie, which do continually pray to God to blesse his Majesty, with our gracious Queene, Prince Henrie, and the rest of his royal Progeny, with long life, a blessed peace, and never ending happinesse, and to continue his holy worde and blessed Peace among us, and to give us all grace with one heart, ever to love and serve him in all true faithfulnesse, I end.

Your loving friend.

T. VV.

A Briefe Discourse upon the Arraignement nad Execution of the 8. Traytors, Digbie, the two Winters, Grant, Ruckwood, Caies, Bates and Johnson, alias Faulks, foure of which were executed in Paules Churchyeard in London, upon Thursday being the 30. of January: the other 4 in the olde Pallace in Westminster, over against the Parliament house, upon Friday next following.

Not to aggrauate the sorrow of the living in the shame of the dead, but to disswade the idolatrously blinded, from seeking their owne destruction, in the way to damnation, I have here briefly set downe a discourse of the behaviour and cariage of the eight persons afore named, from the time of their imprisonment, to the instant of their death: the nature of their offence, the little shew of their sorrow, their visage in prison, and their obstinance to their end. First, for their offence, it is odious in the eares of all humaine Creatures, that it could hardlie be believed, that so many monsters in nature, shoulde carry the shapes of men: Murther, oh, it is the crying sinne of the world, and such an intended Murther as had it taken effect, would have made a worlde to crie and therefore the horror thereof, must needs bee hatefull to the whole world to heare of it.

Men that saw them goe to their execution; did in a sorte grieve, to see such proper men in shape, goe to so shamefull an end, but the end was proper to men of so unproper minds, who to satisfie a blinded conceite, would forget their duties to God and their King, and unnaturally seeke the ruine of their Native Countrie: They are said to be borne unhappie, that are not some way profitable to their Countrie, and then, how accursed are they borne that seeke the destruction of the whole Kingdome

Papists will perhaps idley say, it was a bloody execution, but in respect of their desert, in the blood they entended to have shedde, it was a mercifull punishment; For if Jezabel a Queen for seeking the murther of one private man, was throwne out of a window, and fedde upon by dogs: How can these people bee thought to be cruelly used, that could extend and practice so horrible a villany, as the death of so gracious a King, Queene and Prince, so Noble Peeres, and the ruine of so flourshing a Kingdome.

But since my entent is chieflie to make report of the manner of their demeanors from the prison to the Arraignment, and from thence to Execution I will truly set downe, what I have gathered, touching the same. After their apprehension in the Countrie, and brought up to London, upon the Apparance of their soule treason, before his Majesties most Honorable Councell, they were by their commaundement committed to his Majesties Tower of London, where they wanted nothing, that in the mercy of a Christian prince, was thought fit and indeed too good for so unchristian offenders. For in the time of their imprisonment they seemed to feele no part of feare, either of the wrath of God, the doome of Justice, or the shame of sinne; but as it were, with feared Consciences, senceles of grace, lived, as not looking to die or not feeling the sorrow of their sinnes; and now that no subtille Foxe, or rather Goose, that would faine seame a Foxe, shall have cause to say or thinke, that the justice of the lawe hath not beene truly ministered, acccording to the rules of the divine will, behold here a true report, as I said before of their behaviour, and carriage, from their apprehension, to their imprisonment, and from condemnation to their execution. In the time of their imprisonment, they rather feared with their sinnes, then fasted with sorrow for them; were richly apparrelled, fared deliciously, and tooke Tobacco out of measure, with a seeming carelesnesse of their crime, as it were daring the Law to passe uppon them: but, the Almightie and our most mercifull good God first revealed them. His majesties and his Counsailes carefull head apprended them, the law plainely did diciphper them, justice gave judgement on them, and death made an end of them: but to come to their Araignment, and to deliver the manner of their behaviour, after they went from the Tower by water and come to Westminster before they came into the hall, they made some halfe howres stay, or more in the Star chamber, whether being brought, and remaining til the Court was all ready to heare them, and according to the lawe to give judgement on them, it was strange to notice their carriage even in their verie countenances: Some hanging downe the heade, as if their hearts were full of doggedness, and other forcing a sterne looke as if they would feare death, with a frowne, never seeming to pray, except it were by the dozen, upon their beades, and taking Tabacco, as if that hanging were no trouble to them, saying little but in commendation of their conceited religion, craving mercy of neyther God nor the king for their offences, and making their Consciences, as it were as wide as the worlde; and to the verie gates of Hell, to be the cause of their hellish courses to make a worke meritorious.

Now being come into the hall, and upon the scaffold at the barre standing to aunswere to their inditements, They all pleaded not guiltie, but were all found guiltie, Digby without craving mercie or favour, of either God, or the King made onely five worldy requests, that his wife might have her jointer, his children the lands intailed by his father his sisters theire legasies in his hand unpaid; his debts paid, and for his death, to bee beheaded, and not hanged.

Robert Winter in like manner thinkeing himselfe alreadie halfe a Saint for his whole villanie, said little to any purpose, that eyther made shew of sorrow, or sought mercy, but onely made a request to the king for mercy towards his Brother, in regarde of his offence as he saide, thorough his onely perswasion.

His brother sayed little, but with a guiltie conscience, swallowed up a concealed griefe, with little shew of sorrow for that time.

Grant stubborne in his idolatrie, seemed nothing penitent for his villanie, asked little mercy, but as it were careles of grace received the doome of his defeat.

The younger Winter said little, but to excuse the fowlenes of his fact, in being drawn in by his brother, and not of his own plotting, with little talke to little purpose troubled the time the lesser while.

Ruckwood out of a studied speech would faine have made his bringing uppe and breeding in idolatrie, to have been some excuse to his villanie, but a faire talke could not helpe a fowle deed, and therefore being found guiltie of the treason, had his judgement with the rest of the traytors.

Now after their condemnation and judgement, being sent back to the Tower, there they remayned till the Thurseday following; upon sleddes and hurdles they were drawne into Powles Churchyearde; Fowre of them, vz. Everarde Digbie, the elder Winter, Grant, and Bates, of whome I forgat to speake having no great matter to speake of, but onely that being a villanie, and hoping of advancement by the same, he had the rewarde of a traytor.

Now these four being drawne to the Scaffolde, made one purpose for their execution. First went up Digbie a man of a goodly peersonage, and a manly aspect, yet might a warie Eye in the change of his countenaunce, beholde an inwarde feare of death, for his colour grew pale and his eie heavie, notwithstanding that hee enforced him selfe, to speake as stoutly as hee could, his speech, was not long and to little good purpose onely that his belied conscience, being but indeed a blinded conceit, had led him into this offence, which in respect of his religion alias in deede idolatrie, hee held no offence but in respect of the law he held an offence for which hee asked forgivenesse of God, of the king, and the whole kingdome, and so with vaine, and superstitious consoling of himself betook him to his Latine prayers, mumbling to himselfe, refusing to have any prayers of any, but of the Romish Catholicks, went up the Ladder and with the helpe of the hangman made an end of his wicked daies in this world.

After him went Winter, up to the Scaffold where he used few words to anie good effect, without asking mercie of either God or the king for his offence, went up the ladder, and making a few prayers to himselfe staide not long for his excution.

After him went Graunt, who abhominably blinded with his horrible idolatrie, though he confessed his offence to bee hainous, yet would faine have excused it by his conscience for Religion a bloodie religion, to make so bloody a conscience, but better that his bloode and all such as hee was, should bee shed by the justice of the law, then the bloode of many thousands to have been shedde by his villanie, without lawe or justice but to the purpose, having used a few eidle wordes to ill effect, hee was as his Fellowes before hm, ledde the way to the Halter: and so after his crossing of himself, to the last parte of his tragedie.

Last of them came Bates, who seemed sorie for his offence, and asked forgiveness of God, and the king, and of the whole kingdome, prayed to God for the preservation of them all, and as hee sayed onely for his love to his Maister, drawne to forget his duety to God, his king and Countrie, and therefore was now drawne from the Tower to Paules Churchyeard, and there hanged and quartered for his treacherie. Thus ended that dayes busines.

The next day being Friday were drawne from the Tower to the old Palace in Westminster over against the Parliament house, Thomas Winter the yonger brother, Ruckewoode, Cayes and Faulks the Miner, justly called the Devill of the Vault for had hee not beene a Devill incarnate, he had never conceived so villanous a thought, nor been employed in so damnable an action.

The next day being Friday were drawn from the Tower to the olde pallace in Westminster, Thomas Winter, Rookewoode Caies and Fulkes, where Winter first being brought to the Scaffolde, made little speech, but seeming after a sort as it were sorry for his offence, and yet crossing himselfe, as though those were wardes to put by the Devils Stoccadoes, having already made a wounde in his soule, of which, he had not yet a full feeling, protesting to die a true Catholicke as he said; with a very pale and dead colour went uppe the ladder and after a swing or two with a halter, to the quartering block was drawn, and there quicklie dispatched.

Next came Rouckwood, who made a speech of some longer time, confessing his offence to God, in seeking to shedde blood, and asking therefore mercy of his divine Majestie, his offence to the King, of whose Majiestiee likewise humbly asked forgivenes, his offence to the whole state of whom in generall he asked forgivenesse, beseeching God to blesse the king, the Queene, and all his royal Progenie, and that they might long live to raigne in peace, and happiness over this kingdom, but last of all to marre all the pottage with one filthy weede to mar this good prayers with an il conclusion he praised God to make the king a Catholike, otherwise a Papist, which God for his mercy ever forbid and so beseeching the King to bee good to his wife and children, protesting to die in his Idolatry, a Romish Catholicke, hee went uppe the ladder, and hanging till he was almost dead, was drawne to the blocke, where he gave his last gaspe.

After him came Caies, who like a desperate villaine using little speech, which small or no shew of repentance, wente sloutlie up the ladder, where not staying the Hangmans torture, turne himself of with such a leape, that with the swing, he brake the Halter, but after his fall, was quicklie drawne to the blocke, and thre was quicklie devided into foure partes.

Last of all came the great Devill of all, Faulkes alias Johnson, who shoulde have put fire to the powder. His body being weake with torture and sickness, he was scarse able to goe up the ladder, but yet with much adoe, by the helpe of the Hangman, went hie enough to breake his neck with the fall who made no long speech, but after a sort seeming to be sorie for his offence, asked a kinde of forgivenes, of the King, and the State for his bloodie intent, with his crosses and his idle ceremonies, made his end upon the gallowes, and the blocke, to the great joy of the beholders that the land was ended of so wicked a villanie.

Thus have I ended my discourse uppon the Arraignement, and execution of these eight traitors executed upon thursdaie, and Friday last past in paules church-yard and the old pallace at westminster.

Now thre is certaine report of the execution done on mundaie being the 27. of Januarie in the citie of Worcester, upon one Perkins and his man, for the receiving of traitors. God be blessed for it and continue the justice of law to be executed upon all such rebellious and traitorious wretches as either plot such villanies, conceale such treasons, or relieve such traitors, for since the betraying of the Lord of heaven and earth, was there ever such a hellish plot practised in the world? If the Pope were not a verie Divill, and these Jesuites, or rather Jebusites; and Satanical Semenaries, verie spirites of wicked nesse that whisper in the ears of Eves to bring a world of Adams to distruction how could nature be so senceles or reason so graceles as to subject wit so to will as to run all headlong to confusion? Is this a rule of religion or rather of a legio, where the Sinagogue of Sathan sat in counsaile for the worlds destruction, for the satisfaction of lowzie humour or bloudy devotion or hope of honour, or to make waie to some mad fury to bring the most flourshing kingdome on the earth to the most desolation in the world, to kill at one blow or with one blast, King, Queene, Prince and Peere Bishop, Judge, and Magistrate to the ruine of the land, and utter shame to the whole world, and left naked to the inuasion of anie enimie: is this a holy father that begets such wicked children? Is this religion where is no touch of charitie? or is there anie sparke of Grace, in these priestes that so poison the soules, and breake the neckes of so many people.

Ignorance in the simple and Idolatrie in the subtil, take cerremonies for certainties superstition for religion envie for zeale, and murther for charitie what can that church be but hell where the devill sings such masses: servus servorum saies hee that would be Dominus dominorum servant of servants, that would be maister of maisters; is not he a cunning heards-man, that can make one painted cow, or printed Bull give him more milke, than many a Heard of better kine: are not these sweete Notes to bee taken in the nature of the Popish government, kill princes; sowe seditions, maintaine bawdie houses, blinde the simple, abuse the honest, bereave the innocent, sweare and forsweare, so it be for the popes to profite, the Church will absolve you, and if you misse the marke so hit the mischiefe you shoote at, you shall be a hanging Saint, till you bee taken downe to the Devill. Oh fine perswasions, that infinite sinnes by numbered prayers, inward curses, by outward crossings, an offence against God by a pardon from man, should be beleeved to be helpful. A child cannot conceive it, a wise man cannot disgest it, and surely none but either blind women or mad men can beleeve it. If a man would but a little looke into their idolatries, hee should see a worlde of such mockeries, as would make him both laugh at their fooleries, and abhor their villanies. Their kissing of babies, their kneeling to wooden Ladies, their calling to Saintes that cannot heare them, their praying by the dozen, their taking of penance, their pilgrimages to idols, their shavings and their washings, their confessions and their crossings, and their divelish devises to decive the simple of their comfort. These with a worlde of such trickes, as would make Jacke an Apes a fine jugler; He that could see them with that cleare eye, that can judge betwixt light and darkness, woulde, if they were his friendes, be sorry for them, if his enemies, laugh at them, and howsoever leave them, and say as he may say, that Papistrie is meere Idolatrie, the Pope an incarnate Devill, his Church a Synagogue of Satan, and his priestes the verie locustes of the earth. But let us leave them to their loathsome puddles, and let us be thankefull to Almightie God, for the cleare water of life that in his holy worde, wee receive from the fountaine of his greacious mercie and let us a little looke into the differeence betwixte the Traiterous Papist, that dieth for his vallanie, and the faithful Protestant that dyeth for the truth of his conscience in the beliefe of the worde of God.

The trayterous Papist will pull downe princes, and subvert Kingdoms; murther and poyson whome they can not command; The faithful protestant praieth for princes, and the peace of the people, and will endure a banishment, but hate rebellion. The proud papist will shewe intemperance in passsion, while the humble protestant will embrace affliction with patience. The Protestant cries up to GOD for mercie for his sinnes, the Papist gives authoritie to sinne, when before the offence the pardon is purchased.

I say, was it not a strange speech of Digbie, through the blindnesse of his bewitched witte, that to bring the kingdome into the popish Idolatrie, hee cared not to roote out all his posteritie.

Oh the misery of these blinded people, forsake the true God of heaven and earth to submit their service to the Devill of the world, be Traitours to their gratious Princes to serve a proude ungratious prelate, loose their lands, goods, begger their wives and children, loose their own lives with an open shame, and leave an infamy to their name for ever, onely to obey the command of a cunning Foxe, that lyng in his denne praieth on all the geese that he can light on, and in the proude belief to be made Saints will hazard their soules to goe to the Devill.

But how many millions hath this Devill inchaunted, and how many kinges hath he ruinated, and how many massacres hath he plotted, and how many soules hath he sent to damnation? God for his mercy cut him off or open the eies of all them Christian princes, that they may agree together and pull him down. For during his pride, Princes that are of his Religion, will bee but as Copoieholders to his Countenance, Souldiers that fight not under his banner, shall be as shake rags to his Armie; Lawyers except they pleade in his right, shall have but curses for their fees: Divines, if not of his opinion shall be excommunicated out off his Church, Merchantes that bring not him commodities shall keepe no shops, in his Sanctuarie, nor Beggars that pray not for his Monarchie, shall have any almes in his Basket and therefore I hope, that God will so wipe off the skales from the eyes of the blinde; than both one and other, Souldier and lawyer, Divine and Laye man, rich and poore, will so lay their heades, their heartes and handes, and their purses together, that where as hee hath beene long in rising and could not sitte fast, when hee was uppe, shall take a fall of sodaine, and never rise againe, when hee is downe to which prayer I hope all true Christians will say Amen

FINIS

Account of the Miracle of Garnet's Straw,

Trial of the Conspirators, 1606.

After the execution of Oldcorne and Garnet, the most absurd tales of miracles performed, in vindication of their innocence, and in honour of their martyrdom, were industriously circulated by the Jesuits in England and in foreign countries. Thus it was said,—and the story is repeated by Father More, in his history of the Jesuits*, by Ribadeneira in his Catalogue of Martyrs, and other Catholic historians, —that after Oldcorne had been embowelled, according to the usual sentence in cases of treason, his entrails continued burning sixteen successive days, though great quantities of water were poured upon them to extinguish the flames ;—the sixteen days denoting the number of years that he laboured in propagating the Catholic religion in England. Father More also relates, that from that particular spot, on the lawn at Hendlip, where Garnet and Oldcorne last set their feet before their removal, " a new and hitherto unknown species of grass grew up into the exact shape of an imperial crown, and remained for a long time without being trodden down by the feet of passengers, or eaten up by the cattle." It was asserted too, that, immediately after Garnet's execution, a spring of oil suddenly burst forth at the western end of St. Paul's, on the spot where the saint was martyred.

But among these absurd illustrations of the superstition and credulity of the times, the miracle which was most insisted upon as a supernatural confirmation of the Jesuit's innocence and martyrdom was the story of Father Garnet's Straw. It is related at great length, and with a full detail of circumstances, by Eudaemon-Joannes, by Father

* Mori Hist. Soc. Jesu. p. 335.

† Bishop Hall's Sermon before the King, Sep, 19, 1624.

More, and almost all the earlier historians of the English mission. In Spain, a "Ballad of the Death of Father Garnet," with the legend and figure of the miraculous straw, was circulated generally through the provinces, and excited so much attention that the English ambassador was directed by James to require its suppression by the Spanish government *. The original fabricator of this miracle was supposed to be one John Wilkinson, a young Catholic, who, at the time of Garnet's trial and execution, was about to pass over into France, to commence his studies at the Jesuits' college at St. Omers. Some time after his arrival there, Wilkinson was attacked by a dangerous disease, from which there was no hope of his recovery; and while in this state he gave utterance to the story, which Eudaemon-Joannes relates in his own words, as follows :—"The day before Father Garnet's execution, my mind was suddenly impressed (as by some external impulse), with a strong desire to witness his death, and to bring home with me some relique of him. I had at that time conceived so certain a persuasion that my desire would be gratified, that I did not for a moment doubt that I should witness some immediate testimony from God in favour of the innocence of his saint; though as often as the idea occurred to my mind, I endeavoured to drive it away, that I might not vainly appear to tempt Providence by looking for a miracle where it was not necessarily to be expected. Early the next morning I betook myself to the place of execution, and, arriving there before any other person, stationed, myself close to the scaffold, though I was afterwards somewhat forced from my position as the crowd increased." Having then described the details of the execution, he proceeds thus :—" Garnet's limbs having been divided into four parts, and placed together

• Winwood's Memorials, vol, ii. p. 336.

with the head in a basket, in order that they might be exhibited according to law in some conspicuous place, the crowd began to disperse. I then again approached close to the scaffold, and stood between the cart and the place of execution; and as I lingered in that situation, still burning with the desire of bearing away some relique, that miraculous ear of straw, since so highly celebrated, came, I know not how, into my hand. A considerable quantity of dry straw had been thrown with Garnet's head and quarters from the scaffold into the basket; but whether this ear came into my hand from the scaffold or from the basket, I cannot venture to affirm: this only I can truly say, that a straw of this kind was thrown towards me before it had touched the ground. This straw I afterwards delivered to Mrs. N., a matron of singular Catholic piety, who inclosed it in a bottle, which being rather shorter than the straw, it became slightly bent. A few days afterwards Mrs. N. showed the straw in the bottle to a certain noble person, her intimate acquaintance, who, looking at it attentively, at length said,' l can see nothing in it but a man's face.' Mrs. N. and myself being astonished at this unexpected exclamation, again and again examined the ear of the straw, and distinctly perceived in it a human countenance, which others also coming in as casual spectators, or expressly called by us as witnesses, also beheld at that time. This is, as God knoweth, the true history of Father Garnet's Straw."

Such is Wilkinson's circumstantial account of the miracle. In those days of ignorance and superstition, when the public mind was in a state of great excitement respecting Garnet, it was a story well calculated to attract attention. Among the lower orders of the people in particular, the prodigy was circulated with much diligence, and believed with implicit confidence; while the higher class of Catholics who knew better, or ought to have known better, chose to foster the delusion. The story, which was originally confined to the vulgar, gained ground by frequent repetition, until at last, and within a year from the time of Garnet's death, by that love of the wonderful, and that tendency to exaggeration, which, are the natural results of popular ignorance, it was declared, and currently believed, by Catholics both in England and abroad, that an undoubted sign from heaven had been given for the establishment of Garnet's innocence. Crowds of persons of all ranks daily flocked to see the miraculous straw. The Spanish ambassador saw and believed ; and the ambassador from the Archduke, not only saw at the time, but long afterwards testified what he had seen by a written certificate, which is published *verbatim* by Father More*. In process of time the success of the imposture encouraged those who contrived it, or who had an interest in upholding it, to add considerably to the miracle as it was at first promulgated. Wilkinson, and the original observers of the prodigy, merely represented that the appearance of a face was shown on so diminutive a scale, upon the husk or sheath of a single grain, as scarcely to be visible unless specifically pointed out; but a much more imposing image was afterwards discovered. Two faces appeared upon the middle part of the straw, both surrounded with rays of glory; the head of the principal figure, which represented Garnet, was encircled with a martyr's crown, and the face of a cherub appeared in the midst of his beard. In this improved state of the miracle, the story was circulated in England, and excited the most profound and universal attention ; and thus depicted, the

* More's Hist. Soc. Jesu, p. 330.

miraculous straw became generally known throughout the Christian world. The following representation exactly describe the prodigy in its original and in its improved state. The latter figure formed the frontispiece to the Apology of Eudaemon-Joannes:—

Depictions of Garnet's Straw

"I had thought (says Bishop Hall in a contemporary letter, alluding to the "noise which Garnet' straw had made")—I had thought that our age had too many grey hairs, and with time, experience, and with experience, craft, not to have descried a juggler; but now I see by its simplicity it declines to its second childhood. I only wonder how Fawkes and Catesby escaped the honour of saints and privilege of miracles."

Such, however, was the extent to which this ridiculous fable was believed, and so great was the scandal which it occasioned among the Protestants, that Archbishop Bancroft was commissioned by the Privy Council to call before him such persons as had been most active in propagating it, and, if possible, to detect and punish the impostors.

The archbishop commenced the inquiry in November, 1606, and a great number of persons were examined; but as Wilkinson, who was supposed to be the chief impostor, was abroad, and as the inquiry completely exposed the fraud, though the hand that effected it remained undiscovered, no proceedings seem to have been taken to punish the parties concerned in it. It appeared upon this inquiry, that "Mrs. N., the matron of singular Catholic piety," mentioned with so much parade in the declaration made by Wilkinson at St. Omers, was the wife of one Hugh Griffiths, a tailor, with whom Wilkinson lodged; and the "noble person, her intimate acquaintance," who was supposed to have first seen the face of Garnet in the straw, turned out to be a footman named Laithwaite, in the service of a lady of quality. Griffiths and Laithwaite were separately examined by the archbishop, and varied materially in their accounts of the discovery. The tailor, in his first examination, on the 27th of November, stated that "Wilkinson had brought home the straw from Garnet's execution, and given it to him, and that he had delivered it to his wife, charging her to take great care of it, and to enclose it in something which might prevent the spots of blood upon it from becoming effaced." He further stated, that his wife, with the assistance of Wilkinson, enclosed it in a glass bottle. He at first said that this was done about nine or ten days after Garnet's execution; but in a subsequent examination, he corrected himself, saying that, upon consideration, he recollected that it was done on the very day on which the execution took place; but that, as Wilkinson lodged in the house for seven weeks afterwards, he might have subsequently had it in his possession. At the time of the enclosure of the straw in the bottle, and for some time afterwards, he said that nothing was seen of the face. Griffiths then went on to depose, " that about the 18th of September, nearly five months after Garnet's death, he was looking attentively at the ear of straw (which he gives no reason for not having done before, except that he had not leisure), and thought he perceived a face depicted on it, which he immediately pointed out to his wife and one Thomas Laithwaite, then present." Laithwaite was then examined, who contradicted Griffiths materially, inasmuch as he claimed for himself the honour of having made the first discovery, which was indeed originally ascribed to him by Wilkinson. "I was one day sitting," says Laithwaite*, "by the fire in Griffith's house, and looking intently at the straw, when I thought I saw a man's head upon it. The day. was dark and cloudy, so that, as I sat in the inner part of the room, the appearance was not very distinct; for which reason, I took it to the window, where I discerned the face beyond all doubt. Mrs. Griffiths wondered why I examined the bottle so industriously ; upon which I pointed out the face to her, and afterwards to her husband and to Wilkinson. It was visible to all three of them, and all of them declared that they had never seen it before." Previously to the institution of this inquiry, the straw had been withdrawn or destroyed;

---

* Examination, Dec. 2, 1606.

but several persons were examined by the Archbishop of Canterbury who had repeatedly seen it, and were therefore fully capable of describing it. Among these one Robert Barnes, a gentleman of Cambridgeshire, declared *, " that the straw having been shewn to him by Griffith's wife, he had discoursed of it to several persons when walking in St. Paul's, and told them at the time, as his real opinion was, that it seemed to him a thing of no moment; that he saw nothing in the straw but what any painter could readily have drawn there; that he considered it so little like a miracle, that he never asked the woman how it was done. The face," he said, " seemed to him to be described by a hair or some very slender instrument; and that, upon the whole, he saw nothing whatever wonderful in the thing, except that it was possible to draw a man's face so distinctly upon so very small a space." A painter, named Francis Bowen, who had been shewn the straw by Garnet's devoted friend, Anne Vaux, was also examined by the archbishop. He made a drawing of the straw from recollection, upon the margin of the paper which contained his examination, a copy of which drawing was published in Dr. Abbott's Antilogia, from which work the above illustration of it is engraved. Bowen said " he thought that beyond all doubt a skilful artist might depict upon a straw a human countenance quite as artificially as that which he had seen, and more so; and therefore that he believed it quite possible for an impostor to have fabricated this pretended miracle." With respect to the exaggeration of the miracle after this period, the testimony of Griffiths himself, given in his first examination, is sufficiently conclusive. "As far as I could discover," said he, "the face in the straw was no more like

* Examination, Nov. 27, 1606.
t Examination, Nov. 27,1606.

Garnet than it was like any other man with a long beard; and truly, I think, that no one can assert that the face was like Garnet, because it was so small; and if any man saith that the head was surrounded with a light, or rays, he saith that which is untrue."

Many other persons were examined, but no distinct evidence could be obtained as to the immediate author of the imposture. It was quite clear, however, that the face might have been described on the straw by Wilkinson, or under his direction, during the interval of many weeks which occurred between the time of Garnet's death and the discovery of the pretended miracle in the tailor's house. At all events, the inquiry had the desired effect of checking the progress of the popular delusion in England; and upon this the Privy Council took no further proceedings against any of the parties, wisely considering that the whole story was far too ridiculous to form the subject of serious prosecution and punishment. Some apology is perhaps due to the reader for thus bringing forward in the 19th century the idle and foolish delusions of a former age. But the fable of Garnet's Straw is not altogether a useless legend. It illustrates in a remarkable manner the prevalence of gross superstition, not only among the lower orders of Catholics of that day, but also among well-instructed and enlightened Jesuits, such as L'Heureux and Father More. The latter were no doubt influenced by a strong disposition to remove the imputation which Garnet's conviction had thrown upon the sanctity of their order by thus imposing upon the multitude the belief of a

Divine interference in his favour; but it is most probable that they were also believers in this miracle. "Credulity and imposture," says Lord Bacon*, "are nearly allied; and a readiness to believe and to deceive are constantly united in the same person."

* De Augmentis Scientiarum.

-Jardine, David, Criminal Trials, Volume 2, Part 1, 1835, p.355.

Investigations noted in the Calendar of State Papers Domestic: James I, Parliament, 1603-1610.

The Investigations of Parliament

Martis, 5 Novembris, 1605

Gunpowder Plot.

This last Night the Upper House of Parliament was searched by Sir Tho. Knevett; and one Johnson, Servant to Mr. Thomas Percye, was there apprehended; who had placed Thirty-six Barrels of Gunpowder in the Vault under the House, with a Purpose to blow King, and the whole Company, when they should there assemble.

Afterwards divers other Gentlemen were discovered to be of the Plot.

- Journal of the House of Commons. Volume 1, 1547-1629, 1802.

November, 1605.

Nov. 5.

[Tower.]   First examination of Guy Faukes, under the assumed name of John Johnson. Particulars of his past life; served Thos. Percy; details of the intended Plot; refuses to reveal the names of the conspirators. [G. Plot Bk., No. 6.]

[Nov. 5.]   7. Notes [by Sir Edw. Coke,] on the examination of Johnson, alias Faukes; with memoranda of the contents of Mrs. Vaux's letter [found upon him], &c. Indorsed with notes of Faukes' confessions.

Nov. 5.   8. Proclamation for the search and apprehension of Thos. Percy

Nov. 5.

Lambeth.   Archbp. Bancroft to Salisbury. Thos. Percy was met riding towards Croydon that morning, and reported that "all London is up in arms." [G. Plot. Bk., No. 7.]

Nov. 5.

Ware.   Thos. Swyned, Postmaster at Ware, to the Same. In answer to his letter, informs him that Percy has not passed northward, but that he and his brother came from the North, on Saturday last. [Ibid., No. 8.]

Nov. 5.   Examination of Isabel, servant of -- Cole. Knows Thos. Percy; he visited Carden, a recusant, whom she formerly served; saw him this day, at 8 a.m., come down by Dowgate, and pass towards Colharbour, with his man. [Ibid., No. 234.]

Nov. 5.

Serjeants' Inn.   Lord Chief Justice Popham to Salisbury. Thos. Percy is escaped towards Gravesend. Measures taken for his apprehension. [Ibid., No. 9.]

Nov. 5.

Tower.   Sir Wm. Waad to the Same. Thanks God on the knees of his soul "that this monstrous wickedness is discovered." All his prisoners are safe and shall be well guarded. [Ibid., No. 12.]

Nov. 5.   Same to the Same. The people exclaim against the Spaniards and their Ambassdors. Precautions to be taken against a tumult. [Ibid., No. 13.]

Nov. 5.

Tower.   Same to the Same. His cousin, Sir Edw. Yorke, met Percy going northward in disguise. [Ibid., No. 14.]

Nov. 5.

St. Giles in the Fields.   Justice E. Grange to the Same. Percy's house searched, and John Roberts taken in it. Percy's wife says she has not seen her husband since Midsummer, as he serves the Earl of Northumberland. [Ibid., No. 15.]

[Nov. 5.]   9. "Points and names of persons discovered in the papers found in Percy's house."

[Nov. 5.]   10. "Points mentioned in the papers and letters found in Percy's house, likely to be the priest's, Roberts, which was taken there."

Nov. 5.

St. Martin's, London.   Geo. Southaick to Levinus Munck (Salisbury's Secretary). Has been riding day and night the last 8 days, to discover the plotters. Asks warrants for their apprehension. Their correspondence abroad, &c. [G. Plot Bk., No. 16.]

Nov. 5.   11. Examination of Rob. Rookes, servant of Ambrose Rokewood, of Coldham Hall, Suffolk, as to his master's proceedings.

Nov. 5 ?   12. Notes of persons seen in Amb. Rokewood's house.

Nov. 5.   13. Examination of Elizabeth, wife of Edw. More, as to parties lodging in her house-[Robert] Keyes, [Ambrose] Rokewood, and Chris. Wright.

Nov. 5.   14. Examination of Gideon Gibbins, porter. He and 2 others carried 3,000 billets to the vaults under the Parliament House, which Johnson (Guy Faukes) piled up.

Nov. 5.   15. Examination of Wm. Grantham, servant to Jos. Hewett. Purchase of hats, &c., by [Chris.] Wright.

Nov. 5 & 6.

Serjeants' Inn.   Lord Chief Justice Popham to Salisbury. Has given warrants to arrest two suspicious persons. Mrs. [Elizabeth] Vaux expected something was about to take place, and Gerard and Walley, the Jesuits, make her house their chief resort. [Sir Rich.] Wenman and Lady Tasburgh know of the letter. [See Nov. 18.] Particulars of Chris. Wright, Ambrose Rokewood, Keyes, Winter, Walley, and Strange, the Jesuits. (Footnote *) There are letters from abroad, at Fortescue's house by the Wardrobe. [G. Plot Bk., No. 10.] Incloses,

I. Deposition of Hen. Tatnall. He met 2 gentlemen that morning near Lincoln's Inn, and one said "God's woundes! we are wonderfully besett, and all ys marred." Nov. 5. [Ibid., No. 11.]

Nov. 6.   16. Declaration of John Cradock, cutler. He engraved sword hilts with the Passion of Christ, for Rokewood, Chris. Wright, and another. Catesby and Tyrwhit were often with them.

Nov. 6.   17. Examination of Hen. Griffith, tailor. A letter was brought to his house, a few days before, for Johnson, but he refused it, not knowing such a person.

Nov. 6.

Forenoon. Tower. Examination of John Johnson (Guy Faukes) as to the storing of powder, &c. in the Parliament cellar,-his connections abroad,- whether Mr. Percy would have allowed the Earl of Northumberland to perish, &c. He refuses to inculpate any person, saying, "youe would have me discover my frendes: the giving warning to one overthrew us all;" signed "John Johnson." [G. Plot Bk., No.16A.]

Nov. 6.   The King to the Lords Commissioners [for the Plot]. Proposes interrogatories to be put to the prisoner. Suggests whether he be not the author of a "cruel pasquil" against himself, for assuming the "name of Britain" (King of Great Britain), in which his destruction was prophesied. "The gentler tortours are to be first usid unto him, et sic per gradus ad ima tenditur, and so God speede youre goode worke." [In the King's own hand. Ibid., No. 17.]

Nov. 6.

Afternoon. Answers of John Johnson [Faukes] to the above interrogatories. [Ibid., No. 19.]

[Nov. 6.]   18. Proofs [by Sir Edw. Coke] against Thos. Percy; taken from Johnson's (Faukes) examinations of Nov. 5 and 6.

Nov. 6.   Examinations of Ellen, wife of Andrew Bright, and of Roger Neck, her servant, upon their letting to Percy and his man the vault under the Parliament House. [G. Plot Bk., No. 24.]

Nov. 6.

Ferrybridge.   John Lepton to Salisbury. Has not heard that "that miserable man" (Percy) has gone northward. Has written to the Council at York, to stop him on the Borders, or in the northern ports. One Johnson, a seminary priest, lived near Howden, Yorkshire, and may be the same with "that mercilesse traytor" Johnson (Guy Faukes). [Ibid., No. 36.]

Nov. 6.

Serjeants' Inn.   Lord Chief Justice Popham to the Same. Percy supposed to be in London. The Thames to be guarded. [Ibid., No. 20.] Incloses,

I. List of suspected persons,-Rob. Catesby, Amb. Rokewood, Thos. Winter, [Rob.] Keyes, John and Chris. Wright, and [John] Grant; with notes of where they are likely to be found. [Ibid., No. 20 A.]

[Nov. 6 ?] Note of persons who supped at Wm. Patrick's house with Rob. Catesby, at the beginning of the Term. [Ibid., No. 132.]

Nov. 6. Examination of Rich. Browne, as to his connection with Chris. Wright. [Ibid., No. 26.]

Nov. 6.

Combe. Lord Harrington to Salisbury. Horses have been seized in Warwickshire. Asks directions about the Princess (Elizabeth), fearing she may be seized, should a rebellion take place. [Ibid., No. 21.] Incloses,

I. Mr. Benock to Lord Harrington. All his horses have been seized in the night, by [John] Grant, of Norbrook, and the papists; "it cannot be but some great rebellion is at hand." [Ibid., No. 22.]

Nov. 6.

Coventry. Lord Harrington to Salisbury. Reports of troubles spreading. He has removed the Princess Elizabeth to Coventry, where the people are very loyal. [G. Plot Bk., No. 23.]

Nov. 6.

Warwick. Sheriff and Justices of Warwickshire to the Sheriff, &c., of Worcestershire. Inform them of the late assembly, and that Rob. Winter, Rob. Acton, Rob. Catesby, John Grant, and Amb. Rokewood are gone into Worcestershire. [Ibid., No. 35.]

Nov. 6.

Huddington. 19. Rob. Winter to Mr. Smallpece. Great events are going on. Begs him to stir up his father [in-law, John] Talbot, to pray for them and send them friends. [Half of it torn away. Found in Holbeach House.]

Nov. 6.

Warwick. Sheriff and Justices of Warwickshire to Salisbury. The company that seized the horses are 100 horse strong; two of their servants have been taken and examined. [G. Plot Bk., No. 26.] Inclose,

I. Examination of John Fowes, servant to Rob. Winter. Particulars of the assembling of the plotters at Mr. Talbot's house, whence they went to Lady Catesby's, and thence into Warwickshire. Warwick, Nov. 6. [Ibid., No. 27.]

II. Examination of Rob. Conyers, servant to Amb. Rokewood. He came to meet his master at Mr. Grant's, Norbrook. [Ibid., No. 28.]

Nov. 7.

Warwick. Sheriff, &c., of Warwickshire to Salisbury. Send up examinations. Three trunks of armour taken. Sir Rob. Digby has assisted in taking prisoners. [Ibid., No. 42.] Inclose,

I. Examination of Chris. Ater, servant to Amb. Rokewood. He gives contradictory accounts of himself; came from London to Mr. Grant's, to meet his master. Nov. 6. [Ibid., No. 29.]

II. Examination of Geo. Bartlett, servant to Rob. Catesby. Followed his master from London to Rob. Winter's, in Worcestershire; Grant and Rokewood are intimate with his master; knew nothing of an intended plot. Nov. 6. [Ibid., No. 30.]

III. Examination of Wm. Petty, servant to Rob. Catesby. Came to meet his master at Mr. Grant's, at Norbrook. [Ibid., No. 31.]

IV. Examination of Thos. Carpenter, of Norton, labourer. Particulars of the assembly at Norbrook; a hunting party feigned to be intended; Grant and Wright asked him to join them, and "stand for the Catholique cause," but he refused. Nov. 6. [Ibid., No. 32.]

V. Examination of Rob. Abraham, retainer to Sir Everard Digby. Further particulars; he left the assembly privately, fearing mischief. Nov. 6. [Ibid., No. 33.]

VI. Examination of Fras. Grant, gent., of Norbrook, brother to John Grant. Very many gentlemen have lately resorted to his brother's house. Nov. 6. [Ibid., No. 34.]

Nov. 7 ? List of conspirators; with reports, by James and Simon Digby, of a speech of Sir Everard Digby, on Nov. 5, about an intention to cut Catholics' throats, and of his urging them to go with him, which they refused; with a note that George Prince, servant at the inn at Dunchurch, heard some one say that they were all betrayed. [G. Plot Bk., No. 233.]

Nov. 7.

Westminster. 20. Proclamation denouncing as traitors, Thos. Percy, Robt. Catesby, Ambrose Rokewood, of Coldham Hall, Suffolk, Thos. Winter, brother of Rob. Winter, of Huddington, Worcestershire, Edw. [John] Grant, of Norbrook, John Wright, Chr. Wright, and Rob. Ashfield, conspirators in the Gunpowder Plot. Printed.

Nov. 7.

Westminster. Duplicate of the above. [Proc. Coll., No. 4.]

Nov. 7 ? 21. Address by Geo. Blackwell, Archpriest, to the Roman Catholic priests in England, on the discovery of the Gunpowder Plot. That it is a detestable action, contrary to Scripture, to the decrees of the Councils, and to the orders of their superiors. They are to exhort Catholics to obedience and peaceable behaviour.

Nov. 7.

Tower. Examination of Guy Faukes. The conspiracy began eighteen months before; was confined to five persons at first, then to two; and afterwards five more were added, who all swore secrecy; he refuses, on account of his oath, to accuse any; they intended to place the Princess Elizabeth on the throne, and marry her to an English Catholic. Signed at the foot of each page "Guido Faukes." [G. Plot Bk., No. 37.]

[Nov. 7.] Detailed account of the discovery of the Plot, up to the third examination of Guy Faukes. [Corrected by Salisbury, and written by his Secretary, Levinus Munck. Seemingly drawn up to be read to the Council, with Guy's confession. Ibid., No. 129.]

Nov. 7. Examination of Susan Whynniard. Her house close by the Parliament House, let to Hen. Ferrers, of Warwickshire, was assigned, in March 1604, with her consent, to Thos. Percy, at the entreaty of Mr. [Dud.] Carleton, Mr. Epsley, and others of the Earl of Northumberland's men. She also assigned to him, a year afterwards, the vault under the Parliament House, formerly let to Mr. Skynner, alias Bright. [Ibid., No. 39.]

Nov. 7. Examinations of Roger James and John Shepherd, servants to Mrs. Whynniard, as to the letting of the house and vault, and their occupation and storing by Percy. [Ibid., No. 40.]

Nov. 7. Examinations of Dorothy Robinson, of Spur Alley, and Mr. Jackson, as to Chris. Wright's lodging in their houses. [Ibid., No. 41.]

Nov. 7.   Examination by George Lord Carew of Rob. Wilson, his tenant. He granted a lease of his house to Ambrose Rokewood resort of conspirators there, &c. [Ibid., No. 44.]

Nov. 7.

Doncaster, 9 A.M. T. Fotherley to the Earl of Northumberland. The charge of the Earl's horses and of his money, amounting to more than 3,000£., was committed by Thos. Percy to Lawson. [G. Plot Bk., No. 45.]

Nov. 7.

London.   Wm. Dale to the Earl of Salisbury. Report by Bartholomew Brown, of a speech made by a Page of the Archduke, that there would soon be wars throughout all England. [Ibid., No. 46.]

Nov. 7.

London.   23. John Chamberlain to Dud. Carleton. Hopes Lord [Northumberland] will escape arrest, but being nearly related to Percy, he is desired to remain in his house. Details of the Plot and its discovery. The Earl of Cumberland and Lady Knollys dead. 23. I. Copy of the letter to Lord Monteagle, warning him to be absent from Parliament.

Nov. 7.

Salisbury House.   24. J. Johnson to Mr. Percivall. Informs him of divers houses of recusants in St. John's Street; amongst them, Sir Hen. James's and Thomas Sleep's. Johnson (Faukes) was often at Sleep's house. There is a wonderful resort there, since his apprehension.

Nov. 7 ?   25. Information, that Faukes lodged two months ago, with Mrs. Herbert, now Mrs. Woodhouse, at the back of St. Clement's church. Percy, the two Wrights, Winter, Catesby, and others had secret correspondence with him there. She disliked it, suspecting him to be a priest; he was tall, with brown hair and auburn beard, and had plenty of money.

Nov. 8.

Daventry. 28. Sheriffs of Northamptonshire to the Same. Send examinations of several persons of Ledgers Ashby, relative to a concourse of horsemen there. Inclose,

28. I. Examination of John Myles. Carriage of pistols from Lady Catesby's to Warwick.

Nov. 7.

28. II. Examination of William Boyse. Overheard some horsemen at Lady Catesby's say they would not drink till they came to Lord Harrington's. Nov. 7.

28. III. Examination of Rich. Jackson. Gathering of armed horsemen and money at Lady Catesby's. Nov. 7.

28. IV. Examination of Bennett Leeson. He guided Catesby and others to Dunchurch, and Catesby's man to Rugby. Nov. 7.

28. v. Examination of Martha, wife of Thos. Bates. Her husband left her Nov. 5, taking five or six pistols with him, and ordered her to convey to Lady Catesby's certain trunks of armour, which had lain there since the late Queen's death. Nov. 8.

28. VI. Examination of Chris. Story, Thos. Bates's man, on his delivery of the said trunks and other armour, &c. Nov. 8.

Nov. 8.   29. Sir Fras. Bacon to Salisbury. Sends an examination about the work of a suspected papist. Thinks it "not good to neglect any thing at such a tyme." Incloses,

29. I. Examination of John Drake, servant to Thos. Reynolds, of Holborn, on Mr. Beard's remark about the Plot, that "It had been braue sport, yf it had gone forwards."

Nov. 8.   30. Ben. Jonson [the poet] to the Same. Has done his best to procure a fitting person to perform a certain business [to betray the actors in the Plot?], but many are removed and concealed; some say they must consult the Archpriest; thinks "they are all so enweaved in it as it will make 500 gent. lesse of the religion, within this weeke." Offers his own services, if a better person cannot be found.

Nov. 8.   31. Examination of Henry [Huddleston alias] Hurleston, of Paswick, Essex, son of Sir Edm. Huddleston, as to his previous proceedings; visit at Lady Vaux's; meeting with John Wright, Catesby, and Percy, &c.

Nov. 8.

Warwick.   32. Bailiffs, &c., of Warwick to the Council. Seizure of horses at Warwick Castle. Assembly of persons at Rob. Winter's house; they went to Lord Windsor's, and thence to Dudley Castle; the party sent against them is feeble, because of the absence of the Lieutenants, &c., in London. Their numbers are constantly increasing. At the foot is a list of the chief insurgents. Inclose,

I. Examination of Gertrude, wife of Rob. Winter, as to the persons that came to her house at Huddington. Nov. 6. They went away about sunrise; she heard no talk of rebellion. Nov. 7. [G. Plot Bk., No. 43.]

II. Examination of William Browne, servant to Rob. Winter, on the assembly at Winter's house. Nov. 7. [Ibid.]

Nov. 8.

Toddington. 33. Justices of Bedfordshire to Salisbury. Send up Story, Percy's servant, with examinations. Inclose,

33. I. Examination of John Story, servant to Percy. Proceedings of several conspirators; Percy and Wright passed in haste through Hockliffe, Bedfordshire, on Nov. 5th, where Story was awaiting them, with a relay of horses. Nov. 8.

33. II. Examination of Wm. Johnson servant of Rob. Keyes. His master serves Lord Mordaunt; he ordered him to wait at Hockliffe with a relay of horses, which has not yet been called for.

33. III. Memorandum that Wm. Johnson, being detained at Hockliffe, sent to Lady Mordaunt for directions, but she refused to meddle with any of Mr. Keyes' affairs.

[Nov. 8 ?] Petitions of Faghuy Offerrell and John Offerrell, Irishmen, to the Earl of Devonshire. A servant of Lord Mordaunt's engaged them to serve Rob. Catesby; they never saw him but once, nor had they entered his service; therefore beg they may not be involved in trouble, by his late treason. [G. Plot Bk., No. 239.]

Nov. 8.

Bridgetown. 34. Thos. Tempest to Lady Carew. Intelligence of the conspirators' proceedings in Warwickshire. Old Sir Fulk Greville raises the country for their apprehension. A package of popish vestments, crosses, &c., intercepted. The house at Clopton searched.

Nov. 8.

Sir Thos. Bennet's House. Anthony Visct. Montague to the Earl of Dorset, his father-in-law. Cares not for his imprisonment, but for the imputation of guilt involved; protests his innocence; entreats to be placed with him [Dorset], or at least to have an interview with him. [G. Plot Bk., No. 48 A.]

Nov. 8 ?   35. Deposition of Agnes Fortun, servant to the Duke of York, that Thos. Percy came to the Duke's lodgings about Nov. 1, made many inquiries as to the way into his chamber, where he rode abroad, how attended, &c.

Nov. 8.

Westminster.   Proclamation promising a reward for the apprehension of Thos. Percy. Printed. [Proc. Bk., p. 117.]

Nov. 8.

Gravesend.   36. Rich. Ferrers, Messenger of the King's Chamber, to Salisbury. Percy has been seen riding towards Rochester; the constable of Gravesend has gone to Dover in pursuit.

Nov. ?   37. Note of Percy's secret appearance at the last Stafford assizes. The Sheriff of Staffordshire and Sir Walter Leveson suspected to favour recusants. [See Nov. 12]

Nov. 8.

Tower.   Sir Wm. Waad to Salisbury. Faukes is in a "most stubborn and perverse humour, as dogged as if he were possessed." He promised to give a full account of the Plot, but now refuses. Lord Arundel, Sir Griffin Markham, and one Tresham, long a pensioner of the King of Spain, are suspicious persons. [G. Plot Bk., No. 48 B.]

[Nov. 8.]   38. Interrogatories [by Sir Edw. Coke], for the further examination of Guy Faukes, founded upon his deposition of Nov. 7. Indorsed with other queries relating to the Plot;-what foreign aid was expected; what were the designs of the conspirators as to the Princess Mary, whom, as English born, they intended to make Queen; whether Edw. Neville, titular Earl of Westmoreland, and the titular Lord Dacre, were connected with it, &c.

Nov. 8.

[Tower.]   Examination of Guy Faukes. A plot for the Catholic cause was first revealed to him eighteen months ago, by an Englishman in the Low Countries; details of preparing the vault; as they knew not how to seize Prince Charles,

they resolved to surprise the Princess Elizabeth, and make her Queen; they prepared, in her name, a proclamation against the Union of the Kingdoms, and in justification of their act, but without any declaration as to religion; they would have taken the Princess Mary, but knew not how; had sent down armour into Warwickshire, &c. [G. Plot Bk., No. 49.]

Nov. 8.

[Tower.]   Deposition of Guy Faukes. Thos. Winter first proposed a conspiracy to him; Catesby, Percy, and John Wright were next taken into the scheme, then Chris. Wright, afterwards Sir Everard Digby, Amb. Rokewood, Francis Tresham, John Grant, Rob. Keyes, and many others. Details of the Plot, the same as in the examinations. [Ibid., No. 101.]

[Nov. 8.]   Names of the first five conspirators, and of seven more afterwards admitted; taken from the above examination of Faukes, by Levinus Munck. [G. Plot Bk., No. 133.]

Nov. 9.

Tower.   Sir Wm. Waad to Salisbury. Has persuaded Faukes to disclose "all the secrets of his heart" to his Lordship only, "but not to be set down in writing." Undertakes to procure his acknowledgment and signature to his confession, by degrees. Advises Salisbury to speak with him alone. [Ibid., No. 53.]

Nov. 9.

[Tower.]   Declaration of Guy Faukes [made to Salisbury]. Further details of the Plot. It was communicated to Hugh Owen, the Jesuit, in Flanders. The conspirators met at the back of St. Clement's Inn. Gerard, the Jesuit, gave them the sacrament, to confirm their oath of secrecy, but knew not their purpose. They also met at Walley's [Garnet's] lodgings near Enfield. [On the 10th, this declaration was acknowledged before the Lords Commissioners, and is signed in a tremulous hand "Guido." The signature is supposed to have been extorted by the rack, and the prisoner to have fainted before completing it. Ibid., No. 54.]

Nov. 9.

Stourbridge.   Sir Rich. Walsh, High Sheriff of Worcestershire, to the Council. Further proceedings of the rebels; they were overtaken at Holbeach House, near Stourbridge. Many fled; the rest refusing to surrender, the house was attacked, Catesby, Percy, and the two Wrights slain; Grant, Rokewood, and others taken prisoners. All papers found in their pockets sent up. [Ibid., No. 55.] Annexed are,

39. I. Note of affection from Mrs. Clare to Mr. Lessingham, found in the pocket of Richard Whiting, alias Johnson.

39. II. Note of articles of dress left at the Mermaid and Anchor.

Nov. 9.

Leicester.   Edward Lord Cromwell and the Justices of Leicestershire to the Council. Wm. Andrew, servant to Sir Everard Digby, being told by his master to do something which he thought unlawful, confessed it to Sir Andrew Turpin, Justice of the Peace. Ask directions about him. [G. Plot Bk. No. 56.] Inclose,

I. Examination of William Andrew. Particulars of the meeting at Dunchurch. He withdrew on being ordered to Warwick, to steal horses. Nov. 9, Leicester. [Ibid., No. 64]

Nov. 9.

Rushall.   Sir Edw. Leigh to the Council. Proceedings in Staffordshire in repressing the tumult. Attack on Holbeach House. The two Wrights not killed, as was reported, but wounded. [Ibid., No. 57.] Incloses,

I. Examination of John Flower and Stephen Kirke, servants to Amb. Rokewood. The assembly at Rob. Winter's house at Huddington; on their way to Holbeach, the party asked all those they met to join them; they fled away because they suspected rebellion. Nov. 8. [Ibid., No. 58.]

II. Note of persons in Holbeach House, Nov. 7 and 8, 1605. [Ibid.]

Nov. 9.

Essex House.   40. Sir Edw. Francis to the Earl of Northumberland. Josceline Percy is not in the house; when he comes in, will get all particulars about the man whom [Giles] Greene saw, and described.

Nov. 9.

Essex House.   Sir Edw. Francis to the Earl of Northumberland. Josceline Percy has set down all particulars about his uncle [Thos. Percy's] man; and his own conversation with his uncle. [G. Plot Bk., No. 59.] Annexed is,

I. Statement by Josceline Percy, that on Nov. 3, he went with Davison, his uncle's servant, to seek him; did not find him; saw him several times that day and the next; his uncle appointed a private interview with him, but did not come to it. [Ibid., No. 59.]

Nov. 9 ?

Croydon, Saturday.   41. Earl of Northumberland to the King. Is sorry for having offended him. Fears his displeasure will lead the world to cast imputations on his character. Intreats His Majesty to save his loyalty from suspicion.

Nov. 9.

Valence. 42. Sir Nich. Coote to Salisbury. Sends up the examination of a fisherman at Barking. Incloses,

42. I. Examination of Rich. Franklin. His master, Hen. Paris, has transported goods and soldiers to Calais, on behalf of Rich. Fuller, alias Johnson, and was engaged by him to carry some persons to France.

Nov. 9 ? Note of Faukes, alias Johnson, hiring a boat from [Hen.] Paris, of Barking, to carry him and another man, disguised, to Gravelines. Paris waited 6 weeks there to bring them back. [G. Plot Bk., No. 130.]

Nov. 9.

Warwick. Justices, &c., of Warwickshire to Salisbury. Send the examinations of many suspected persons. Have assembled their troops. Some of the rebels were burned to death, in drying gunpowder at Holbeach. [Ibid., No. 59 A.] Inclose,

I. Examination of James Garvey, servant to Sir Everard Digby. He was sent by his mistress in search of his master, when he was apprehended; Sir Everard had horses at Coughton, at Thos. Throckmorton's house. Nov. 8. [Ibid., No. 51.]

II. Examination of Wm. Kyddall, servant to Rob. Tirwhit, of Kettleby, Lincolnshire. Proceedings of John and Chris. Wright; Kyddall brought John Wright's little girl to him at Lapworth, Warwickshire, and again at London; J. Wright sent him back to Lapworth, where he was going when apprehended. Nov. 8. [Ibid., No. 52.]

III. Examination of Matthew Batty, late servant to Lord Monteagle, on his being found riding near Warwick; will not go to church; refuses to say whether he would join the Pope against the King. Nov. 9. [Ibid., No. 60.]

IV. Examination of Rob. Askew, servant to Rob. Catesby, on his acquaintance with the conspirators. Nov. 9. [Ibid., No. 61.]

V. Examination of Thos. Maunder, servant to Rob. Winter. Movements of his master and the other conspirators; he feared mischief, and left them. Nov. 9. [Ibid, No. 62.]

Nov. 9. 43. Examination of Rich. Parker, servant to Rob. Catesby. Movements of his master and the other conspirators; is a Roman Catholic.

Nov. 10. Elizabeth Vaux to Sir John Roper, her father. Is amazed at his suspecting her of knowing anything of the Plot. Confident that none of her letters can implicate her. Her son would have gone to London about his match with Lady Suffolk's daughter, had not Sir George Fermor and his lady brought news of "this pitifull and tragicall intendment." [G. Plot Bk., No. 226.]

[Nov. 10 ?] The Same to Sir Rich. Verney, Sheriff of Warwickshire. Earnestly entreats him to give a pass for Lancashire to two gentlemen from her house, whom she describes, and who, she fears, are apprehended. His niece Mary would rather give her portion than have the younger of them called into question. Mrs. Huddleston, who is with her, begs that her husband may go up to London with the Lord Lieutenant. [Ibid., No. 227.]

Nov. 10. 44. Geo. Southaick to Levinus Munck. Movements of English Catholics in France, Charles Sutton, Dr. Bagshawe, &c. Mr. Baptista came to Lady Vaux's, to find Jarrett [Garnet], Superior of the English Jesuits. Told the Ambassador two months ago, that a plot was brewing. Incloses,

44. I. Notes of priests who have had meetings in Paris, or have been written to in England.

Nov. 10.

Allexton. Lord Cromwell to Salisbury. Services of the Leicestershire magistracy. Turpin, steward to Sir Rob. Tirwhit, of Lincolnshire, supposed to know much of the conspiracy. [G. Plot Bk., No. 63.]

Nov. 10.

Aberston. Sir Thos. Denys and Sir Benj. Ticheborne to the Same. Send examinations of Rich. Wranford and Wm. Bassett, taken up for sending for a priest to Bassett's brother. [Ibid., No. 65.]

Nov. 10.

Drakelow. Sir Thos. Gresley to the Council. Begs favour for Wm. Handy, servant to Sir Everard Digby, who surrendered himself. [Ibid., No. 66.] Incloses,

I. Examination of Wm: Handy. The meeting at Dunchurch; horse stealing; arming of the conspirators; he fled from them at Holbeach. [Ibid., No. 67.]

Nov. 10. 49. Warrant for payment of the wages and allowance of liveries to ten additional Warders of the Tower, to be appointed by the Lieutenant, it being thought expedient to increase the number.

[Nov. 10.]

Sunday Afternoon. Earl of Northumberland to the Council. Hears that Percy is wounded. Begs that a good surgeon may be sent to take charge of him, "for none but he can shew me clere as the day or darke as the night." [G. Plot Bk., No. 225.

Nov. 11 ? Same to Salisbury. Sends an old servant who can tell Percy's proceedings, whereby he hopes to get some of his lost goods again. [Ibid., No. 224 A.]

Nov. 11 ? Sir Wm. Lane to the Same. Sends the preceding note by the old servant, who will tell of Percy's abuses in his trust. [Ibid., No. 224 B.]

[Nov. 11.] 50. Same to the Same. Has delivered to the Earl [of Northumberland] his Lordship's verbal answer to his letter. Fotherley is coming up with the Earl's money.

Nov. 11.

York.   51. Sir John Ferne to the Same. Proceedings for the arrest of Perkinson, the companion of Tho. Percy. As no christian name was specified, he has issued warrants to arrest five gentlemen of that name, and also others intimate with Percy. Mr. Lepton passed northward in search of Percy, who had been at York Oct. 30, and had had conference with one Collingwood, a lewd recusant.

Nov. 11.   Examination of Rob. Reve. Has neither seen Rokewood nor Wright for a year past. [G. Plot Bk., No. 71.]

Nov. 11.

[White Webbs, Enfield Chace.]   Israel Amice and Thos. Wilson to the Council. Have searched Dr. Hewick's house, called White Webbs, in Enfield Chace. Found Popish books and relics, but no papers nor munition. The house has many trap doors and passages. Walley was not found, but Jas. Johnson, whom they have confined as an obstinate papist, and three women, all whose examinations they send. [Ibid., No. 70.] Inclose,

I. Examination of James Johnson. The books, &c., found belong to the wife of Thos. Jennings; his master, Mr. Meaze, of Berkshire, [alias Garnet,] took the house for his sister, Mrs. Perkins [alias Mrs. Anne Vaux]; names of visitors there. [Ibid.]

II. Examination of Elizabeth, wife of Wm. Shephard, coachman to Mrs. Perkins. Mr. Jennings lives in London; her mistress spent a month at White Webbs lately; mass has not been performed at the house. [Ibid.]

III. Examination of Marg. Walker. Three gentlemen came to White Webbs, the day the King left Royston; she is a Catholic. [Ibid.]

IV. Examination of Jane Robinson. Mass was said at White Webbs 3 months ago, but she knows not the priest's name, &c. [Ibid.]

Nov. 11.   Sir Fras. Hastings to Salisbury. Reports a speech of Foxwell, a notorious recusant, predicting danger to the Parliament. [G. Plot Bk., No. 72.

[Nov. 11.] Declaration of Dr. Wm. Hill. Foxwell, a recusant, pardoned for high treason in the late reign, predicted danger to the Protestants this Parliament, to Thos. Hind, parson of Babington, co. Somerset. [Ibid., No. 231.]

Nov. 11.   "Information concerning goods of y° traytors," i.e., notes by John Boorne, servant to Sir Wm. Turpin, of debts which were owing to Sir Everard Digby and Francis Tresham, on Nov. 9. [Ibid., No. 73.]

Nov. 12.

Sir Thos. Bennet's House. Anthony Visct. Montague to the Earl of Dorset. Protests that no warning was given him to absent himself from Parliament. Relates a conversation with Catesby. His request for a private interview [see Nov. 8] was not because he had anything to disclose, but that he might defend himself. [Ibid., No. 74.]

Nov. 12.   52. Lewis Duke of Lenox to Sir Thos. Lake. To draw a grant to Sir Edw. Harrington of the rangership of Lyfield Forest, shortly to fall void, by the attainder of Sir Everard Digby.

Nov. 12.

Warwick.   Justices, &c., of Warwickshire to Salisbury. Have apprehended and sent up Mrs. Grant, Mrs. Percy, and the wives of other conspirators. Divers servants of rebels taken, also Mr. Huddleston, and some persons known to be priests. The gaol and many houses full of prisoners. Send their examinations, and some others taken by Sir F. Greville, and detained too long by mistake. Danger from the flocking into the country of mounted and armed recusants. [G. Plot Bk., No. 75.] Inclose,

I. "Kalender of the names of the persons apprehended within the saide countie, knowne and suspected for the late conspirasye and insurrection," including 3 gentlemen, 7 suspected priests, 9 wives of conspirators, and 27 servants. [Ibid., No. 134.]

II. Examination of Rob. Higgins, servant to John Grant. Proceedings of his master and others on Nov. 6th; mass sometimes performed in the house. Warwick, Nov. 10. [Ibid., No. 68.]

III. Examination of Edw. Bickerstaff, servant to John Grant. His master would not let him go to church; visitors at the house; mass said by a priest named Yorke, &c. Warwick,

Nov. 10. [Ibid, No. 69.]

Examinations taken by Sir Fulk Greville, at Beauchamps-court, as follows:-

IV. Rich. Westbury, of Norbrook, on the assembly at Norbrook, Nov. 7.

V. Rich. Yorke, gent, on recent movements of Rob. Winter.

VI. Wm. Snowe, servant to Rob. Winter, on his master's movements.

VII. Marmaduke Ward, of Newby, Yorkshire, gent. He was going with Mrs. John Wright, his sister-in-law, to Winter's house when taken; knew nothing of the Plot.

VIII. Robert Askew, of Lapworth. He has left Catesby's service; was come to see his father.

IX. Thos. Rokewood, of Clopton, gent. He was going to Worcester to pay for a hawk, but returned, because he heard the town was disquieted.

X. Rob. Townsend, of Broughton, Suffolk, gent. On his connexion with the Rokewoods, &c.

XI. Wm. Johnson, Rokewood's servant. Was going to Worcester, but found the town disturbed.

XII. Rob. Keye, of Drayton, Northamptonshire, gent. He heard that Amb. Rokewood was taken, and came to see him; Mrs. Rokewood is his kinswoman.

XIII. Fras. Prior, trumpeter. Refuses to answer; was taken up as an idle person, and associate of the conspirators.

XIV. Rich. Dey, of Tilton, Leicestershire, servant to Sir E. Digby. Suspected the ill intent of the assembly, and left them.

XV. Wm. Udall, servant to the Same. Similar to the last. [G. Plot Bk., No. 47.]

Nov. 12.

Daventry. Justices of Northamptonshire to the Council. Houses of Ann Lady Catesby and Thos. Bates searched, but nothing found. Arms discovered in a garner and in a ditch near. Robt. Warren, John, son of Thomas Bates, and Chris. Story, Bates's man, taken. [Ibid., No. 76.] Inclose,

I. Examination of Wm. Rogers, of Daventry. Was sent to Lapworth, 14 Oct., to fetch John Wright, to meet certain parties at the Bell Inn, Daventry. Nov. 12. [Ibid., No. 77.]

II. Examination of Matthew Young, keeper of the Bell Inn, Daventry. Guy Faukes and Bates's son came to his inn a month before, and held a meeting there with others of the conspirators. Nov. 11. [Ibid.]

III. Examination of Rob. Warren, servant of Amb. Rokewood. Mrs. Rokewood's coach was sent to Lady Catesby's at Ashby Ledgers, and also the children of Catesby and of Sir Hen. Brown. Nov. 12. [Ibid.]

IV. Examination of Chris. Story, Thos. Bates's man. Armour brought to his master's house in Mrs. Rokewood's coach, and in a basket sent by the carrier. Nov. 12. [Ibid.]

V. Examination of John, son of Thos. Bates, of Ledgers Ashby. Went to London to enter the service of Catesby, but he having left town, was obliged to return. Nov. 12. [Ibid.]

Nov. 12.

Coldham Hall. Justices of Suffolk to the Council. Rokewood's house, and that of his servant, Edm. Cosen, have been searched, but neither he nor any treasonable papers found. It is declared on oath that Rokewood has not been seen since 31st Oct. Ports of Suffolk are guarded. [G. Plot Bk., No. 78.]

Nov. 12.

Newcastle. Sir Wm. Selby and Sir Wilfrid Lawson to Salisbury. Have searched Prudhoe Castle in hopes of discovering Thos. Percy, but in vain. The country quiet. [Ibid., No. 79.]

Nov. 12.

Newcastle. The above, and other gentlemen of Northumberland, to the Same. Send a packet of letters directed to the Earl of Northumberland, at Tynemouth Castle, "that if the said Earle be in his Mats good favour, it may be delivered to his hands; otherwise that it may be disposed of as shall seem best." [Ibid., No. 80.]

Nov. 12. Gentlemen of Monmouthshire to the Earl of Worcester, their Lieutenant. The King's proclamations have been read in all marketplaces in the county. Search ordered for suspicious persons, and watch set in the ports and chief highways. Though the county abounds with recusants, they seemed ignorant of the Plot. [Ibid., No. 81.]

Nov. 12 ? Notes of such Justices of Peace of Worcestershire and Warwickshire as were absent when the rebellion broke out, and of the difficulties of those who remained. Sir Walter Leveson, of Staffordshire, who married Wm. Coles' daughter, would not help them, though near Holbeach. Stephen Littleton has escaped. Robt. Winter married Mr. Talbot's daughter. [Ibid., No. 131. See Nov. 8.]

Nov. 12 ? 54. Objections by Sir Edw. Leigh and Sir Gilb. Puckering, against certain propositions of Sir Wm. Whorewood, Sheriff of Staffordshire, for the apprehension of Winter and Littleton.

Nov. [12.] 55. Statement by Nich. Fortescue as to the armour in his house at Cookhill, co. Worcester. Most of it has been in his hands 5 years. He has not seen Winter for 8 years, and was not summoned to join the rising.

Nov. 12.

Hursborne. Wm. Oxenbridge to Sir Rob. Oxenbridge. Speeches of Booth, Sir Arthur Hopton's servant, on Nov. 5th, about "strange matters" to be done that day; he railed against English preachers. [G. Plot Bk., No. 82.]

Nov. 12.

Bedford. Examination of Thomas Race, porter, of London. Was sent, Nov. 9th, by Sir John Roper, with a letter to his daughter, Mrs. Vaux, at Harrowden, Northamptonshire. She sent a reply to her father by him, and told him she was very free from those matters whereof her father had written to her. [See Nov. 10. Ibid., No. 83.]

Nov. 12. 56. Declaration of Edw. Brymstede, late factor at Lisbon. His intercourse there with Foster, an English Jesuit, who tried to pervert him to Romanism, argued on the lawfulness of king-killing, and prophesied speedy destruction to James I., unless he tolerated Catholics. Many English children brought up as Catholics, in Spain and Portugal.

Nov. 12 ? 57. Interrogatories [by Chief Justice Popham] to be put to the principal conspirators.

Nov. 12. 58. Examination of John Winter. Knew nothing of treason intended; left the party at Holbeach, and surrendered himself at his brother's house, Huddington.

Nov. 12. 59. Examination of Thos. Winter. He met the other conspirators at his brother's house; Catesby told them the Parliament had confirmed the laws against the Catholics, and that they armed in selfdefence; they expected no foreign aid and had no general head; he had never sworn secrecy; they had no priest amongst them; he was with Lord Monteagle at the last prorogation of Parliament.

Nov. 12.   60. Examination of John Grant. Knew nothing of the treason till after he was apprehended; he and others meant to go to Liverpool, to take shipping.

Nov. 12.   61. Examination of Harry Morgan. Knew nothing of the treason till the day before his apprehension, when Catesby told him of an abortive plot; heard him and Percy speak of taking the Princess Elizabeth; confessed seizing the horses at Warwick Castle.

Nov. 12.   62. Examination of Fras. Tresham as to his interviews with his cousin Catesby, Thos. Winter, and Fathers Walley and Gerard, the Jesuits. Declines to state what passed between them; has not been to Mrs. Vaux's nor to Lord Mordaunt's for a year.

Nov. 13.   63. Declaration of Fras. Tresham. Catesby revealed the Plot to him on Oct. 14th; he opposed it; urged at least its postponement, and offered him money to leave the kingdom with his companions; thought they were gone, and intended to reveal the treason; has been guilty of concealment, but as he had no hand in the Plot, he throws himself on the King's mercy.

Nov. 13.

Tynemouth Town. 64. George Whitehead to the Earl of Northumberland. Sir Hen. Wodrington, by warrant from the Council, has seized Tynemouth and Alnwick Castles, and threatens Prudhoe and Cockermouth. Asks directions.

Nov. 13.   68. Commission to the Lord Chamberlains and Vice-Chamberlains of the King and Queen's Households, to administer an oath of supremacy, of which the form is subjoined, to all who receive wages from the King or Queen.

Nov. 13.

Paris.   69. Dud. Carleton to John Chamberlain. Money affairs. Lord Norris's health improving. The Gunpowder Plot reported in France to be a fable. Much warmth between the two religions, since the return of the Jesuits.

Nov. 13.

Sir Thos. Bennet's House. Anthony Visct. Montague to Earl Dorset. Rectifies a mistake in his former letter [see Nov. 12,] about the time of his conversation with Catesby. Hears "the miserable fellowe that shoulde have bin the bluddy executioner of that woefull tragedie was called Guie Faux." If so, he was in his service a few months, some time ago. [G. Plot Bk., No. 86.]

Nov. 13.

Worcester. Sir Rich. Walsh, High Sheriff of Worcestershire, to Salisbury. Several gentlemen hurt (at Holbeach House) are dead; viz., Rob. Catesby, Thos Percy, John and Chris. Wright. Thos. Winter is recovering. "Rokewood, Grant, Morgan, and others, grievously brunt with powder," are now out of danger. [Ibid., No. 87.]

Nov. 13.

Worcester. Same to the Same. Will send up by Sir Hen. Bromley such prisoners as may travel without injury. Commends the zeal of Sir John Folliott and Humphrey Salway. [Ibid., No. 88.]

Nov. 13.

Warwick. Justices of Warwickshire to the Same. By Barth. Hales, "a very forward and careful man in these late uproars," they send up Mrs. Grant, and other female prisoners. Mrs. Mounson, of Mallerthorp, co. Lincoln, and Mrs. Higgins, wife of Grant's bailiff, are detained. [Ibid., No. 90.]

Nov. 13.

Worcester. Sir Henry Bromley to the Same. A principal conspirator seized; asks directions as to bringing him and other prisoners to Court. [Ibid., No. 89.]

Nov. 13.

Warwick. Sir Rich. Verney, Sheriff of Warwickshire, to Salisbury. Upright conduct of Mrs. Grant; hopes she disapproved her husband's proceedings. [G. Plot Bk., No. 91.]

Nov. 13.

Harrowden. Wm. Tate to the Same. Search at Lord Vaux's house at Harrowden; his mother, Mrs. Vaux, gave up all her keys; all the rooms, especially his closet, narrowly searched, but no papers found. She and the young Lord strongly deny all knowledge of the treason; the house still guarded. [Ibid., No. 92.] Annexed are,

I. Examination of Fras. Swetnam, baker to Mrs. Vaux. He went on Nov. 5 to Wellingbourne, with Matthew [Batty], Lord Monteagle's servant, who bought 20 lbs. of gunpowder. [Ibid., No. 93.]

II. Examination of Patrick Kent, of Harrowden, innkeeper. Batty lodged at his house the night of Nov. 5, and left on the 6th for Kettering. [Ibid.]

Nov. 13.   Examination of Giles Greene, as to his last seeing Percy, hiring lodgings at Westminster for him, &c. [Ibid., No. 95.]

Nov. 13.

London.   Wm. Stallenge to Salisbury. Particulars of Mr. Littleton and Mr. Tracy, who travelled from Sherborne to Salisbury, in October. [Ibid., No. 96.]

Nov. 13.   Geo. Southaick to Levinus Munck. Sutton has returned from Rome, and has particular business with priests in England. Gerard, the Jesuit, gave the sacrament to Percy and others. Is embarrassed from having but one warrant to apprehend [Arthur] White, Browne, Gerard, and Charnock. Suggests the seizure of Hen. and Thos. Shelley, of Mapledingham, Hampshire, and of Mr. Reves; and search of And. Hilton's house at Burton, Westmoreland, where Freysarde and Owen lurk. [Ibid., No. 97.]

[Nov. 13.] 70. "Kalender of letters come about this treason" by [Levinus Munck.] In addition to many noted above, the following are named which are missing:-

Nov. 5. Contents of Mrs. Vaux's letter, "fast and pray that that may come to pass which we purpose, which yf it doe, wee shall see Totnam turned French."

One of "two letters from Fotherley, the Earl of Northumberland's servant, to his lord, concerning his treasure coming up from his audytt."

Nov. 8. "A paper reporting that at Clopton there hath ben with Ambrose Rockwood, John Grant, Mr. Winter, Mr. Ross, Mr. Townshend, Mr. Cee, Mr. Wright, Sir Edward Bushell, Robert Catesbye."

Nov. 12. "Lord Herbert, out of Monmouthshire, to my Lord. Privy searches appointed in those parts, and all wayes, ports, havens, and ferryes layd, so that none can escape. Proclamations published upon 10 Novemb."

Nov. ?   71. Hackett's report touching the movements, &c. of Sir Hen. Hastings, of Branston, Hen. Hastings, and their people in Leicestershire, about the time of the treason

Nov. 14.

Holy Island.   73. Sir Wm. Bowyer to the Council. Has put 20 soldiers into the fort at Holy Island, Capt. [Sir Wm.] Reede being on guard there.

Nov. 14.

Holy Island.   74. Sir Wm. Reede to the Same. Has received the soldiers. He and they will hazard their lives before any mischief shall come to the King.

Nov. 14.   Information from Sir Geo. Fermor [taken by Chief Justice Popham]. Lord Vaux sent for him Nov. 6, and Mrs. Vaux requested him to ride to London with her son, to treat for his marriage with the Earl of Suffolk's daughter; but she afterwards wished him to postpone the journey, because Sir Griffin Markham's man told her there were broils in London, &c. [G. Plot Bk., No. 98.]

Nov. 14.

76. I. Declaration of Vincent Earle that two gentlemen described, walking near Holborn, said Lord Northumberland would do well if Percy were dead, and that Rob. Newport, one of the Earl's servants, was an arrant papist. Newport lives with Wm. Mylwarde, of Caversham near Reading.

Nov. 15.

Lambeth.   77. Earl of Northumberland to the Council. Argues the course of his life, unambitious and given to private pleasures, such as gardening, building, &c. as presumptions of his innocence; also his scanty supply of arms, horses, and servants. He knew none of the plotters excepting Percy.

Nov. 15.

3 A.M.   Sir Rich. Verney to Salisbury. His house has been set on fire a second time, but hopes to keep his prisoners safe. [G. Plot Bk., No. 99.]

Nov. 16.

Carlisle.   78. Gentlemen of Cumberland and Westmoreland to the Council. They are ready to watch for the arrest of Thos. Percy, and his adherents. Quiet state of those counties.

Nov. 16.

Berwick.   79. Sir Wm. Bowyer to Salisbury. Means for guarding Berwick and Holy Island. Has laid watches for Percy. He is said to be in Scotland; many of the Borderers were prepared to join him.

Nov. 16.

Carlisle.   80. Sir Wilfrid Lawson to the Same. Cumberland and Westmoreland quiet. Percy's connexion therewith.

Nov. ?   81. Lord Dunfermline to Salisbury. Surprise and horror at the Gunpowder Treason; hopes for the rigorous prosecution of the offenders. Praises the King and Council. Recommends that the prisoners be confined apart, in darkness, and examined by torch-light, and that the tortures be slow and at intervals, as being most effectual.

Nov. 16.

Tower.   82. Sir Wm. Waad to the Same. Sends a note of what room is left in the Tower. "My Lord Mordaunt is fallen into an extreeme pensivenes, not without great cause." Will provide bedding for the prisoners expected.

Nov. 16.

Edinburgh. 83. Sir Jas. Sempill to the Same. Congratulations on escape from "that Catholique blast." Met with Percy on his journey northward. A Jesuit has said mass at Lord Temple's. Answers many enquiries about his [Salisbury's] religious principles.

Nov. 16.

[Tower.]   Declaration of Guy Faukes. Catesby had advised Lord Montague not to come to Parliament, because he could do no good there. Lord Mordaunt was to be absent at the opening, because he would not attend the sermon; Lord Stourton to be detained by accident. Tresham was very anxious to have Lord Monteagle warned; they wished to warn the Earl of Arundel, but though under age, he was eager to be present. They intended to secure the absence of the Catholic Lords, by telling them that strict laws were framing against Catholics, which they could not prevent, &c. [G. Plot Bk., No. 101.]

Nov. 17.

Lambeth.   Sir Wm. Lane to Salisbury. The Earl [of Northumberland] refrains from writing himself, but trusts for protection to Salisbury's justice and friendship. He is a man of so excellent temper that it were a pity he should incur the stain of disloyalty. [Ibid., No. 102.]

Nov. 17.

Tavistock. 84. William Earl of Bath to the Same. Joy at the deliverance of the King and Parliament from the Powder Treason. Desires to know if his former proxy will be available for the next Parliament. Had prepared to quell any risings in Somerset or Cornwall.

Nov. 18.

Westminster. 85. Proclamation for searching for and apprehending Robt. Winter and Steph. Littleton; with description of their persons.

Nov. 18.

Westminster. 86. The King to Lord Treasurer Dorset. To make stay of granting any lease, &c. of Pipewell Manor, which will be forfeited by Fras. Tresham, if convicted of a share in the late horrible conspiracy, Sir Thos. Lake being a suitor for the same.

Nov. 18. 88. Anne Lady Markham to [Salisbury]. Hen. Huddleston can tell him best about Gerard, and Sir Everard Digby about Walley. Knows not where Mrs. Vaux is. Chris. Parker, an embroiderer, and Brian Hunston a painter, removed with Gerard or imprisoned. The "Plot hath taken deep and dangerous root;" many will not believe "that holy good man" [Gerard] was an actor in it. Death of her father.

Nov. 18. Examination of Elizabeth Vaux. Does not know Gerard the priest. The visitors at her house were Rob. Catesby, Sir Ever. Digby, Hen. Huddleston, Sir George and Lady Fermor, and Greene and Darcy, priests; heard of the broils in London by Sir G. Fermor and Sir Griffin Markham's brother's servant; wrote to Lady Wenman last Easter, and said that "Tottenham would turn French," &c. [G. Plot Bk., No. 103.]

Nov. 18. Copy of the above, annotated [by Sir Edw. Coke.] [Ibid., No. 104.]

Nov. 18. Declaration of Lady Tasburgh. Mrs. [Eliz.] Vaux wrote the letter to Lady Wenman, bidding her be of good comfort, for there should soon be toleration for religion; Sir Rich. Wenman was displeased with his wife's acquaintance with Mrs. Vaux. At the back, are notes [by Sir Edw. Coke] of examinations of Rob. Keyes' wife. She serves Lord Mordaunt's children; had a month's holiday; met her friends on Nov. 7, at her cousin Rokewood's; knows Dobbes, Lord Mordaunt's man. Also of examination of [Henry] Morgan's wife. Her husband and she were sworn to secrecy at Grant's; he left her a fortnight ago, and said he should never see her more; she knows Thos. Bates, Mr. Catesby's man. [Ibid., No. 105.]

[Nov.] 89. Notes [by Chief Justice Popham] of Dobbes, Shenston, and Bath of Ashby, suspicious persons. Marg. Ash says the two Moatfords are priests, and call themselves Croft and Grey. One serves Lord Sandys' daughter as footman, and says mass there.

[Nov. 19]

[Westminster.] 90. Proclamation warranting Sheriffs to prosecute rebels into other counties.

Nov. 19. Geo. Southaick to Levinus Munck. Intreats a new warrant, his former one having expired. [G. Plot Bk., No. 106.] Incloses,

I. Warrant to aid the bearer in the apprehension of suspicious persons, for 10 days only. Whitehall, Nov. 8. [Ibid., No. 107.]

Nov. 19. 93. Examination of Jane Lady Lovel. Knows Rob. Catesby and Sir E. Digby slightly, but none other of the conspirators; Broughton was formerly her servant; Phil. Roper, Mr. Norris, and Mr. Iseley, have been at her house.

Nov. 19. 94. Examination of Sir Everard Digby. Catesby told him better days were coming for Catholies; advised him to take a house in Warwickshire or Worcestershire; he borrowed Thos. Throgmorton's; came down, Nov. 4, to hunt with Sir Robt. Digby; the conspirators joined them; Catesby told him the King and Salisbury were dead, urged him to join the Catholic cause, and said they had many adherents; he was with them two days, but finding they had few supporters, left them and was taken.

Nov. 20.

Tower. 95. Second examination of the Same, confronted with Guy Faukes. Confesses his previous knowledge of the Plot, which he dared not reveal because he had sworn secresy.

Nov. 20 ? 96. List [annotated by Popham] of Plot prisoners in Worcestershire and Staffordshire.

Nov. 21 ? Extracts from examinations, to prove what meetings have been held amongst the Gunpowder conspirators and priests since Midsummer last; what preparations they had made; that the assembly at Dunchurch was on pretence of hunting: the plan of insurrection, &c. [G. Plot Bk., No. 240.]

Nov. 21. 97. Earl of Northumberland to Salisbury. Requests that Rob. Davison and Wm. Tailbois, two of Percy's servants, and Laurence Rushford, may be apprehended; and that Percy's study at Alnwick may be sealed, as there are bonds there belonging to himself. Begs that his Auditor may be examined upon Percy's conduct.

Nov. 21.   Examination of Wm. Ellis, servant to Sir Everard Digby. Rob. Catesby, Thos. Winter, and Sir Oliver Manners are intimate with his master; proceedings in Warwickshire; seizure of horses, arms, &c.; Browne, a seminary priest, was often at his master's. [G. Plot Bk., No. 108.]

Nov. 22.   Examination of Mich. Rapier, servant to Sir Everard Digby. Is a recusant; has served Sir Oliver Manners, Lady Catherine Gray, and Sir Hen. Bellasis; private masses said by Duckett, Fairfax, or Fisher, Brown, and Darcy, priests; all the conspirators received the sacrament at Rob. Winter's house, Nov. 7th; their proceedings; general hope of Catholics that times would mend. [G. Plot Bk., No. 111.]

Nov. 22.

Ryegate.   99. Giles Arkenstall to Salisbury. Being employed to transport wheat into Spain, has had access to certain religious houses of English priests there. Can give information of their proceedings. George Dowlies's work is printed in English, to be sent into England.

Nov. 22.

Co. Worcester.   Examination of Wm. Cole, brother-in-law to Rob. Winter. Was sent by R. Winter on a message to the Countess of Shrewsbury; his intercourse with the two Winters, Grant, Percy, and other conspirators; left London Nov. 5, on hearing of the stir excited by the Plot, to secure his wife whom he had left at John Grant's, but finding Grant's house under guard, travelled to and fro till his apprehension; denies all knowledge of the Plot. [G. Plot Bk., No. 110.]

Nov. 23.   100. Suggestions [by Lord Chief Justice Popham] for questions to be put to the Earl of Northumberland, as to his promising to join the Catholics; his intercourse with Percy; communications with Sir Walter Raleigh, &c.

[Nov. 23.] 101. The above, with other interrogatories [by Sir Edw. Coke], in the form in which they were actually put to the Earl.

Nov. 23.

Lambeth.   Replies of the Earl to the above and similar interrogatories. In the late Queen's time, the King allowed him to give hopes to the English Catholics, which he did, but went to further; his association with Percy was only on business matters; heard of the King's nativity being cast in Paris, but never saw it. [Ibid., No. 113.]

Nov. 23.   Addition to the above, in the Earl's own hand, relating to the King's nativity. [Ibid., No. 113 A.]

Nov. 23. 104. Sir Everard Digby to Salisbury. Is willing to tell all he knows, but can remember nothing more than he has already confessed, except that Catesby intended to send the Earls of Westmore- land and Derby to raise forces in the North, and would send information to France, Spain, Italy; &c., of their success. Begs that the King will have compassion on his family.

Nov. 23.

Tower. Confession of John Winter to the Council. He joined the assembly in Warwickshire, in ignorance of their intent; left them at Holbeach, and surrendered himself to the officers at his brother's house. [G. Plot Bk., No. 109.]

Nov. 23.

[Tower.] Confession of Thos. Winter. Full particulars of the Plot, from its first development till he was made prisoner at Holbeach House; with a marginal note [by the King.] [G. Plot Bk., No. 114.]

Nov. 23. Examination of John Hoppisley. He introduced Percy to Mr. Whynniard, from whom the house near the Parliament House was hired. [Ibid., No. 115.]

Nov. 23. 105. Declaration of Wm. Symonds, rector of Halton-Holegate, dioc. Lincoln, respecting the seditious speeches of Parker the recusant.

Nov. 23.

Barmoor. 106. Sir Wm. Selby to Salisbury. Has arrested Fergus Story, a friend as intimate with Tho. Percy as Rushford or Wm. Ord. Has also arrested four Davisons, not knowing which of them was the follower of Percy.

Nov. 24. 109. Bill of Mr. Wilson's charges, for the apprehension and bring- ing to Court of Jas. Johnson, and for the guarding of White Webbs, Enfield.

Nov. 25. 110. Warrant to pay to Thos. Heton sums due for the diet and apparel of priests and other prisoners, kept in his charge at Wisbeach.

Nov. 25.

Lambeth. 112. Earl of Northumberland to Salisbury. Repeats the requests of his former letter [Nov. 21], especially about sealing up Percy's study. As the bonds are from Sir Hen. Wodrington, who is made Keeper of Alnwick, he fears their falling into his hands.

Nov. 25.   Examination of Thos. Winter. Money was advanced to the conspirators by Tresham, &c. Lord Northumberland was first thought to favour Catholics, but Percy reported the contrary, and that "for matter of relligion" he "trobled not much himselfe." [G. Plot Bk., No. 116.]

Nov. 25.   Note by Thos. Winter, of a message sent to him by Lord Monteagle, Catesby, and Tresham, relative to the Plot. [The name of Lord Monteagle is half scratched out, and half pasted over with paper. Ibid., No. 117.]

Nov. 25.   Examination of Rich. Trewman, servant to Robt. Winter. Assemblage at his master's house, arming, &c. [Ibid., No. 118.]

Nov. 25.   Examination of Thos. Maunder, servant to Rob. Winter. Was persuaded to be a recusant, by Hammond, a priest, living in his master's house, who often said mass there; proceedings of his master; the assembly at Dunchurch, &c.; books and other things hid in a secret place in his master's house. [G. Plot Bk., No. 119.]

Nov. 25.   Examinations of Matthew Power, Humph. Streylley, Hugh Powell, Edw. Herbert, and Thos. Caple, touching the seditious speeches of Thos. Booth, on Nov. 5; predicting great alterations to take place that day, and railing against protestant ministers. [Ibid., No. 120.]

Nov. 26.   Examination of Thos. Booth, as to his uttering these speeches. [Ibid.]

Nov. 26.   113. Declaration by Thos. Holcomb, of his hearing one out of three persons who passed under the scaffold on Tower Hill say, "I'le actte it upon that croked wryche (wretch), in the habett of a gentlewoman."

Nov. 27.   Examination of Wm. Handy, servant to Sir Everard Digby. Has been converted to popery by Fairfax, alias Fisher, alias Percy, a priest; mass at Thos. Throgmorton's said by Darcy, alias Walley [Garnet], an old priest; other private masses in different places; one Littlejohn serves the old priest; particulars of Walley; "Mrs. Ann Vaux doth usually goe with him whithersoever he goethe;" assembly at Dunchurch, &c.; mass and sacrament administered by Hart, a priest. [G. Plot Bk., No. 121.]

Nov. 27.   Examination of Nathaniel Torporley, about his casting the King's nativity for Mr. Heriot, who lived at Essex House, the Earl of Northumberland's. [Ibid., No. 122.]

Nov. 28.   Examinations of Thos. and Edw. Ockley, retainers of Rob. Winter. They were sent for by him to join the assembly on Nov. 5, but stole away at Stourbridge. [Ibid., No. 123.]

Nov. 28.

Coventry. 114. Mayor, &c., of Coventry, and Lord Harrington to Salisbury. Respecting Mr. Cowper, a minister, who stated in a sermon, that the papists had contrived nine plots against the King and State.

Nov. 28 ? 115. Notes [by Salisbury] of the parties to be examined for proofs against Greenway, Garnet, Baldwin, Stanley, Owen, and Creswell.

Nov. 28 ? 116. Notes [by Sir Edw. Coke] of interrogatories to be put to Faukes, Winter, and Tresham, as to foreign aid expected; the conduct of the Earl of Northumberland; a project for the Earl of Salisbury's murder, &c.

Nov. 29.

Tower. Examination of Fras. Tresham. Knew not of Spanish forces to be sent over to help the Catholics in England; knew that in the late reign, Thos. Winter went into Spain, on an employment with which Lord Monteagle, Catesby, Father Garnet, alias Walley, the Jesuit, and Father Greenway were acquainted. [G. Plot Bk., No. 124. A slip of paper is pasted over the name of Lord Monteagle.]

Nov. 29. Interrogatories for the Earl of Northumberland, to be answered in writing; similar to those of Nov. 23rd. [G. Plot Bk., No. 125.]

Nov. 30. Examination of Rob. Keyes. Was admitted into the Plot by Catesby, 18 months past, and took the oath; wished Lord Mordaunt to be warned; Catesby said he would, by tricks, keep him and other Catholic Lords away, but rather than fail, would blow them all up, were they dear unto him as his own son; had charge of the house at Lambeth, where the powder was kept; Percy boasted that he had told the Earl of Northumberland a lie, to get money from him. [Ibid., No. 126.]

Nov. 30. Examination of Wm. Turner, carter to Rob. Winter. Drove a cart with armour from Huddington to Lord Windsor's, where more armour was put in. [Ibid., No. 128.]

Nov. ? 117. Petition of Walter Burford and Edw. Musgrave, of Wapping, Peter Kenton, of Dover, and Rob. Colthurst, of Newcastle, to Salisbury, for redress of wrongs inflicted upon them when trading to Spain.

Nov. ? 118. Petition from the English merchants trading to Spain and Portugal to the Council for redress; they complain of the injuries they receive in their trade, and of their persecutions for religion, contrary to treaty.

[Nov.]   119. Note of concessions promised by the King of Spain to Sir Chas. Cornwallis, in behalf of the English merchants trading to Spain. [See Span. Corresp., Nov. 25.]

Nov. ?   120. Robert Bennet, Bp. of Hereford, to Salisbury. Informs him that Ric. Abington, of Bromyard, an obstinate recusant, was lying at a house called Poplar, near Blackwall; and that he keeps in his house a Jesuit named Stansby, alias Drury.

Nov. ?

[King's Bench Prison.]   121. Rob. Hogg to [Salisbury ?]. Advertisements that several of Amb. Rokewood's men in the prison know of hidden money, plate, and horses; can tell more, if set at liberty.

Nov. ?   122. Notes for a Thanksgiving Sermon, after some "heavy and dreary tragedy" [the Gunpowder Plot ?].

Nov. ?   125. List of all the recusants in England, indicted during the past year: total number, 1,944.

Source: James I: Volume 16

November, 1605, Calendar of State Papers Domestic: James I, 1603-1610 1857 Pages: 238-264

January-February, 1606.

Jan. 3.   4. Anne Lady Markham to Salisbury. Hopes soon to see Gerard the priest, and will keep him in view till she can let Salisbury know where he is. Had the watch at Harrowden been kept two days longer, he would have been starved out. Is obliged to act very cautiously, lest her party should suspect her of betraying them. Richard, the butler, is in the Gatehouse, but in prisons, money will help to send letters to friends.

Jan. 8.

Edinburgh.8. Earl of Dunfermline to the Same. Though the Powder Treason was not openly supported abroad, the conspirators had intelligence with persons dependent on foreign princes. The Earl of Dunbar diligent at the Council. The Earl of Mar expected when it meets at Linlithgow, for the censure of some troublesome ministers, against whom the King has conceived greater offence than they are worthy of. The town is free from plague, &c.

Jan. 8.

Florence. 9. Tobie Matthew to Dud. Carleton. Presumes the sickness of Lord Norris prevented Carleton from being in England time enough to be suspected of implication in the Powder Plot, on account of his connection with Northumberland. His own travels in Italy; names of Englishmen there.

Jan. 8. 12. Confession of John Talbot. Came to his cousin Talbot at Pepperhill, 7th Nov.; told him of Winter's rising, and that his brother Talbot was ordered by the Sheriff to be in readiness to serve the King.

Jan. 9. 13. Examination of Sir Ever. Digby. Took the oath from Catesby, but was excused by him from taking the sacrament upon it.

Jan. 9. Examination of Guy Faukes. Sir Edw. Baynham was sent by Catesby to the Pope, to complain of the persecutions of Catholics, and was to be ready in Rome to negotiate for help, if the Plot succeeded. [G. Plot Bk., No. 163.]

Jan. 9. Examination of Thos. Winter. Manner of taking the oath of secresy; Gerard, alias Lee, the priest, gave them the sacrament afterwards, but knew not of the Plot. [Ibid., No. 164.]

Jan. 10. Voluntary declaration of Hen. Morgan, late of Norbrook, co. Warwick. Has seen Greenway at Winter's and Grant's; he was with the conspirators on Nov. 6, attired in "coloured sattin done with gould lace," but left them. [G. Plot Bk., No. 165.] Annexed is,

I. Note by Amb. Rokewood of seeing Catesby and Percy converse at Winter's house with a gentleman, who then rode away. [Ibid.]

Jan. 13. Examination of Thos. Bates, servant of Rob. Catesby. Was sent from Mr. Grant's of Norbrook to Coughton, Thos. Throgmorton's house, hired by Sir Ever. Digby, with a letter to Father Farmer, alias Walley [Garnet]; he shewed the letter to Greenway, who returned with Bates to Winter's house, and had an interview with Catesby; thinks Greenway is at Mr. Abington's, in Worcestershire. [G. Plot Bk., No. 166.]

Jan 15.

Whitehall. 19. Earl of Salisbury to Lady Markham. Though loath to prosecute the Jesuits, yet finding they have been principals in the conspiracy, accepts her offer to apprehend Gerard the priest, and sends her a blank warrant for his capture. Her fidelity may advantage her husband. Gerard, Walley, and Greenway are the guilty priests.

Jan. 15.

Westminster. Proclamation for the apprehension and discovery of John Gerard, Henry Garnet, and Oswald Tesmond. Printed. [Proc. Bk., p. 120.]

Jan. 17. Examination of Rob. Winter, of Huddington, Worcestershire. Past associations with the conspirators; on Nov. 7th Father Hammond, though knowing their share in the Plot, confessed and absolved them all, and gave them the sacrament; when he and Stephen Littleton fled, they sent twice to Father Hall for help. [G. Plot Bk., No. 168.]

Jan. 17. Examination of the Same. Was told of the Plot by Catesby at Oxford a year ago, and took the oath of secresy; Catesby said he would save such of the Catholic nobility as he could, and would proclaim the Princess Elizabeth Queen. [Ibid., No. 169.]

Jan. 17. Examination of Thos. Winter. Went to Rome in Christmas, 1599; had the Plot succeeded, Hugh Owen would have instructed Sir Edward Baynham to inform the Pope, and get help from him; admission of Rob. Winter into the Plot; taking the sacrament at Huddington. [Ibid., No. 170.]

Jan. 17. Note by Amb. Rokewood that Catesby and Thos. Winter told him that they had acquainted Rob. Winter with the Plot. [Ibid., No. 171.]

Jan. 17. Examination of Stephen Littleton, of Holbeach, co. Stafford. His share in the insurrection. Greenway was sent for to Huddington; escaped with Rob. Winter, from Holbeach, and since then, they have lain hid in barns and poor men's houses in Worcestershire. Went with Thos. Winter to Mr. Talbot's, but did not hear what passed. Winter said that Mr. Talbot was grieved with their proceeding. Took the sacrament at Huddington, but will rather die than reveal what passed between him and Hammond the priest. [G. Plot Bk., No. 172.]

Jan. 17. 24. Examination of Sir Everard Digby. Catesby told him that the Papists' throats would be cut

Jan. 17. 25. Examination of John Grant. He and Rob. Winter were sworn into the Plot a year ago, at Oxford. Rob. Winter said it was a dangerous matter, but for his oath's sake, he would not reveal it.

Jan. 18. Examination of Rich. Cudberd, mariner, of Scarborough, and cook in a ship called "the Gift of God." Interview at the English college in Seville, in October last, with Father Westmoreland, who told him he would find England in a different state at his return, from that in which he left it. [G. Plot Bk., No. 173.]

Jan. 19.

Durham. 28. Wm. James, Dean of Durham, to the Same. Has committed "a base huswyfe, a recusant," for speeches before the Gunpowder Plot. Begs that recusants' conveyances of their lands about the time of the Plot, may be annulled by Parliament.

Jan. 19.

Charlton, Worcestershire. Fras. Dingley to the Same. Encloses information which Alex. Gower, servant to Rob. Winter, forgot to name in his examination before Sir Hen. Bromley. [G. Plot Bk., No. 174.]

Jan. 20. Declaration of Guy Faukes. Talked with Catesby about noblemen being absent from the meeting of Parliament; he said Lord Mordaunt would not be there, because he did not like to absent himself from the sermons, as the King did not know he was a Catholic; and that Lord Stourton would not come to town till the Friday after the opening. [Ibid., No. 175.]

[Jan. 20.] 29. Directions [written by Levinus Munck] to Sir Hen. Bromley, Sheriff of Worcestershire, for searching Henlip House, Worcestershire; to pull down the wainscoat, bore the ground, drill the boards and chimney corners, examine the attics and roof, &c., in search of concealed hiding-places.

Jan. 20. Lease, in reversion to Dr. John Hammond, of the site of the manor of Chartley Beomond, co. Surrey, and others. [Ind. Wt. Bk., p. 49.]

Jan. 21. Rob. Winter to the Lords Commissioners [for the Plot]. His remonstrances with Catesby against the Plot. Purport of their conversations. Catesby bribed the Littletons to join the meeting at Dunchurch. Details of the insurrection. He refused to write to his father-in-law Talbot, to persuade him to join them, because he knew he would not. Wrote to Mr. Smallpeece, but did not send the letter. (See Nov. 6, No. 19.) After they left Holbeach, they sent to Father Hall for help, which was delayed. Was absolved, and took the sacrament at Huddington. [G. Plot Bk., No. 176.]

Jan. 21. Voluntary declaration of Amb. Rokewood. Confessed he told Hammond, Nov. 7th, in confession, that he was sorry he had not revealed the Plot, it seeming so bloody. Hammond absolved him, without remark. [Ibid., No. 177.]

Jan. 21. Declaration of Hen. Morgan. In his confession to Hammond, Nov. 7th, said he knew not the conspirators' intent, but joined them for the cause of religion. Hammond told him that whatever he did in the Catholic cause was right, and absolved him. [Ibid, No. 178.]

Jan. 21.

Edinburgh.31. Earl of Dunfermline to Salisbury. The Council have met at Linlithgow, and the refractory ministers were arraigned and convicted of treason, by Assize men, chosen beforehand. Hopes his Majesty will not often exact such services, for Puritanism is so predominant, that more discontent will be caused than good done.

Jan. 23. 35. John Gerard, Jesuit, to the Duke of Lenox. Protests his ignorance of the conspiracy. Begs the Duke to influence the King to grant him a speedy trial, that his innocence may be fully established. Appeals to the dying testimony of the other conspirators, and to Sir E. Digby, who knows that he knew nothing of the Plot two days beforehand. Incloses,

35. I. Same to Salisbury. To the same purport as the above, and requesting an audience. Jan. 23.

35. II. Same to Sir Everard Digby. Implores him to exculpate him from any knowledge of the conspiracy. Protests his ignorance "without any equivocation, and the words thereof so understood by me as they seem to others." Relates a conversation between them on Nov. 2nd, which he begs Digby to confirm. Has always disapproved violent courses. Jan. 23.

Jan. ? 36. Mary Lady Digby to Salisbury. Thanks him for procuring the letter from the Council, ordering the Sheriff of Buckinghamshire to restore part of her property. Implores his intercession for the life of her husband.

Jan. 23. 37. Same to the Same. Is in distress because the Sheriff of Buckinghamshire refuses to obey the letter and restore her furniture, &c., in spite of her bond to deliver it when demanded, and also detains her husband's money. Entreats mercy for her husband.

Jan. 23. 38. Sir Henry Bromley, Sheriff of Worcestershire, to the Same. His measures for searching Henlip House. Difficulties of the search. Mr. Abington and all the household deny any knowledge of the priests. Had given up hopes of finding any one, when two men crept from a secret place, and surrendered through hunger and cold. Thinks they are Owen and Hall. [They were Owen and Chambers.]

Jan. 24. Examination of Geo. Vavasour. Denies certain speeches about his affection for Thos. Strange, and about the rebellions of Protestants, which Thos. Audley, John Pett, John Jefferys, and John Johnson, confronted with him, declared they heard him utter. [G. Plot Bk., No. 179.]

Jan. 24. 39. Informations of Rob. Hasselgrave and Rob. Ballmer, sailors, taken before Chief Justice Popham, relative to certain discourses of an Englishman, at the English College of Seville, on alterations in England, and an expected revival of Popery.

Jan. 25.

Newcastle. 41. Sir Wm. Selby and Sir Wilfrid Lawson to Salisbury. Same subjects as the preceding. Six of those executed at Newcastle were followers of Thos. Percy.

Jan. 25. 42. Minutes by John Locherson of a conversation, which he overheard in the Tower, between Rob. Winter and Guy Faukes, on the probabilities relating to their trial and execution; that Lord Monteagle was said to have begged for some of them, &c.; their regret at their failure in the Plot, and that no apology was published in its justification.

Jan. 26. Examination of Guy Faukes on the above conversation. [G. Plot Bk., No. 180.]

Jan. 26. 44. Examination of Rob. Winter on the same conversation and on other points. Father Walley was at his house twice last summer. Has not written to Andrew Windsor for a year, but saw him in November at Mr. Talbot's and Mr. Abington's.

Jan. 27.

Gloucester. 46. Mayor, &c. of Gloucester to Salisbury. Have apprehended a man calling himself Valentine Palmer, but whom they suspect to be Gerard, alias Brooke, the Jesuit, and who confesses that he once served Percy.

Jan. 30.

Holt Castle. 52. Sir Hen. Bromley to Salisbury. Has taken Garnet and Hall, and conveyed them to his own house, to restore their strength for their journey to London. Particulars of other prisoners taken in "this wearisome action." A priest sent to Worcester and examined by Mr. Attorney Fleet, whose services he commends. Incloses,

52. I. John Fleet to the Same. Has committed to gaol the priest, and John Green, in whose house he said mass. Mr. Abington's abuse of him, and his own good services detailed. Worcester, 30 Jan.

Jan. 30 ? 53. Notes of evidences by Sir Hen. Bromley, that before Jan. 26, Garnet and Hall were at Mr. Abington's house, with his knowledge, and were well acquainted with the conspirators.

Jan. 31. 54. Substance of Sir Edw. Poole's motion in Parliament, concerning thanks to Lord Monteagle; precautions against recusants, &c.

Jan. 31.   55. Thos. Wilson to Salisbury. Matters in progress in Parliament. Sir Edw. Poole's speech relative to Lord Monteagle, the thanksgiving, and precautions against recusants.

Source: James I: Volume 18, January-February, 1606,

Calendar of State Papers Domestic: James I, 1603-1610 1857 Pages:277-294

On the Commemoration:

January 1606

Gunpowder Plot.

A learned and religious Speech. -

Sir Edw. Mountague moveth, That an Act may be made, that there may be an everlasting Memory of Thanksgiving. -

No extraordinary Blessing in Scripture, but an extraordinary Sign : -

The Covenant with Noe, the Rainbow: - Jacob and Esau : - ix. Hester, Hamon, and Mordecay: - Keeping of Days of Deliverance of the Jews. -

Yearly Thanksgiving.

Offereth a Bill, intituled, A Bill for a publick Thanksgiving to be given to Almighty God, every Year, on the fifth Day of November: - First Reading.

Hotham's Estate.

1. Reading : - The Bill for Enabling of John Hotham Esquire, the Father, and John Hotham, his Son, to convey certain Lands, for a Jointure of such Wife, as John, the Son, shall marry.

Yearly Thanksgiving on 5 Nov.

2. Reading: - The Bill for a publick Thanksgiving to be given to Almighty God, every Year, on the fifth Day of November: - Committed to Mr. Secretary Herbert, Sir Edw. Mountague, Mr. Solicitor, Sir Fr. Hastings, Sir Herbert Crofts, Sir Roger Aston, Sir Fr. Bacon, Sir Vincent Skynner, Sir Rob. Wingfield, Sir James Perrot, Sir Tho. Ridgeway, Sir Geo. St. Poll, Sir John Bennett, Sir Tho. Hobby, Sir Antho. Rous, Sir Geo. Moore, Sir Roger Owen, Sir Fr. Barrington, Mr. Winch, Sir H. Billingsley: - And presently met in the Committee Chamber; but adjourned till the next Morning, in the same Place.- House of Commons Journal Volume 1

23 January 1606/ p.258-259.

Yearly Thanksgiving on 5 Nov.

Mr. Solicitor reporteth from the Committees for the Bill of publick Thanksgiving, that they had amended the Bill, not only in Circumstance, but in Substance: The Amendments twice read ; and the Bill, with the Amendments, upon the Question, ordered to be ingrossed.

Ingrossetur

-House of Commons Journal Volume 1, 24 January 1606, p.258.

Annual Thanksgiving on the 5th November.

Hodie 1a vice lecta est Billa, An Act for a Publick Thanksgiving to Almighty God, every Year, on the 5th of November.

This Bill was brought this Day from the Lower House; and presented to the Lords, by Mr. Secretary Herbert, Sir Frauncis Hastings, and others; with this Message, That the Knights, Citizens, Burgesses, and the whole Commons of that House, having entered into Consideration of the great Blessing of God, in the happy Preservation of His Majesty and the State, from the late most dangerous Treason (intended to have been attempted by the Instigation of Jesuits, Seminaries, and Romish Priests), had framed and passed the said Bill in that House (as the First Fruits of their Labours in this Session of Parliament), which they did very earnestly recommend unto their Lordships.- House of Lords Journal Volume 2, 25 January 1606, p. 362-363.

Feb. 4. Examination of Edward Lord Stourton. Intercourse with the conspirators. Reasons for not coming up to the opening of Parliament. [G. Plot Bk., No. 181.]

Feb. 4. Examination of Henry Lord Mordaunt. Intercourse with the conspirators. Rob. Keyes' wife taught his children. Wrote to Lord Compton for leave of absence from Parliament because he was seeking evidence about his assart lands. [Ibid., No. 182.]

Feb. 5.

Wickham. 64. Sir Hen. Bromley to Salisbury. Is bringing up the prisoners, but Garnet's weakness compels them to travel slowly. Incloses,

64. I. List of the prisoners, viz.: Abington, Garnet, Hall, Owen, Chambers, and two servants.

Feb. 5. Lease to Francis, Earl of Cumberland, of lands, co. Cumberland, parcel of the Duchy of Lancaster. [Ind. Wt. Bk., p. 42.]

Feb. 13.

Whitehall. 86. Interrogatories to be put to Garnet, alias Walley, alias Darcy, alias Farmer, and to Edw. Hall, alias Oldcorne, Jesuits. Their intercourse with the conspirators; foreign negotiations; the book of equivocation; doctrines of Rome about obedience to a heretic king; lawfulness of the late treason, &c.

Feb. 13.

[Whitehall.] 87. Examination of Hen. Garnet upon some of these interrogatories. Has been 20 years Superior of the Jesuits in England; was appealed to, on Nov. 6th, for help by the conspirators, but refused it, because they acted foolishly and wickedly; denies all knowledge of the Plot; never was at White Webbs, &c.; corrected the Book of Equivocation, but would not have it printed; its doctrines are those of divines, but have not been approved at Rome

Feb. 13.

[Tower.] Examination of Edw. Hall. Came to Mr. Abington's house Jan. 20th; Humphrey Littleton came to him from Stephen Littleton and Rob. Winter, to beg him to help them to a place of safety, but he thought it was a scheme to intrap him, and declined. [G. Plot Bk., No. 183.]

Feb. 13. Examination of Jas. Stanley, scrivener, of Cornhill, London. Catesby hired a house in Mr. Churchill's name, at Erith, where there were frequent secret meetings held. Valentine Wilkinson and his wife, Mr. and Mrs. Compton, and Mr. and Mrs. Gwyn frequent it. [Ibid., No. 184.]

Feb. 17.

St. Omer. 97. Giles Schondonck to Father Baldwin. Has seen [Dr.] Cecill's book, and is surprised that whilst condemning the Gunpowder Plot, it approves the designs of those 5 who are said to have sworn to kill Cecil [Earl of Salisbury]; the tale is improbable, for the 5 persons accused are either ill or oppressed with sorrow. Regrets that Garnet and Vincent are taken. No Jesuits implicated in the examinations.

Feb. 20.

[Tower.] 109. Examination of Thos. Strange, Jesuit. Was not at Mrs. Vaux's about the 5th of November; has not seen Gerard, the Jesuit, lately; has said he hoped the King was not excommunicated, as it would give foreign princes a pretence to attack him; Garnet is his superior; never wrote to Davies before his coming from St. Omer, nor inquired after "stirring spirits," to whom to reveal "the main project;" knew of no oath of secresy.

Feb. 20.

[Tower.]   Examination of Edw. Oldcorne. This is his true name, but he is sometimes called Hall, Vincent, or Parker. [G. Plot Bk., No. 185.]

Feb. 23.   Examination of Geo. Chambers. Was at Mr. Abington's on Nov. 2nd; stayed there some days, and thence went about amongst Catholics in the neighbourhood, whom he refuses to name; is not a priest, but refuses to say whether he is a lay Jesuit. [G. Plot Bk., No. 186.]

Feb. 23.

[Tower.]   111. Report [by John Locherson,] of a conversation overheard in the Tower between Garnet and Hall. Greenway escaped; Garnet hopes to get over to Father Parsons; Mrs. Anne [Vaux] in town, and can let them hear from their friends; Garnet bribes his keeper, and advises Hall to do the same; Garnet will be compelled to confess the meetings at White Webbs, but will deny that he was there lately, or that the servants there know him, lest they seize the servants and torture them to confess; will explain the prayers he wrote for Catholics at Parliament time, by their fear of severe laws; Sir Wm. Waad's hatred of Jesuits; hopes they will not ask him about the letters which Lord Montague [Monteagle ? See p. 297] sent by Sir Edw. Baynham; is persuaded he shall wind himself out of this matter.

Feb. 23 ?   Hen. Garnet to --. Wishes a pair of spectacles to be repaired. Has confessed being at Coughton with Greenway, when Bates came to ask help, but said that he refused it, and urged them to desist; will be compelled to confess White Webbs; asks where Mr. Anne [Vaux] is. (Footnote *) [G. Plot Bk., No. 241.]

Feb. 24.   Examination of Edw. Oldcorne, alias Hall. Went with Garnet, Jan. 19th, to Mr. Abington's; an old servant, whose name he refuses to give, put them into their hiding-place. [Ibid., No. 137.]

Feb. 25.   117. Interlocution between Garnet and Hall, reported by Edw. Forsett and John Locherson. Garnet sees that the Lords wish to justify Lord Monteagle; fears their hearing why he, Garnet, came to Coughton; they have disagreed in their confessions about coming to Mr. Abington's; Garnet charged with composing prayers for the success of the Plot; Jas. Johnson has been on the rack for 3 hours, whereas Faukes confessed after being racked half an hour. [Modern copy of Archbp. Sancroft's transcript, in the Bodleian Library, Oxford.]

Feb. 25.   Examination of Jas. Johnson. Entered Mrs. Perkins', alias Vaux's, service 6 years ago; was engaged by Robert Skinner; found out her true name 3 years ago; the taking and furnishing of White Webbs; Mr. Skinner there with his mistress; describes the visitors there, Mr. Meaze, Mr. Perkins, Mr. Jennings [alias Brookesby], Catesby, the Winters., &c. [G. Plot Bk., No. 188.]

Feb. 26.

Tower.   Examination of Jas. Johnson. Having seen Garnet, confesses that he is the person who came to White Webbs under the name of Meaze, and was afterwards called Farmer. [Ibid., No. 189.]

Feb. 26.

Tower.   Examination of Edw. Oldcorne, alias Hall. Never saw Chambers till they were taken prisoners together; never met Garnet near Enfield House, and knows no such place as White Webbs; met Garnet Jan. 19, and went with him to Mr. Abington's. [G. Plot Bk., No. 190.]

Feb. 26.   Examination of Thos. Abington, of Henlip. Went to Mr. Talbot's Jan. 19th; knew not that the horse he rode belonged to Hall the Jesuit; it was his sister-in-law's, and bought from Rob. Winter; the apparel found in the chest belongs to himself and his brother Richard; does not know whether Chambers is servant to Hall. [Ibid., No. 191.]

Feb. 26.   Examination of Nicholas Owen. Will not say whence he came to Mr. Abington's on Jan. 19th; does not know Garnet nor Hall; nor whether Chambers, whom he has known some years, is Hall's servant. [Ibid., No. 192.]

Feb. 26.   118. Proceedings of the bailiff of Stratford-on-Avon, as escheator of the borough, against certain conspirators in the Gunpowder Plot, viz.: Summons, dated Feb. 20, from William Wyatt, bailiff, for 24 jurors to meet at Stratford, on Feb. 26.

Feb. 27.

Tower.   Examination of Jas. Johnson. Catesby came to White Webbs 3 or 4 years before, under the name of Roberts; knows not how his mistress supports the house; remembers no other visitors than those he named before. [G. Plot Bk., No. 193.]

Feb. 27.   122. Report by Edw. Forsett and John Locherson, of a conversation overheard in the Tower between Garnet and Hall. They detailed particulars of their examinations, and consulted that they might not contradict each other. Mr. Attorney rallied Garnet about Mrs. Brookesby's child, christened at White Webbs.

Feb. 27.   123. Declaration by Thos. Strange, Jesuit, that he did not meet Father Garnet on St. Bartholomew's day last; with a sentence added by Garnet that Strange did so meet him.

Feb. ?   128. Petition of Officers of the Customs of the Port of London to the King, for redress against certain merchants who, since the beginning of Parliament, refuse to pay their fees, on the ground that the customs are let to farm. Suggestions for remedy thereof.

Feb. ?   129. Warrant to the Treasurer of the Chamber, and Captain and Officers of the Guard, to deliver to Thos. Cotty, 2s. per diem and yearly livery, the same as to the Yeomen of the Guard, for his services in assisting the Sheriff of Worcestershire to take divers traitors in Staffordshire, and to bring them to the Tower.

Source: James I: Volume 18, January-February, 1606,

Calendar of State Papers Domestic: James I, 1603-1610 1857 Pages:277-294

March, 1606.

March 1.

Durham.   2. Dean James to Salisbury. George Jarvis, from Berwick, a seminary priest, sent to him by the Earl of Dunbar, is suspected to have had some share in the "horrible and barbarous intended treason." Incloses,

2. I. Examination of Geo. Jarvis, relative to his education, and where he abode and exercised his profession, since he came into England; he will mention no places but Mr. Haggerstone's, of Haggerstone, and Mr. Carr's, of Itell.

March 1.

York.   6. First examination of John Healey. His education and travels. Refuses to attend Divine Service, and denies that he was ever required to pray for Thos. Percy and that action; or that he said there was "yet another barrell to broach." [See March 11.]

March 1.   Examination of Nich. Owen. Has served Garnet four years; was at Mr. Throgmorton's house at Coughton, when the insurrection broke out; Garnet said mass at Coughton, Nov. 1st., and was at Henlip, six weeks before the search; Garnet and Hall usually dined and supped with Mr. and Mrs. Abington; he served Garnet at Henlip, and had often been with him at White Webbs. [G. Plot Bk., No. 194.]

March 1.

Tower.   Examination of Geo. Chambers. Serves Hall, the Jesuit; has been several times at Henlip; saw Garnet and Hall there, Jan. 19; has only been once at White Webbs with his master; Hall has a black horse, bought of Rob. Winter. [Ibid., No. 195.]

March 2.

Tower.   7. Report by Edw. Forsett and John Locherson, of a conversation overheard in the Tower between Garnet and Hall. They confess to each other. Garnet is sure Littlejohn [Nich. Owen] will not betray him; asks Hall what was said to him of White Webbs. Garnet says they shall do, if it be not discovered that Mr. Abington knew of their being in his house; hastens away to read or write a letter.

March 3.   Salisbury to Sir Hen. Bruncard. Father Garnet's share in the Powder Treason detected. Lords Mordaunt, Stourton, and Montague will be called before the Star Chamber, to account for their intended absence from Parliament. Stourton and Montague were continually with Mordaunt last summer. The King is disposed to leniency with them and the other great man [the Earl of Northumberland. Irish Corresp. 1606, March 3.]

March 3.

[Tower.]   Hen. Garnet to Anne Vaux. Has received the linen, &c. Desires a loan of 11£., as he and Mr. Hall have not paid their fees. Could not read her last letter. She is to come to his keeper's mother for directions. If she come to the Tower, she may see him, but not speak to him. Catesby wrongs him if he says he approved of the Plot. If any of the Society's money can be procured, he wants beds for James, John, and Harry, who have been tortured. [G. Plot Bk., No. 242.]

March 4 ? Anne Vaux to Hen. Garnet. Sorry he could not read her letter. Will come to the garden to see him, if he will appoint the time. [Almost illegible. Ibid., No. 243.

March 4.   11. Hen. Garnet to Anne Vaux. Full detail of his proceedings. His taking refuge in Henlip House, with Hall. Their sufferings in their place of concealment. Discovery and apprehension by Sir Hen. Bromley. Kind treatment at Sir H. Bromley's house, on the road, and at the Tower. His several examinations and conversations with Chief Justice Popham, Sir Edw. Coke, and Sir Wm. Waad. Is threatened with torture. If he suffers, it will be for not having betrayed what he tried in vain to prevent. [Dated Shrove Tuesday (March 2nd), but indorsed, and probably finished March 4.]

March 5.   Examination of Edw. Oldcorne, alias Hall. Bought a horse of Rob. Winter and sold him again; has spoken twice or thrice with Garnet in the Tower, through the door; Garnet said he would not confess Hall's being at White Webbs; he had frequented White Webbs with Garnet, Gerard, and others, for several years, &c. [G. Plot Bk., No. 196.]

[March 5.] 13. Note by Levinus Munck concerning - Spiller, alias Bellamy, who accompanied Guy Faukes on his last return to England, and has a brother in the Exchequer. [See Feb. 28.]

March 5.   15. Examination of Hen. Garnet. Denies any private conferences with Hall in the Tower, though Hall confesses them; Hall may accuse him falsely, but he will not accuse himself.

March 6.   16. Examination of Hen. Garnet. Confesses that he came to Mr. Abington's house, Henlip, Dec. 4th, and remained there till apprehended, with Hall, Chambers, and Owen; White Webbs was taken by him for their meetings; Mrs. Anne Vaux, alias Perkins, he, and Brookesby, bore the expenses; had a conference with Faukes last Easter, in Thames Street; met Catesby and others at Sir Everard Digby's, Nov. 1st, and met Catesby in Moorfields at Whitsuntide; wrote to Father Baldwin to commend Sir Edw. Baynham as a soldier.

March 6.   Examination of Edw. Oldcorne. Sent for Garnet from Coughton to Mr. Abington's; Tesmond came, Nov. 6th, from Huddington to Henlip, and told them of the Plot and its failure, and of the rising; they refused to join it; Tesmond was angry, and set off to rouse Catholics in Lancashire. In their conferences in the Tower, Garnet told him that if Catesby accused him (Garnet) of the Plot, he wronged him; that he hoped his being at Coughton was not known, as that was the worst thing against him; that Lord Monteagle (Footnote *) had written letters by Sir Edw. Baynham; that he (Garnet), on Nov. 1st, had taken the lead in private prayers for the destruction of heresy. [G. Plot Bk., No. 197.]

March 6.

Tower.   Examination of the Same. Declines to say whether Chambers is his servant; Garnet told him he might acknowledge White Webbs, as the Lords had promised not to harm the parties there; they met at White Webbs twice a year, to confess and renew their vows; particulars of his Tower conversations with Garnet. [Ibid., No. 198.]

March 9. 27. [Earl of Salisbury] to the Earl of Mar. Divers priests were concerned in the Gunpowder Treason, but none have been apprehended except Walley, who confesses his privity, but says that he dissuaded from it. Importance of convincing the world that he is punished for treason, not for religion; the King will have the three Lords tried in the Star Chamber, not by common law. Differences in the Parliament concerning enactments against papists, and as to the punishment of non-communicants. Two subsidies granted; more asked for. Abuses of Purveyors suppressed.

March 11.

York. Information of Phil. Thirlewell, of Hexham, Northumberland, as to the speeches of John Healey, servant to Lancelot Carnaby, on praying for Percy and his company, and on "another barrell yet to be broached." [G. Plot Bk., No. 199. See March 1.]

March 11. Examination of Anne Vaux. Keeps White Webbs at her own expense; since August last has visited her friends; came to London with Mrs. Abington; Catesby, Winter, and Tresham have been to her house; Wm. Shepherd, Rob. Avery, and Rob. Marshall have left her service; went to St. Winifred's Well, with Lady Digby and others whom she will not name; knew nothing of the Plot; told Garnet she feared that the horses at Winter's and Grant's were for mischief, and begged him to prevent it. He spoke to Catesby, who said they were for the Low Countries; was at Coughton Nov. 1, but knows nothing of the prayer there. [Ibid., No. 200.]

March 12. Note by Anne Vaux. Is sorry to hear that Father Garnet was privy to the Plot, as he made many protestations to the contrary. [Ibid., No. 201.]

March 12. Voluntary declaration of Edw. Oldcorne. His conversation with Humphrey Littleton, that the rightfulness of Catesby's Plot was not to be judged by its good or ill success. [Ibid., No. 202.]

March 12.

London. 39. John Chamberlain to Dud. Carleton. Sir Walter Cope has spoken for Carleton to Lord [Salisbury], who will not allow him to go abroad, nor attend Parliament, till Lord [Northumberland's] cause is decided. Two witnesses declare that he (Carleton) was "privy to the hiring of the house for the main blow."

March 12.

Tower. 40. Examination of Hen. Garnet. The letter sent by Sir Everard Digby was to say they were going into Wales; last July, Tesmond, alias Greenwell, revealed Catesby's project to him; Catesby promised him he would not proceed without asking directions from the Pope, how to relieve English Catholics; Catesby or Winter told the Plot to Tesmond, but as he was told it in confession, he ought not to reveal it, even to the Pope; efforts by foreign Ambassadors to obtain relief for Catholics from the King; Father Parsons wrote to him last Michaelmas, to ask what plots the Catholics had on hand; did not answer the letter; burnt all his letters from Rome, and kept no copies of his answers.

March 13. 41. Declaration by Garnet, that since the King's accession, he had tried to persuade Catesby not to plot against Government, that course being forbidden by the Pope. In June, 1604, Catesby and Winter told him of a sure plot they had, but gave no particulars; Greenwell told him they had something in hand, but he (Garnet) disapproved of it; could not persuade Catesby that it was unlawful to take arms.

March 13. 42. Voluntary confession of Hen. Garnet. About a year before the late Queen's death, he received two briefs from Rome, one addressed to the lay Catholics, and one to the priests, bidding them not consent to any successor to the Crown who would not submit to Rome; he kept them secret during Elizabeth's reign, and burnt them on her death, but had shewed them to Catesby, who considered that they authorized his proceedings. There was a league between the Pope and the Kings of France and Spain, to establish a Catholic successor to Queen Elizabeth, by means of an armed force, but her death put an end to the project.

March 13. 43. Thos. Strange [to the Lords Commissioners]. The first news of the Plot was brought by Hen. Huddleston to Harrowden, on 4th November, Mr. Jarret [Gerard] and Mr. Singleton present; he left Harrowden and went to Henlip.

March 13. Examination of Edw. Oldcorne. Garnet shewed him at White Webbs, the Pope's bull, excommunicating all Catholics that should take the part of any Protestant successor to the Throne. [G. Plot Bk., No. 204.]

March 14.

Tower. 44. Examination of Hen. Garnet. On arrival of the two briefs above named, he showed them to Catesby, Percy, and Winter, at White Webbs; but finding all quiet on the Queen's death, he burnt them; Greenwell told him the design of the Plot, but refused to tell particulars, being bound to secresy.

March 17.

Austria.   53. Wm. Joys to Rob. Waverley. Glad to hear of an attempt to release English Catholics from servitude. Sorry for Catesby's death in the good cause. Is prepared to risk his life for it, and will soon come over to England.

March 18. 56. Examination of Rich. Gibson, concerning the speeches of John Healey relative to his being requested to pray for the late intended treason, and saying that "there was a barrell to broche which was not yet knowne."

March 19. 59. Salisbury to Sir Hen. Wotton, Ambassador at Venice. Praises the course he took with the Papal Nuncio. People may now see that the severe laws against Catholics are not made against them merely for their religion, but for treason; since Garnet, the Provincial of the Jesuits, not only confesses his knowledge of the Gunpowder Plot, but thinks it justifiable. Parliament has made severe laws against the papists, and granted the King liberal supplies

March 21 ?

[London.] Anne Vaux to Hen. Garnet. Asks if the spectacles will fit his sight. The Attorney [General] says he (Garnet) acknowledges that he knew of the Plot, but was not a practiser in it. Requests directions. Other friends will write to him, if they can do so safely Life without him "is not life but deathe." [G. Plot Bk., No. 244.]

March 23. Declaration by Garnet of the address of the two papal briefs (see March 14); that the "matter of Spain" was in the winter 1601-2; particulars of his intercourse with Fras. Tresham. [G. Plot Bk., No. 205.]

March 23. Further declaration by Garnet of his intercourse with Tresham, 1600-1603. [Ibid., No. 206.]

March 23. Examination of Wm. Vavasour, servant to Fras. Tresham. A paper which, in a note affixed, he had affirmed to be written by his mistress for his master, and by him witnessed and taken to Sir Walter Cope for the Earl of Salisbury, he now confesses to be in his own handwriting, dictated to him by his master, shortly before his death, when too weak to write himself. [Ibid., No. 207.]

March 24. Examination of Anne, widow of Fras. Tresham. Her husband dictated the declaration to Salisbury sent by her to Sir Walter Cope, without instigation of any person, and Wm. Vavasour wrote it. [Ibid., No. 209.]

March 24. Sir Edw. Coke to Salisbury. Particulars of the two preceding examinations. Tresham has acted upon his book of equivocation, by affirming "manifest falshoods, in articulo mortis." Gladdis, Mr. Abington's man, has confessed the plot by which his master was to have excused himself. [Ibid., No. 208.] Incloses,

I. Declaration by Fras. Tresham to the Lords Commissioners, retracting his former confession that Walley (Garnet) had any connection with the Spanish negotiation; and declaring that he knew not that he had any, nor had he seen nor heard from him for 16 years. Dec. 22. [Ibid., No. 210.]

I. Anne Tresham to Sir Walter Cope. Requests him to deliver the above declaration to Salisbury. [Ibid., No. 211.]

March ?   72. List of relics, church stuff, &c. belonging to Mrs. Brookesby and Mrs. Anne [Vaux.]

March 24. Examination of Anne Vaux. Francis Tresham, her cousin, often visited her and Garnet at White Webbs, Erith, Wandsworth, &c., when Garnet would counsel him to be patient and quiet. They also visited Tresham at his house in Warwickshire. Subscribed as true, by Garnet. [G. Plot Bk., No. 212.]

March 25. Edw. Oldcorne to the Lords Commissioners. Sets down, in order, the conversations between himself and Garnet in the Tower, as before detailed, with a few added particulars; viz., that when Garnet was in the Gatehouse, he received a letter, written with orange juice, telling him that Tesmond was gone over the sea and that Greenway would follow, and that in his examination, he had denied sending Winter and Tesmond into Spain, and would not confess that Lord Monteagle knew of the mission; also that he thought the examiners wished to "save my Lord Monteagle's credit." Oldcorne begs that Mr. Abington may not be punished for entertaining them. [G. Plot Bk., No. 214.]

March 26. 87. Declaration by Hen. Garnet. Gives the substance of the two briefs and of the letter to the Nuncio, the object of which was to establish a Catholic succession in England; the Nuncio was ordered, whenever "that miserable woman died," [Queen Elizabeth], to let the Pope know at once, and to publish the bulls in England.

March 27. Sir Edw. Coke to Salisbury. Requests him to return Mrs. Anne Vaux's examination of March 24. [G. Plot Bk., No. 215.]

March 27. Sir Wm. Waad to the Same. To know whether Garnet should not ride to Guildhall to his trial. Requests to have a part of the bar railed off for himself. [Ibid., No. 216.]

March 27.

London. Abington, Hall, and Strange sent to Newgate, to be conveyed to Westminster for trial. Arraignment of Garnet; he comforts himself with sack to drown sorrow. The Council of Scotland have issued a declaration of the causes of the imprisonment of ministers there

March ? Thos. Abington to Salisbury. His obligations to his Lordship's late father; his substance spoiled by imprisonment; begs relief. [G. Plot Bk., No. 238.]

March ?

Fleet Prison. 91. Thos. Abington to the Council. To be released from prison, that he may recover the losses sustained by destruction of his house.

March 28 ? 93. Notes [by Sir Edw. Coke] of parties implicated in the treason, and of the examinations, &c., by which they are implicated.

March 28 ? 94. Salisbury to [Sir Edw. Coke]. Sends directions from the King on the trial of the Gunpowder Conspirators. He is to shew that their practices began on the Queen's death, and before the severe laws against the Catholics; to disclaim that any one of them wrote the letter to Lord Monteagle, and to praise his conduct, as the King did in his own book, because he has been suspected to have a hand in the Plot; also to make [Hugh] Owen, the Jesuit, as foul as possible.

[March 28.] 95. Narrative of charges against Father Garnet, and his answers to them on his trial. French. [Fuller than in the printed narrative of the trial.]

March 29.

[Tower.] Sir Wm. Waad to Salisbury. Cannot prevail on Garnet in certain particulars. Sets down what he has written on equivocation. [G. Plot Bk., No. 217.] Incloses,

I. Statement at full by Henry Garnet of his sentiments relative to equivocation. It is justifiable only when used for a good object. Is reluctant to judge in the case of Fras. Tresham's equivocation, as he did it to save a friend; but that which is lawful in life may also be done in death. Would consider himself justified in equivocating in death, relative to Gerard's share in the treason, if by so doing, he could clear him; but thinks all treason should be revealed, by any means short of breaking the secresy of the confessional. March 29. [Ibid., No. 217 A.]

-Source: James I: Volume 19 March, 1606 ,

Calendar of State Papers Domestic: James I, 1603-1610, 1857 Pages: 294-307

April, 1606.

April 1 ? 1. Questions propounded to Darcy [Garnet], Provincial of the Jesuits in England, respecting excommunication, heretics, the Gunpowder Plot, the authorship of a book against the King, &c., with answers thereto. Latin.

April 1. 2. Declaration of Hen. Garnet. Considers the penal laws against Catholics as no laws; true treason is that which is made such by just laws; if the law be unjust, then there is no treason; inferior Jesuits are not bound to reveal secrets of confession to their superior; equivocation lawful only when a man is not bound to confess the truth.

April 1. 3. Attested statement by Sir Wm. Waad, that Garnet affirms that if any one undertake to kill the King, he is not bound to confess it, unless there be proof to convict him.

April 1.

Essex House. 4. Sir Allan Percy to Dud. Carleton. Nothing new has transpired from Garnet's trial. Parliament about to assemble. Illness of the Lord Chancellor and Earl of Devonshire. Is going to join his brother [the Earl of Northumberland] whose affairs are not hopeful; for though there was nothing said of him at the arraignment, yet there was a show as though they could say more than they would. Strange is to be arraigned before the execution of Garnet. A great quarrel between three gentlemen, on occasion of drinking the Earl of Southampton's health.

April 2.

London. 5. John Chamberlain to the Same. Particulars of Garnet's trial; the King, Lady Arabella, and many others present. The French King and Duke of Bouillon agreed. Danger of the Earl of Devonshire.

[April 2.] Hen. Garnet to Anne Vaux. Directions for the disposal of herself. Mr. Hall dreamt there were two tabernacles prepared for them. [G. Plot Bk., No. 245.]

April 3. Anne Vaux to Hen. Garnet. Acknowledges the receipt of the spectacles. Wishes Mr. Hall had dreamed there was a third seat for her; asks fuller directions. [G. Plot Bk., No. 246.]

April 3. 11. Hen. Garnet to Anne Vaux. Full directions as to her proceedings, residence, &c., when set at liberty; her vow of obedience ceases if she goes abroad. Arranges the pecuniary matters of the Jesuit mission, and its temporary management. Sorry that Catholics are scandalized at his conduct. Was so pressed in his late examination that he determined to confess the whole truth, rather than undergo torture, or trial by witness, and therefore acknowledged that Greenwell told him the Plot in confession. He "sought to hinder it more than men can imagine, as the Pope can tell;" has written to declare to the King his detestation of it; will die "not as a victorious martyr, but as a penitent thief." Indorsed [by Sir Wm. Waad], "Garnet to Mrs. Vaulx, to be published after his death, by her and the Jesuytes."

April 4. 12. Hen. Garnet's declaration, written to be shewn to the King. Protests the Gunpowder Plot to be "altogether unlawful and most horrible;" ought to have revealed it but did not, partly to spare his friends, and also in hopes of preventing it. Has offended God, the King, and the state, and begs forgiveness of all.

April 9.

Serjeants' Inn. 20. Chief Justice Popham to the Same. Montague House has been searched, but several persons escaped out of it. If Gerard be in England, he might be one of them. Money bags found in Rich Carey's house; he is under guard, and Barlow, a priest, taken. Rich. Fulwood disposes of the moneys. Recusants not to be allowed to flock together in London.

April 21. 39. Hen. Garnet to Anne Vaux. Details his multiplied misfortunes; his own apprehension and arraignment; his conversations overheard; his letters intercepted; her apprehension; Greenwell taken; Erith and the other house ransacked; Hall executed; and now Richard and Robert taken with a cypher letter and the key of the cypher also. Below is a drawing of a cross, the letters I. H. S., and a pierced heart, inscribed "Deus cordis mei, et pars mea Deus in æternum."

April 24.

Rutland. 42. Examinations of Eliz. Tilton, Eliz. Courtney, John Chambers, John Tampion, John Digby of Seaton, Rutland, Thos. Ager of Deene, Northamptonshire, and Chris. Blunston, as to Fairfax, and other priests, who were entertained at the houses of John Digby and John Brudenells.

April 25.

Tower. 44. Examination of Hen. Garnet. His burning the Pope's bulls; proposal to make some nobleman Protector; Greenwell's confession of the plot to him; neither saw nor wrote to Greenwell since Nov. 6, nor agreed with him not to discover some noblemen. Fulwood came to him at Coughton, but left him before he went to Henlip. All this he affirms on his priesthood.

April 25. 45. Examination of John Healey, servant to Lancelot Carnaby. Sicklemore said the rising in Warwickshire was for the Catholic cause, and bade Catholics pray for its success, and not be faint-hearted. Particulars of private masses in Northumberland and Lincolnshire, and of the priests who celebrated them.

April 27.

48. I. Information of Hen. Guevara against John and Michael Davison, of Bittleston, as to their resistance when he came to their house to search for Percy. 1605, Nov. 18.

April 28. Exposition and defence of equivocation, by Henry Garnet. When asked if it were well to deny on his priesthood that he had written to Greenwell or had conference with Hall, knowing his denial to be false; replied that in his opinion, and that of all the schoolmen, equivocation may be confirmed by oath or sacrament, without perjury, "if just necessity so require." [G. Plot Bk., No. 218.]

April 29.

Tower. 50. Thos. Phelippes to Salisbury. Exculpates himself from any connexion with Garnet and the conspirators in the Powder Plot. [See Feb. 1606.]

April ?

Tower. 51. Account of the proceedings of Thos. Phelippes, addressed by him to the Lieutenant [of the Tower]. Begs the King's consideration of him. His intercourse with Owen was only a stratagem on behalf of Government, in the late Queen's time; particulars of it; presents received by him from Spain; he renewed his correspondence with Flanders, after his first trouble, only in hope of obtaining largesse from Spain; wrote not to Owen but to Mancididor ; his acquaintance with Freeman; knows nothing of Garnet, nor received money from Baldwin. Paget's malice causes his troubles. [Dr. Wm.] Gifford writes that the Pope is working for the King's disquiet; wishes to serve the King by his correspondence, or to retire.

[April 29.] 52. Proofs [alleged by Sir Edw. Coke in the House of Commons] of the complicity of Hugh Owen, in the Gunpowder Plot, as prefixed, viz.:-

Confession of Guy Faukes that he went into Flanders, and disclosed the whole Plot to Hugh Owen and others, who liked it well, and said that Thos. Morgan had proposed the very same thing, in Queen Elizabeth's time. Owen promised that Sir Wm. Stanley should come over with his English troops, if it succeeded. 1606, Jan. 20.

Testimony of Charles Ratcliffe, that Hugh Owen, Father Baldwin, and Colonel Jaques had written to the Archpriest and the English Jesuits, urging caution in "the great important business."

Confession of Thos. Winter, that Rob. Catesby sent him over to Flanders to find a fit agent for the Powder Plot; Father Owen commended Faukes, for secrecy, resolution, and valour. 1605, Nov. 25.

[April.   55. Narrative of the Gunpowder Plot, from its first discovery to the seizure of the conspirators at Holbeach House. French. [The letter to Lord Monteagle is here said to be written by Fras. Tresham.]

April ?   56. Preamble of a grant to Lord Monteagle of land, value 200£. per annum, for his services in the detection of the Gunpowder Plot.

-Source:James I: Volume 20, April, 1606 Calendar of State Papers Domestic: James I, 1603-1610 1857 Pages: 308-314

May, 1606

May 2.

London.   4. Dud. Carleton to John Chamberlain. Sir Thos. Stukeley in town; has bought a manor of Lord Lisle. Garnet's execution postponed from May-day to May 3, for fear of disturbances. His surprise when told he was to die; he shifts, falters, and equivocates, but "will be hanged without equivocation." Reception and departure of the Spanish Ambassador; he did not plead for Garnet, lest the King should insist on the delivery of Owen. Earl of Devonshire's funeral. Intended promotions.

May 3.   5. Narrative [by a Romish eye-witness] of the execution of Father Garnet. Latin.

May 3.   Portrait of Henry Garnet, engraved by Johan Wirix, subscribed: "Si quid patimini propter justitiam, beati.-Henricus Garnetus, Anglus, e Societate Jesû, passus." [G. Plot Bk., No. 218 A.]

May 3.

Portrait by the Same, of Garnet's head, in the midst of an ear of wheat, [as it was said to have appeared to a Romanist, when looking at a straw taken as a relic from his scaffold.] Circumscribed "Miraculosa effigies R. P. Henrici Garneti, Sotis Jesus, Martyris Angliæ, 3 Maii, 1606." [Ibid., No. 218 B. See Flanders Corresp., 18 Jan. and 4 Feb. 1607.]

Garnet's Straw, The Penny Magazine, Vol. 4, 1835, p.245.

May ?   6. Detail [by Levinus Munck, corrected by Salisbury,] of the secret negotiations of Guy Faukes and Rob. Winter with the King of Spain and Constable of Castile, to induce them to support the Catholic cause, on the accession of James I. States that nothing was proved, from any of the examinations, inculpating any foreign prince in the Gunpowder Plot.

[May 13.]   23. Act of Attainder of the Conspirators in the Gunpowder Treason.

May 21.   27. Examination of John Tucker, shipmaster, relative to the speeches of Robt. Moore during his passage to England. Jesuits and priests are now allowed by the Pope to deny their profession, or to swear and forswear anything to heretics, for their own preservation. The Gunpowder Plotters would have been sainted at Rome.

Source: James I: Volume 21

May, 1606 Calendar of State Papers Domestic: James I, 1603-1610,1857,315-319

August-November, 1606.

August 14.

[London.] 8. Dud. Carleton to the Earl of Northumberland. Begs that as the gates of Court are shut to all connected with his Lordship, he will make him one of his country farmers.

August 20.

[Tower.] 9. Earl of Northumberland to Dud. Carleton. Can bear his own misfortunes, because he is innocent, but regrets those of his dependants who suffer for his sake. Thinks the Court the best sphere for Carleton, but has no hope of ever helping him there. Objects to his turning clown. Will allow him a small pension, to keep him from sinking.

August 20.

London. 10. Dud. Carleton to John Chamberlain. Fears to accept offers from the Earl of Northumberland. Lord Northampton troubled that the King never sent to visit him in his illness, although he sent to Lord Salisbury, when he was only ill one day.

Sept. 15.

Tower Hill. 20. Sir Allan Percy to Dud. Carleton. Private affairs. Disputes with Lord Northumberland; Salisbury's health improves. The King is at Hampton Court, to receive a son of the Duke of Lorraine. Extents issued on the Earl of Northumberland's lands. The Countess of Northumberland pleads so hard for her husband, that Salisbury will not see her again. Sir Walter Cope much consulted. Whitelock's pension augmented.

Sept. 15. 21. Examinations of Eliz. Upcher, John Wakering, and others, of Kelden, co. Essex, on the speeches of Esdras, alias Thomas Simson, Vicar of Kelden, as to his connexion with Tirrel, who was privy to the Gunpowder Plot; his preaching popish doctrines, &c.

-Source: James I: Volume 23
August-November, 1606
Calendar of State Papers Domestic: James I, 1603-1610, 1857 Pages: 328-336
-Wenceslaus Hollar, 1641

A Scary Event Sends Lasting Ripples out Through Time

"The verie relating or mentioning thereof dawnteth my hart with horror, even shaking the verie pen in my hand, whilst I think what a shake, what a blast, or what a storme (as they termed it), they ment so suddenly to have raised for the blowing up, shivering into pieces, and whirling about of those honourable, anointed and sacred bodies, which the Lord would not have to be so much as touched."

-A Comparative Discourse of the Bodies Natural and Politique, 1606, Cited in: -Williams, Richard, Frederick James Furnivall, William Richard Morfill, Ballads from Manuscripts,, Vol.2, 1873, p.xxxiii.

The Artifacts of Iconography are Assembled to Convey the Significance of the Deliverance

-Image: "Powder Plot 1 W.E. exc. 1605, From: Gerard, John, <u>What Was the Gunpowder Plot, 1897</u>, frontispiece. (According to Gerard the image was created within five months of the "Great Deliverance.")

Right after the plot, the wonder of providence, the mystery of the deliverance was given form by the application of the iconography of the eye of God. The source for this association was the "Old Testament" of the Bible, which describes how the people of Israel had employed it to give shape and form for their mysterious deliverances.

The eye is shown coming from above with a beam of light emerging from the eye shining down upon Guy Fawkes. Fawkes is shown with his icon, the lantern, and sometimes his matches and boots with spurs. This method of presentation has lasted for centuries. The iconographic depictions of the deliverance are often found stitched into the Book of Common Prayer to accompany the Liturgy for November 5, Powder Plot Day. These icons made an important impression upon the largely illiterate public. Perhaps the masks of bonfire Guys today are descendents of these early icons.

Constructing Celebration

The Bibilcal Foundations of Celebration

Here are relevant verses from the Bible which were used to construct the icons of remembrance.

Psalm 66

¹Make a joyful noise unto God, all ye lands:

²Sing forth the honour of his name: make his praise glorious.

³Say unto God, How terrible art thou in thy works! through the greatness of thy power shall thine enemies submit themselves unto thee.

⁴All the earth shall worship thee, and shall sing unto thee; they shall sing to thy name. Selah.

⁵Come and see the works of God: he is terrible in his doing toward the children of men.

⁶He turned the sea into dry land: they went through the flood on foot: there did we rejoice in him.

⁷He ruleth by his power for ever; his eyes behold the nations: let not the rebellious exalt themselves. Selah.

⁸O bless our God, ye people, and make the voice of his praise to be heard:

⁹Which holdeth our soul in life, and suffereth not our feet to be moved.

¹⁰For thou, O God, hast proved us: thou hast tried us, as silver is tried.

¹¹Thou broughtest us into the net; thou laidst affliction upon our loins.

¹²Thou hast caused men to ride over our heads; we went through fire and through water: but thou broughtest us out into a wealthy place.

¹³I will go into thy house with burnt offerings: I will pay thee my vows,

¹⁴Which my lips have uttered, and my mouth hath spoken, when I was in trouble.

¹⁵I will offer unto thee burnt sacrifices of fatlings, with the incense of rams; I will offer bullocks with goats. Selah.

¹⁶Come and hear, all ye that fear God, and I will declare what he hath done for my soul.

¹⁷I cried unto him with my mouth, and he was extolled with my tongue.

[18]If I regard iniquity in my heart, the Lord will not hear me:

[19]But verily God hath heard me; he hath attended to the voice of my prayer.

[20]Blessed be God, which hath not turned away my prayer, nor his mercy from me.

-Bible, King James Version, "Psalm 66, 1-19

From the Story of King Asa of Judah

[6]Then Asa the king took all Judah; and they carried away the stones of Ramah, and the timber thereof, wherewith Baasha was building; and he built therewith Geba and Mizpah.

[7]And at that time Hanani the seer came to Asa king of Judah, and said unto him, Because thou hast relied on the king of Syria, and not relied on the LORD thy God, therefore is the host of the king of Syria escaped out of thine hand.

[8]Were not the Ethiopians and the Lubims a huge host, with very many chariots and horsemen? yet, because thou didst rely on the LORD, he delivered them into thine hand.

[9]For the eyes of the LORD run to and fro throughout the whole earth, to shew himself strong in the behalf of them whose heart is perfect toward him. Herein thou hast done foolishly: therefore from henceforth thou shalt have wars.

-- Bible, King Jame's Version, "2 Chronicles 16:6-9,"

Psalm 33

[18]Behold, the eye of the LORD is upon them that fear him, upon them that hope in his mercy;

[19]To deliver their soul from death, and to keep them alive in famine.

[20]Our soul waiteth for the LORD: he is our help and our shield.

[21]For our heart shall rejoice in him, because we have trusted in his holy name.

[22]Let thy mercy, O LORD, be upon us, according as we hope in thee.

-Bible, King Jame's Version, "Psalm 33," 18-22.

Proverbs 33

[12]The eyes of the LORD preserve knowledge, and he overthroweth the words of the transgressor.

--Bible, King James Version, "Proverbs," 33:18.

Psalm 94

[7]Yet they say, The LORD shall not see, neither shall the God of Jacob regard it.

[8]Understand, ye brutish among the people: and ye fools, when will ye be wise?

⁹He that planted the ear, shall he not hear? he that formed the eye, shall he not see?

¹⁰He that chastiseth the heathen, shall not he correct? he that teacheth man knowledge, shall not he know?

¹¹The LORD knoweth the thoughts of man, that they are vanity.

--<u>Bible</u>, King James Version, "Psalm 94",7-11.

Proverbs 15

³The eyes of the LORD are in every place, beholding the evil and the good.

-<u>Bible,</u> King James Version, "Proverbs 15," 3.

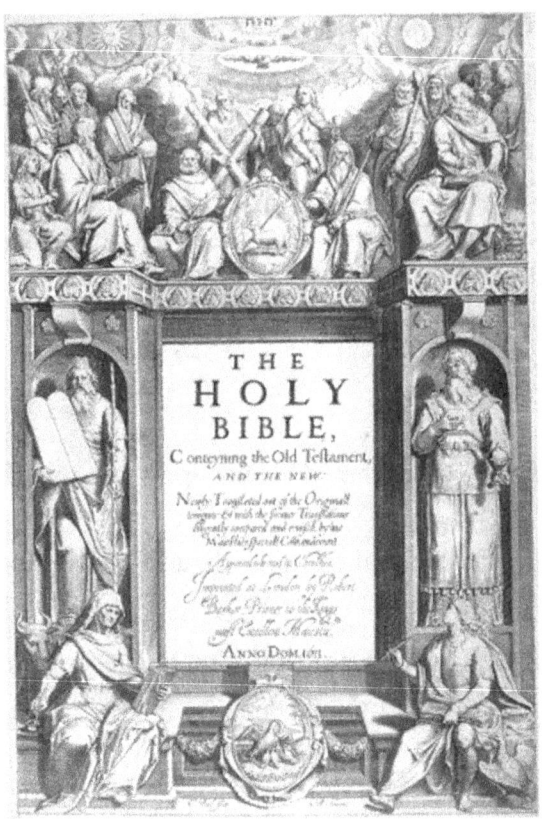

King James' Bible, 1611

Frontispeece "Discovered" from Novembris Monstrum, A.B.C.D.E., 1641

Though not appearing till later, "Frontispeece Discovered" is a good example of the development of the iconography of the deliverance which began in 1605.

The Devill plots, the Pope will owen
The Jesuits must act or none
One God doth See and Smile, and Blast,
What hell, and Rome, and all forecraft.

'tis not the blackness of the Pit
Can cloud this eye from seeing it,
Tis not the deepenesse of The Pit,
Can straine this Arme from reaching it,
Tis not the terror of the Pit
That feare this Smile from daring it,
This eye can chase the thickest mist,
This arme can conquer, when it lift,
One looke, one touch, one Smile can quell
The Pride and Pollicy of Hell….

   -A.B.C.D.E., <u>Novembris Monstrum,</u> 1641.

Paradise Lost, John Milton, 1667

John Milton was born in 1608, three years after the plot. He was both surrounded at an early age with, and contributed to, the iconography of the plot through his writings. The iconography of the Eye of God is found in <u>Paradise Lost.</u>

> Now had the almighty Father from above,
> From the pure empyrean where he sits
> High throned above all highth, bent down his eye,
> His own works and their works at once to view

--Milton, John, <u>Paradise Lost</u>, 3.56-59, 1667.

Video Rideo- I See and Laugh to Scorn

This slogan is an important element which successfully ties the Great Deliverance of 1605 to the traditions of the Old Testament of the <u>Bible</u>. It is often attached to the beam of light that comes down from the eye of God to illuminate the plotter Fawkes. It forcefully brings the message that Providence is an important and real force in the world, protecting the chosen people of England just as it had protected the Hebrews of the <u>Bible.</u>

As for Laughing:

Psalm 2

2 Why do the heathen rage, and the people imagine a vain thing?

2 The kings of the earth set themselves, and the rulers take counsel together, against the Lord, and against his anointed, saying,

3 Let us break their bands asunder, and cast away their cords from us.

4 He that sitteth in the heavens shall laugh: the Lord shall have them in derision.

5 Then shall he speak unto them in his wrath, and vex them in his sore displeasure.

Psalm 37

37 Fret not thyself because of evildoers, neither be thou envious against the workers of iniquity.

2 For they shall soon be cut down like the grass, and wither as the green herb.

3 Trust in the Lord, and do good; so shalt thou dwell in the land, and verily thou shalt be fed.

4 Delight thyself also in the Lord: and he shall give thee the desires of thine heart.

5 Commit thy way unto the Lord; trust also in him; and he shall bring it to pass.

6 And he shall bring forth thy righteousness as the light, and thy judgment as the noonday.

7 Rest in the Lord, and wait patiently for him: fret not thyself because of him who prospereth in his way, because of the man who bringeth wicked devices to pass.

8 Cease from anger, and forsake wrath: fret not thyself in any wise to do evil.

9 For evildoers shall be cut off: but those that wait upon the Lord, they shall inherit the earth.

10 For yet a little while, and the wicked shall not be: yea, thou shalt diligently consider his place, and it shall not be.

11 But the meek shall inherit the earth; and shall delight themselves in the abundance of peace.

12 The wicked plotteth against the just, and gnasheth upon him with his teeth.

13 The Lord shall laugh at him: for he seeth that his day is coming.

14 The wicked have drawn out the sword, and have bent their bow, to cast down the poor and needy, and to slay such as be of upright conversation.

15 Their sword shall enter into their own heart, and their bows shall be broken.

Job 22," 17-21.

From rhe speech of Eliphaz Job's comforter

17 Which said unto God, Depart from us: and what can the Almighty do for them?

18 Yet he filled their houses with good things: but the counsel of the wicked is far from me.

19 The righteous see it, and are glad: and the innocent laugh them to scorn.

20 Whereas our substance is not cut down, but the remnant of them the fire consumeth.

21 Acquaint now thyself with him, and be at peace: thereby good shall come unto thee.

Psalm 37

11 But the meek shall inherit the earth; and shall delight themselves in the abundance of peace.

12 The wicked plotteth against the just, and gnasheth upon him with his teeth.

13 The LORD shall laugh at him: for he seeth that his day is coming.

14 The wicked have drawn out the sword, and have bent their bow, to cast down the poor and needy, and to slay such as be of upright conversation.

15 Their sword shall enter into their own heart, and their bows shall be broken.

16 A little that a righteous man hath is better than the riches of many wicked.

17 For the arms of the wicked shall be broken: but the LORD upholdeth the righteous.

-Bible, King James Version,

The Eye of God:

Deuteronomy 26:7

7 And when we cried unto the Lord God of our fathers, the Lord heard our voice, and looked on our affliction, and our labour, and our oppression:

8 And the Lord brought us forth out of Egypt with a mighty hand, and with an outstretched arm, and with great terribleness, and with signs, and with wonders:

Psalm 102:19-20

19 For he hath looked down from the height of his sanctuary; from heaven did the Lord behold the earth;

20 To hear the groaning of the prisoner; to loose those that are appointed to death;

Deuteronomy 11

11 But the land, whither ye go to possess it, is a land of hills and valleys, and drinketh water of the rain of heaven:

12 A land which the Lord thy God careth for: the eyes of the Lord thy God are always upon it, from the beginning of the year even unto the end of the year.

--<u>Bible,</u> King James Version

Discovery of Fawkes, Raymond Shist, 1788

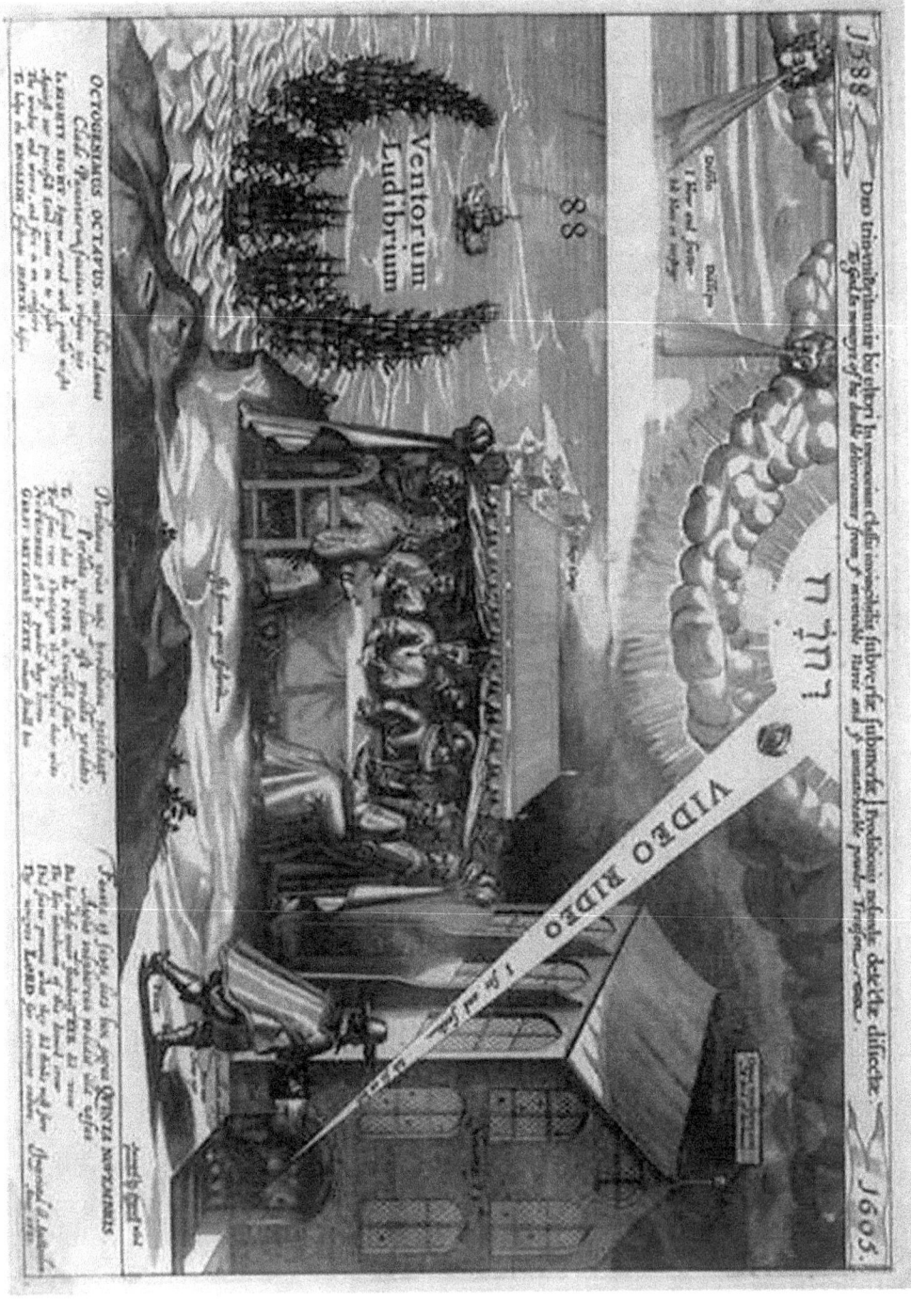

"The Double Deliverance of England from the Spanish armada and Gunpowder Plot," Samuel Ward, 1621.

"The Double Deliverance of England from the Spanish armada and Gunpowder Plot," Samuel Ward, 1621

Here we see the Eye of God aiding in the discovery of Guy Fawkes who is shown with his Iconic lantern. The beam of light is inscribed "Video Rideo," I see, I laugh.

On the left side reference is made to the other grand act of mysterious providence, the defeat of the Spanish Armada which was wrecked by a storm at sea thus saving England.
In the middle the Pope and his cardinals and the devil plot, personifying the threat posed by the political papacy in their pursuit of the Counter Reformation. In the print is found the inscription in three languages:

"Deo Trin-Vni Britanniae bis ultori, in Memoriam Classis invincibilis subversae, submersae; Proditionis nefandae detectae, disiectae."
"To God, in memory of his double deliverance from ye invincible Navy, and ye unmatcheable Powder-treason."
"Octogesimus octavus, mirabilis annus,
Clade Papistarum faustus ubique piis,
Perditione prius, nunc proditione petebant;
Perdita perditio est, prodita proditio.
Fausta et festa dies, lux aurea quinta Novembris,
Anglis sulphureum prodidit ilia nefas."

"In Eighty-eight, Spayne, arm'd with potent might,
Against our peaceful land came on to fight;
But windes and waves and fire in one conspire,
To help the English, frustrate Spayne's desire.
To second that, the Pope in counsell sitts,
For some rare stratagem they strayne their witts;
November's 5th, by powder they decree
Great Brytane's state ruinated should bee.
But Hee, whose never-slumb'ring Eye did view
The dire intendments of this damned crew,
Did soone prevent what they did thinke most sure.

Thy mercies, Lord! for evermore endure."

Offending the Spanish ambassador, this engraving was responsible for having Ward brought before the Privy Council and subsequently emprisoned.

-Samuel Ward, The Double Deliverance of England from the Spanish armada and Gunpowder Plot, 1621.

Volpone; Or, The Foxe. Ben Jonson January 1606- February 1607

Volpone: An Early Reaction to the Plot

Image: Benjamin Jonson, after Abraham van Blyenberch, 1617

Ben Jonson, a convert to Catholicism, had many encounters with the government although one of his most important patrons was Robert Cecil. Carefully avoiding the censors, Jonson crafted his play Volpone; Or, The Foxe immediately following the discovery of the plot. He had been noticed as being present at a meeting of the conspirators prior to the plot and because of that association he is thought by some to have been one of Cecil's spies. Jonson, however, had suffered greatly for offending powerful figures with his writing, being imprisoned at Tyburn where he was branded with the letter T and being placed on trial as a recusant along with his wife. Richard Dutton (2008) makes a convincing argument that Volpone was written as an attack upon Robert Cecil, (whose nickname was "The Fox") that would have been recognized as such by the community of British writers and intellectuals. (Dutton also notes that Jonson's play Catiline can also be interpreted as a similar attack upon Cecil.) As such these introductory pieces published with the play are of great importance. In them Jonson hints at the play's purpose and even includes a portion of a letter that he had written to Robert Cecil.

Ben Jonson

January 1606- February 1607

Volpone; Or, The Foxe.

Comick-poet to imitate justice and instruct to life, as well as puritie of language, or stirre up gentle affections. To which, upon my next opportunity toward the examining & digesting of my *notes,* I shall speake more wealthily, and pay the World a debt.

In the meanetime *(most reverenced* SISTERS) as I have car'd to be thankfull for your affections past, and here made the understanding acquainted with some ground of your favors; let me not dispayre their continuance, to the maturing of some Worthier fruits, wherein, if my MUSES bee true to me, I shall raise the dispis'd head of POETRY againe, and stripping her out of those rotten and base ragges, wherewhich the *Times* have adulterated her forme, restore her to her primitive habite, feature and majesty, and render her worthy to be imbraced, and kist, of all the great and Maister *spirits* of our World. As for the vile, and slothfull, who never affected an act, worthy of celebration, or are so inward with their owne vicious natures, as they worthely feare her ; and thinke it a high point of policie to keepe her in contempt with their declamatory and windy invectives : Shee shall, out of just rage, incite her Servants (who are *Genus irritabile*) to spout inke in their faces that shall eate farder than their marrow, into their fames ; and not CINNAMUS the Barber, with his art, shall be able to take out the brands, but they shall live, and be read, till the Wretches die, as Things worst deserving of themselves in chiefe, and then of all mankind.

From my house in the Black-Friars this II. of February. 1607. AD UTRAMQUE ACADEMIAM,

To My Deare friend, Mr. Beniamin Jonson, upon his FOXE.

If it might stand with Justice, to allow
The swift conversion of all follies ; now,
Such is my Mercy, that I could admit
All sorts should equally approve the wit,
Of this thy even worke : whose growing fame,
Shall raise thee high, and thou it, with thy Name.
And did not Manners ; and my Love command
Mee to forbeare to make those understand,
Whom thou, perhaps, hast in thy wiser doome,
Long since, firmely resolv'd shall never come
To know more than they do; I would have showne

To all the world, the Art, which thou alone
Hast taught our tongue, the rules of Time, of Place,
And other Rites, deliver d with the grace
Of Comick stile, which onely, is farre more,
Than any English Stage hath knowne before.
But since our subtle Gallants thinke it good
To like of nought, that may be understood,
Least they should be disprov'd; or have, at best,
Stomachs so raw, that nothing can digest
But what's obscene, or barkes: Let us desire
They may continue, simplie, to admire
Fine Clothes, and strange words; and may live, in age,
To see themselves ill-brought upon the Stage,
And like it. Whilst thy bold, and knowing Muse
Contemnes all praise, but such as thou wouldst chuse.

THE PROLOGUE

Now, luck God send us, and a little wit
Will serve, to make our PLAY hit;
(According to the palates of the season)
Here is rime, not emptie of reason:
This we were bid to credit, from our Poet,
Whose true scope, if you would knowe it,
In all his Poemes, still, hath beene this measure,
To mixe profit, with your pleasure ;
And not as some (whose throates their envie fayling)
Crie hoarsely, All he writes, is rayling :
And, when his Playes come forth, thinke they can flout them.
With saying, He was a yeare about them.
To these there needs no Lye, but this his creature,
Which was, two monthes since, no feature ;
And though he dares give them five lives to mend it,
'Tis knowne, five weekes fully fend it:
From his owne hand, without a Co-adjutor,
Novice, Journey-man, or Tutor.
Tet, thus much I can give you, as a token
Of his Playes worth, No egges are broken,
Nor quaking Custards with feirce teeth affrighted,
Wherewith your route are so delighted;
Nor hales hee in a Gull, old ends reciting,
To stop gappes in his Loose writing ;
With such a deale of monstrous, and fore action :

As might make Bethlem a faction :
Nor made he his Play, for iests stolne from each Table,

But makes jests to fit his Fable ;
And, so presents quick Comoedy, refined,
As best Criticks have designed,
The Lawes of Time, Place, Persons he observeth,
From no needefull Rule he swerveth.
All gall, and coppresse, from his inke, he drayneth,
Onelie, a little salt remaineth ;
Wherewith, hee"ll rub your cheekes, till (red with laughter)
They shall looke fresh, a weeke after.

-Johnson, Ben, <u>Ben Jonson , His Volpone: or, The Foxe,</u> Ed.: Vincent O'Sullivan, 1898.
(January 1606- February 1607)

Making the Commemoration Official

Calendar of State Papers Domestic: James I, 1603-1610, January 1606

Gunpowder Plot - A learned and religious Speech. -

Sir Edw. Mountague moveth, That an Act may be made, that there may be an everlasting Memory of Thanksgiving. -

No extraordinary Blessing in Scripture, but an extraordinary Sign : -

The Covenant with Noe, the Rainbow: - Jacob and Esau : - ix. Hester, Hamon, and Mordecay: - Keeping of Days of Deliverance of the Jews. -

Yearly Thanksgiving.

Offereth a Bill, intituled, A Bill for a publick Thanksgiving to be given to Almighty God, every Year, on the fifth Day of November: - First Reading.

-James I: Volume 18, January-February, 1606, Calendar of State Papers Domestic: James I, 1603-1610 1857 Pages:277-294

Noah's Thanksgiving

¹³And it came to pass in the six hundredth and first year, in the first month, the first day of the month, the waters were dried up from off the earth: and Noah removed the covering of the ark, and looked, and, behold, the face of the ground was dry.

¹⁴And in the second month, on the seven and twentieth day of the month, was the earth dried.

¹⁵And God spake unto Noah, saying,

¹⁶Go forth of the ark, thou, and thy wife, and thy sons, and thy sons' wives with thee.

¹⁷Bring forth with thee every living thing that is with thee, of all flesh, both of fowl, and of cattle, and of every creeping thing that creepeth upon the earth; that they may breed abundantly in the earth, and be fruitful, and multiply upon the earth.

¹⁸And Noah went forth, and his sons, and his wife, and his sons' wives with him:

¹⁹Every beast, every creeping thing, and every fowl, and whatsoever creepeth upon the earth, after their kinds, went forth out of the ark.

²⁰And Noah builded an altar unto the LORD; and took of every clean beast, and of every clean fowl, and offered burnt offerings on the altar.

²¹And the LORD smelled a sweet savour; and the LORD said in his heart, I will not again curse the ground any more for man's sake; for the imagination of man's heart is evil from his youth; neither will I again smite any more every thing living, as I have done.

²²While the earth remaineth, seedtime and harvest, and cold and heat, and summer and winter, and day and night shall not cease.

-<u>Bible,</u> King James Version, Genesis 8, 13:22

1605 Shilling

Robert Bowyer, "Book I, Stanford MS," 1606-1607.

Robert Bowyer reports on the Bill making November 5 an official day of Thanksgiving

23 Jan.

Sir Edward Montague, in a speach well penned, but not affected did declare how greate a deliverance his Majestie and the Realme latelie had from the entended treason: and moved that the same having happened through Gods greate favor there may be some provision whererby the rememberance of his goodnesse in this behalf be continued to posterity: this he perswaded to be necessarie, by declaring that God having provided for the continuance of his Churche by the preservation of Noe, and his family commanded a rememberance therof, and to that purpose placed the Raine bow in the firmament and so discended to Gods other blessings towards his church and people in aunciet time and their thanckfull rememberance of the same by building of Alters and other like signes which he particularly and breife did mencion or rather touche : and in conclusion offered a bill intituled An act for a publique thanksgiving unto God every yeere on the 5h of November *primo lecta* and herin he wished the howse would proceede before anie other matter. Mr. Speaker taking this bill began with himself to peruse it and soddainly staied, and moved the house that a private bill might be readde whilest he overlooked this so delivered by Sir Edward Montague, whereunto the howse assented, and then was readde An bill intituled, An act to enable John Houther the father and John Houther the son to make a jointure to the wife of John the son: *primo lecta*: Then was the foresaide bill of thankesgivinge, offered as afore by Sir Edward Montague, readde, and presentlie the howse required the same to be readde the second time which was doon, and then also committed and the Committees directed by the howse foorth with to repaire into the Committee chamber: whether they immediately went accordinglie where they continued together untell halfe hower after 12 of the clocke at which time the Speaker sent the Serieant to wish them to come away if they weare ready, for that the howse had staied longer than their other occasions required beyond the ordinary hower for them, but for that they returned aunswere that they had not concluded of all points in such sort as they desired, but requested to be forborne and that they might meete the next day in the same place before the setting of the court the howse yelded thereunto and so arose......

24 Jan. 1605

Mr. solicitor brought in againe the bill of thanksgiving before offered by Sir Edward Montague with some alteracions in forme agreed on by the Committees, which alteracions weare readde: which bill so altered by consent of the howse was put to engrossing.

-Bowyer, Robert,"Book I, Stanford MS," <u>The Parliamentary Diary of Robert Bowyer, 1606-1607</u>, Ed. David Harris Wilson, 1971. P.4-7.

Here begins the Official Annual Commemoration of the Great Deliverance.

The history of this official commemoration, which remained in the Book of Common Prayer until the last half of the 19th century, can be found in: Lathbury, Thomas, Guy Fawkes: or, A complete History of the Gunpowder Treason, 1839.

Thanksgiving Act, James I, 1605

1605

1605- Thanksgiving Act

In the Third Year of King *James*

An ACT for a publicke Thanks-giving to Almighty God, on the fifth day of November every Year.

For as much as Almighty God hath in all Ages shewed his Power and Mercy, in the miraculous and gracious deliverance of his Church, and in the protection of Religious Kings and States And that no Nation of the earth hath been blessed with greater benefits then this Kingdom now enjoyeth, having the true and free protection of the Gospel under our most Soveraigne Lord, King James, the most Great, Learned, and Religious King that ever reigned therein, inriched with a most hopeful and plentiful Progenie, proceeding out of his Royal loynes, promising continuance of this happiness and possession to all posterity: the which many Malignant and Devillish Papists, Jesuites and Seminary Priests much envying and fearing, conspired most horribly, when the kings most excellent Majesty, the Queen, the Prince, and all the Lords Spiritual and Temporal, and Commons would have been assembled in the Upper-house of Parliament upon the fifth of November, in the year of our Lord one thousand six hundred and five, suddainly to have blown up the said whole house with Gunpowder; an invention so inhumane, barbarous, and cruel, as the like was never before heard of, and was (as some of the principal Conspirators hereof confess) purposely devised and concluded to be done in the said house, that where sundry, necessary, and Religious Laws for preservation of the Church and State were made, which they falsely and slanderously term cruel Laws, enacted against them and their Religion, both place and persons should all be destroyed and blown up at once, which would have turned to the utter ruine of this whole kingdom, had it not pleased Allmighty God, by inspiring the Kings most excellent Majesty with a Divine Spirit, to interpret some dark phrases of a Letter shewed to his Majesty, above and beyond all ordinary construction, thereby miraculously discovering this hidden treason not many hours before the appointed time for the Execution thereof: Therefore the Kings most excellent Majesty, the Lords Spiritual and temporal, and all his Majesties faithful and loving Subjects, do most truly acknowledge this great and infinite Blessing to have proceeded meerly from God his great mercy, and to his most holy name do ascribe all honor, Glory and Praise: and to the end, this unfeigned thankfulness may never be forgotten, but be had in a perpetual remembrance, that all ages to come may yield praises to his Divine Majesty for the same, and have in perpetual memory, This joyful day of deliverance.

Be it therefore enacted by the Kings most excellent Majesty, the Lords Spiritual and Temporal, and the Commons in this present Parliament assembled, and by the Authority of the same, that all and singular Ministers in every Cathedral and Parish Church or other usuall place for common Prayer, within this Realm of England, and the Dominions of the same, shall always upon the fifth day of November, say morning Prayer, and give unto Almighty God, thanks for this most happy Deliverance.

And that all and every Person and Persons inhabiting within this Realm of England, and the Dominions of the same, shall always upon that day, diligently and faithfully resort to the Parish Church or Chappel accustomed, or to some usual Church or Chappel where the said Morning Prayer, preaching or other service of God shall be used, then and there to abide orderly and soberly, during the time of the said Prayers, preaching or other service of God there to be used and ministered.

And because all and every person may be put in mind of this Duty, and be the better prepared to the said holy Service, Be it enacted by authority aforesaid, that every Minister shall give warning to his Parishoners publickely in the Church at Morning Prayer, the Sunday before every such fifth day of November, for the due observation of the said Day. And that after Morning Prayer or preaching upon the said fifth day of November, they read distinctly and plainly this present ACT.

FINIS.

-As cited in: <u>England's warning-peece:or The History of the gun-powder treason:inlarged with some notable passages not heretofore published. Whereunto is annexed the Act of Parliament for publick thanksgiving upopn the fifth day of November yearly.</u> By T.S.

Let the Sermons Begin

Almost immediately following the plot in 1605 the tradition of reading a Gunpowder Plot Sermon to Parliament began. I include here the first two sermons. Other notable sermons will be found in the Sermons Volume. Sermons set the tone and content for celebration and are important indicators of changing philosophies and interests.

SERMON AT ST PAUL'S CROSS ON GOOD FRIDAY. From a Drawing in the Pepysian Library. This Cross was erected about 1450, and re-modelled in 1595.

St. Paul's Cross, London, Site of Presentation of many sermons, Chambers, W.&R., The Pictorial History of England, 1858).

The Sermon Preached at Paules Crosse, the tenth day of November, Being the next Sunday after the Discoverie of this late Horrible Treason, William Barlow(e), November 10, 1605.

1605

November 10

William Barlow(e)

The Sermon Preached at Paules Crosse, the tenth day of November,

Being the next Sunday after the Discoverie of this late Horrible Treason,

By the Right Reverend Father in God, William,

By Gods permission, Lord Bishop of Rochester.

ESAY 59.5.

They hatch Cockatrice egges but weave the Spiders Webbe.

London

Printed by I.VV. for Mathew Law,

1606

The Preachers friend to the READER

Gentle Reader, if thou thinkest the Preacher of this Sermon, was upon purpose appointed to relate the discovery of this late Tragi-comical treason, (Tragical, in the dreadful intention: Comicall in the happye and timely Detection thereof) thou art deceived: but being three weekes before requested, to supply the roome amongst other Bishops for the Parliament, if it had continued: this occurrent happened in the interim some foure or five dayes before the Sabboth, wherein he was to Preach, whereby he thought it fit, (though he had purposed a Scripture of that day for his Text) to change a Gospel into a Psalme: which notwithstanding, albeit out of the Psalmes, may well bear the name of *Evangelium*, not onely in respect of David the Author (who writ more like an Evangelist then a Prophet, and therefore the Fathers conclude him to be *Homo in veteri, non de veteri Testamento*, a man that lived in the Time, but not after the Manner of the olde Lawe, more like a Christian than a Jew) but also the Matter, which the Scripture (suitable to this Accident) will afford: which truly may be called *Evangelium Regni*, the Gospell or Tydings of this Kingdome, and could not but be acceptable to the Hearer, if the Messenger thereof were accepted (for *multum interest quid a quoque dictator*) and herin Reason & Religion should be, because [Beautiful are those feet (saith Paul) which bring glad tidings of good things:] Now what Newes so good, as that in the Prophesie of Esay, to tell Sion, *Regnauit Deus tuus*, Thy God hath shewed himselfe a King; and what message more gladsome than with Nahum to tell Judah, that the man of Belial is taken, and that the sonnes of wickednesse shall be utterly cut off. How gratefull, or distastefull it was to the Auditorie, the present Hearers can best report: but whether to the censorious reader (who useth to examine every Periode & sentence with a curious touch in an exact balance) it will be either currant or refuse, is a question, which none but he, which brings the assay and scales can assoile, and yet if he will withal, remember the shortness of the time for the gratulation, the dreadfulness of the danger, the fresh escape whereof could not but leave an impression of horror in the Preachers minde (able to have confounded his Memorie,) who should have bin one of the hoisted (?) number, the late receiving of the Instructions which in that short space could not be many: hee will perhappes not bee so rigide in his Censure, as either preiudice to the person, or opinion of his owne abilities to have performed it better, would cause him to be. And, as I heard, the Preacher himselfe frankely confesse, that unlesse the Kings Majestie his most excellent Speech, with the right honourable Lord Chancellour his grave Oration (both of them in the Parliament house the day before,) and divers circumstances sensibly conceived and imparted to him over night, by the Earle of Salisbury, his Majesties principall Secretary, had not succoured him, he had failed even in that slender performance, which was then offered to the Eare, and here is presented to thy View.

Farewel

PSAL. 18 50.

Great Deliverances giveth he unto his King, and sheweth mercy to his annointed David and to his seede for ever.

The whole Psalme, as the title sheweth, 2. Sam. 22.1. is Davids or Triumphing Song, after his many rescues and victories: and is one of those, which Psalme 32.7. he calleth *Cantica liberationis*, the Songes of Deliverance: for it seemeth that God and David had entered a covenant each with other, Psalme 89.2 ratified on each parte with an othe, God for his parte tooke his oath, Psalme 89.35, *I have sworn by my Holines, that I will never faile David*: David againe for his parte sware unto the Lord, Psalme:32.2, and vowed a vow unto the Almighty, not to cease day & night, to performe all meanes for the setting foorth of Gods praises, & of that vow, this book of Pslames is everlasting witness. wherein he generally verifieth what in one place he spake de te *Canticum meum simper*, Pslam 71.8, *My song shall always be of thee*. In this, above the rest, hee inlargeth himselfe in that kinde, which hee beginneth with love. *I will love thee most dearely O Lord my strength,* verse I. (for praises not issuing from a loving affection, are eyther Flatteries or Hypocrisies) and endeth verse 49. *I will prayse thee O Lord among the Nations;* (for benefites acknowleged, not ending with praises to God, argue either a prophane ingratitude, or an arrogant presumption.) Of both these, namely, his affection and acknowledgement, this verse is the *Epiphonema*, or the closing blast of this triumphing Trumpet, wherein, as if hee wanted winde to sound out, by particular enumeration, all his severall Deliverances, (for so himselfe confesseth, Psalme 40.5. *Thy mercies exceeded all account, I would declare them, and speake of them, but I am not able to expresse them*:) therefore, as if this verse were the etc. or total summe of all the particular Items hee would have you take this for all, Great deliverance, etc

Which he setteth out, first intensive, shewing what hey are in their owne nature (*magnificasti salutes*) because petty benefices become not GOD to give for Psalme 2.8. *Aske of me,* saieth hee, *and I will give thee no lesse then the Heathen to possesse, and thine enemies to crush.*

Secondly, extensive, how these are diffused or communicated (to David and his seede) for GOD hoardeth not uppe his blessings but distributes them abroad, James 1.17. *Everie good gifte commeth downe from the Father.*

In the parte intensive, concurre two partes; First, the double quantitie, both that which they call *discreta*, the pluralitie of the number [Deliverances] as also that which they call *continua*, the magnitude thereof [great] Secondly, the double qualitie, as well internall and essentiall [salutes, healthes, wholesome Deliverances:] as outward and accidentall, [*magnificasti*] deliverances, beseeming a Great God whome Saint Basil calleth, a most magnificent King.

The part extensive, is personall and successive, the Person [David] First, as an eminent person [a King.] Secondly, as a sacred person [Annointed] Thirdly, as a person appropriate unto God [his King, his Annointed] The sucession indefinite and infinite, [unto his seed] the number not defined [for evermore] the time not limited.

And both these generall paretes, hee deriveth from these two qualities which God, by a reiterated speech challengeth unto himselfe above all other attributes. Psalm 62. 11. *Power unto God, and unto thee, O Lorde, mercie,* In the part Intensive [great Deliverances] there is Gods power, both *Potentia virtutis*, Ephes. 6.10. *The power of his might* (for weakenes cannot make manie rescues) then *Potential claritatis*, Coloss. 1.11. The *power of his glorie,* [Magnificasts] for Gods Deliverances cannot be obscured.

In the part Extensive, there is Gods mercie [sheweth mercyes] First, that which is called, Luke, 1.78. *Misericordia viscerum*, his emboweled merecie, wherewith hee tenderly and specifically affected David: For which cause, in the title of this Psalme, (as the Latines read it) hee is called *Puer Domini*, the Lordes Darling, or tenderling, and so much himselfe confesseth 22. verse, *saluum me fecit quoniam voluit me,* Because he had a favour unto me. Secondly, that which Divines call, *Misericordia facta*, not onely affecting David, but also acting and perfourming mercies unto him (for so it is here [*Misericordiam faciens*] doing mercie unto David) Thirdly, that which the Scripture calleth *Misericordia custodita,* Exod. 34.7. His treasured mercy, *Reserving mercy for thousands*, etc. Not onely to David, but lineally and laterally, [to his seed] and that [for ever] for many generations.

These are the partes of this Scripture, the summe whereof is, that admiration of David, Psalme 31.19 *Quam magna multitudo dulcedinis tua?* There is the part Intensive *which thou hast done to them that feare thee*, etc. There is the parte extensive. Of these in their order

The first part.

The first part wee observed, is the Pluralitie & the Qualitie of these Deliverances: they be *plures* and they be *salutes*: both which with the Fathers, ye may call the two handes of God, vz. Latitude and Fortitude: the first in the pluralitie, *Giving to all men*, aboundantly, 1. Tim. 6.19. that is, *Manus expansa*: The second in the qualitie, defending what he gives powerfully, there is *Manus extensa*. Or in Saint Paules Metaphor, *The fulnesse of Gods riches*. First, *Divitiae gratia*, Ephes. 1.17. Giving frankely and liberally. Secondly, *Divitiae bonitatis*, Roman. 2.4. In that the thinges which he giveth, be [*Salutes*] For so it is, Mat. 7.11. Your heavenlyFather shall give unto you *bona*, good things and this comes nearer to Davids sense, who, when he meditates of his Deliverances from God, still attributes them to Gods right hand. Psalme 73.23. I was always with thee, and thou upheldest me *with thy right hand*: but herein he observeth two things: First, *Plenitudo dextrae*, Psalme 16. 11. the plenty of that hand. Secondly, *salutare dextrae*, Psal. 20.6. the wholesomnesse of that hand. For the first vz. the pluralitie: it is not with God as Esau spake of his Father Isaac, Genes. 27. 38. *Hast thou but ONE blessing my Father?* As if God had but one way to save, or as hee said, i. Kings 20.2: that he were a God of the Mountaines onely, that is, coulde ridde us from high & eminent daungeres and not a God of the Valleis: (yes, and of the vaultes too we may say,) for with him, sayeth David, there *is coporosa redemptio*. Psalm 131.7. all maner of wayes to redeem. And therefore as there being diverse kinds of sinnes, andfor every of them he hath mercies answerable and proportionable, an abilitie to redeeme *Israel from all his sinnes* Psal. 131.8. as for great sins she hath *magnam misericordiam*, and for many sins, *multitudinem miseria um*. psal. 51.1. (so proportionable to every mans dangers, or miseries, are Gods deliverances. Be they great as Psalme 71.20, great adversities hast thou shewed unto me, etc. Behold here Great deliverances, Are they Many? as Psalme 25.17. *Tribulationes multiplicasti*, my sorrowes are multiplied, there is with him, *Multitudo Salutum*, Pl. 94.19. In the Multitude of the sorrows which I had in my heart, thy comfortes have refreshed mee. Particularly, to fore-prise a daunger, hee hath *Salutem prevenientem*, Psalme 21.3. Thou diddest prevent me with thy goodnesse, to meete with a daunger when it commeth, hee hath *Salutem preparantem*, Psalme 18.43. Thou diddst Girde mee with strength unto the battle, to assist at a pinch in the daunger, hee hath *salutem suscipientem*, Pslame 118.13. I was thrust at fore that I might fall *sed Dominus suscepit me*, but the Lorde upheld me, to stay a relapse after an escaped danger, hee hath *salutem confortantem*, Psalme 89.21. My hand shall holde him uppe, and my arme shall stabish him. And this pluralitie might David above all other acknowledge, and so he did, when Psalm 118.14 he confessed, that God had so many wayes delivered him, *Ut totus factus esset in salutem*, as if hee intended nothing else but to deliver him. For *Salus* being eyther *Redimens* rescuing from daunger, or *Redimiens*, Dignifying or Crowning with Honour. Dignifying or Crowning with Honour: the first, 1. Samuel 13.41. shall Jonathan die, *qui salutem tam magnam fecit*, which hath given us so great Deliverance, that is, *Salus redimens*, For the second, Psalme 2.5. His Glory is greate in *tua salute*, Why? *Glory and Honour hast thou laide upon him*, There is *Salus*

Redimiens, in both these, David had his share from God more then any other. For the first, his Rescew from the Beares pawe, the Lions jawe, Saules jaue line, Goliahs speare, Achitophels counsel, Doegs slaunder, Schemi his reviling, the mouth of the sword, the murren of his people, the multiplicitie of his sinne, the rebellion of his sonne, (no meane nor ordinarie dangers) is an evident demonstration, and accordingly he confessed it, when Psalme 54.7. hee sayeth, hee hath delivered mee from all my feare: For the second, his Honours were as many as his daungers, the favour with his Prince, the love of the people, the designed heritage of a Kingdome, the glorious wearing of a Crowne, the triumphant victories over his enemies, the secure establishing of his Kingdome in his sonne while he lived: these *Salutes* it pleased GOD to afforde him, and with an othe to assure him; *I will make him my first borne higher than the Kinges of the earth:* himselfe putteth them both together, Psalme 104. verse 4. *Prayse the Lorde, O my soule, which saveth thy life from destruction*, there is the first *Salus*, his acquitall from daunger: *which crowneth thee with mercy and loving kindnesse*; there is the second, his requital with Hounour. And so much for the pluralite [Deliverances,] the summe whereof, is that of our Prophet in Psalme 34, verse 19. *Manie are the troubles of the righteous, but the Lord delivereth them out of all*, this is *Plenitudo dextrae*.

The Second part.

Now we come to the Quality, that is, *salutare dextrae*, For as GODS Deliverances are many, so they bee *Salutes*, they have health in them, they bee as David sayeth, Psalme 21. Verse 3. *Benedictiones dulcedinis* sweete blessings *Usque in delicias amamur*, sayeth Seneca: this is GODS *Syntaxis*, (as the vulgar English reades, Psalme 28. verse 8. The wholesome Deliverance of his annointed. It is not so with the sonnes of men, in whom there may be helpe *sed non est salus in eis*: Psalme 146.3. there is no health in their helpe: trust them not. Munera *qua putas, insidia sunt*, their Deliverances are not without some annoyance, Even the verie Salutre of the tongue, like the Saliva thereof, hath some venome in it, Psalme 28.3. *They speake friendly to their neighbours, but imagine mischiefe in their hearts,* But their reall Deliverances, much more noxious: For as it is in the *Apologue* (to which the Poet alludeth) of the Combat betweene the Staggs and the Horse, viz. That, the Horse being too weake for the Stagge, "required the helpe of the man, which hee easily obtained; who getting upon the Horse backe, drived the Stagge to flight, but after that, *non equitem dorso, non fraenum depulit oze*," he could never since quit his backe of the ride, nor his mouth from the bit: so is it with the helps of worldly Potentates, *beneficia viscata*: as the birde having escaped the snare, percheth upon the trees for refuge, and there she findes bird-lime to intangle her, from whence she cannot flie, but with losse of her feathers, if not of her members: so is it with the helps of States and Nations, aske their helpe in distresse they will graunt it; but withal, eyther they exact a tribute, which exhausteth the Treasury, or impose conditions, which infringe the Liberty, or require a future aide, which weakeneth the Power, or betray upon advantage, which redoubles the Misery, or upbraide the benefite, which exulcerates the minde. This is *Saluatio ab Optimatibus*, (as the Latines reade) Jeremy, 25.35. which as the usurers loane (to speake for the capacity of the Citty) freeth a man from the prison for the time, but invellops him in bondes more miserable, more durable than the prison. Herein differing from God, for his blessing, sayeth Salomon, giveth riches, yea and Deliverances; *nec addit inolestiam*, and joineth no sorrowes with them. For if it be *salutare ex Sion*, Ps. 53.6. *Then shall Jacob rejoice, and Israel shall be glad.*

And thus much for the word *Salutes*, the summe whereof is, Psalm 85.9. that if it be *Salutare Domini* there concurre with it, *omnes Salutes* Glory, Mercy, Righteousness, Peace, as the Prophet there noteth. The conclusion that in psalme 3.8. *Domini est salus*, it is the Lord onely that gives true Deliverance, and withal a blessing upon his people. And this for the Pluralitie and Qualittie of the Deliverances.

Now we come to the Quantitie, [Great] wherein wee will not goe further than this Psalme, nor there speake of his *Salus coronans*, eyther the Celsitude of his honour, verse 35. *He hath set me up on high places*: nor of the Amplitude of his honour verse 45. *Thou hast made mee the head of the heathen, a people remote & unknowne,* nor of his Triumphs over his enemies, verse 42. *Driving them, as the winde the dust before him trampling them as the clay in the streets under him:* (though this bee also the *Salus coronans* of our dread Soveraigne and glorious King) but onely shew the greatnesse of the dangers which David escaped, as more sutable to this late horrible occurent, both in respect of the dangers themselves as first, *Dolores mortis*, verse 4. *the pangs of death* which the imminent expectation put him unto (for the expectation of death, is more bitter then death it selfe. Secondly, *Laquei mortis funes inferni*, verse 6. daungers in the darke, treasons in secret, treacheries of the Vaults. Thirdly, *aquae multe*, one danger in the necke of another, verse 16. And also of the Authors, as verse 4. *Torrentes iniquitatis*, streames of wickednesse, a concurrence of Conspirators. Secondly, (which is our late case) vers. 48.*Vir injuriarum*, or rapina, a cruell bloodthirsty wretch, like our Vault-enginer. All these of Davids were great indeed, but compared to this of our gracious King: (the last, I trust, for a worse there cannot be) but as a minium to a large, whether we consider therein, eyther the Plot it selfe, or the Con-comitance with it, or the Consequeces of it.

Plot

First in the *Plot*, observe I pray you a cruell Execution, an inhumane crueltie, a brutish immanitie, a divelish brutishness, & an Hyperbolicall, yea an hyperdiabolicall divelishness.

First, Cruelty in the effusion of blood cursed both of God and man for *Cursed art thou from the earth* saith God to Cain, Genes. 4.11. for one mans blood spilt. Cursed be the rage for it was cruell, saith Jacob of his sonnes, Gen. 4.9.7. in the slaughter of the Shechemites.

Secondly, Immane crueltie in the multitude of the slaine, to make himselfe drunke with blood of so many Worthies, and so innocent (for by the reporte of militarie men) his provision was so large, that if fire had beene given, (beside the place it selfe at the which hee aymed) the Hall of Judgement, the courtes of Recordes, the Collegiate Church, the Cittie of Westminster, yea, White-Hall the Kings house, had beene crushed and overthrowne, such heapes hee had layde in, of Billets, Faggots, huge stones, Iron crowes, Pike-axes, great Hammer-heades, besides so many barrels of Gun-powder, five and thirtie in number small and great, as I am credibly informed.

Thirdly, his bruitish immanity in the manner of the death, not man-like to kill, but beast-like to discorpe, and teare parcel meale, the bodies of such personages, *Ferina rabies est*, saith Seneca, *dilaniare non occidere*.

Fourthly, his divelish verse, first, for the materials of the death intended (Gun powder) which they say none but the divell, the King of the sulphurious pit did invent: secondly, for the firie massacre it should have made, not from heaven, as the fire that came downe from above upon Jobs substance, Job. 1.165. For which cause it is there called *Ignis Dei*, but under the earth, out of a Cave, as kindled and sent from the infernall pit. The apostle sayeth, *That the member which sets on fire, Rotam generationis*, James, 3.6. *The whole course of generation* (as should have done) *it selfe is set on fire by Hell*.

Fifthly But this (?) more then divelish, for this Divell of the Vault, contented not himselfe with the death of the bodie, but reached in his Project at the second death, of the soule; by taking away many, so suddenly in their sinnes unrepented with their minds un-prrepared. I trust that this escape will make many to like the better of the prayer against suddaine death, for though I doubt not, but if it had beene effected, that this whirling blast would have been unto our sacred King(so Relisious in his profession, so innocent from wrong, so cleare in his conscience) as the Whirle-wind and fiery chariot of Elias, to have carried upp his soule to heaven, and that God in his mercy, woulde have made this Deluge of Bloode, as a *Baptismum sanguinis*, a baptism of Martyrdome, to have washt away our sinnes; and as a Holocaust, an whole burnt sacrifice, to propitiate his wrath for our Transgressions, yet as much as in this Fury it lay, he would have sent us all to hell.

Secondly, And still I say, a Rage more than divelish: for the Divell when hee is described to have Apoc. 12.12. to bee in his extreamest rage, yet then hee is saide, verse 4 to have drawne with his tayle, but the third part of the starres, and that from heaven to earth, but this Divell, with his traine would at once have pulled down all the glorious Starres, both fixed, and erratical (those that are fastened to the Court, and those which come and goe as they are called and dismissed) yea even the Sunne & the Moone themselves not from heaven to earth, but to the bottomlesse pit, as much as in him lay.

Thirdly and still I say, more than divelish: For as the Fathers (alluding unto that speech of the King of Sodome, *Da mihi animas, caetera cape tibi* Genes. 14.21.) doe well obseve, that the divell is contented with the soules of men, for if Job would have cursed God to his face, Job. 1.11. he would not have cared, though his substance and honour had beene encreased, and his life continued, but this Satanicall miscreant must have body and goods, and life, and soul and all.

Lastly, marke in this Plot a production without a match (and yet it shoulde have beene effected with a *match*) but I meane, a Treason without a Paralell; a slaughter beyonde comparison. For the Treason, the nearest that I find to it, is that in the Roman Historie of the Schoolmaster among the Falerians, whose Citty Camillus besieged, who having the sonnes and youth of all the Nobility, and the Chiefe of that Cittie in his tuition, drawing them into the fieldes a little without the Walles, under pretence for their recreation, betraide them all at once into the handes of Camillus: and yet herein there is a great disparison, for they were but children, but in this case olde and young, parents and progenie, all at once, should have been betrayed, they were alive, and so might be eyther raunsomed or recovered, or if slaine yet they should have seen their death: but here without ransom or recovery, or seeing who had hurt them (for so the letter boasts) a death suddaine and invisible: there but the sprowtes of one Cities Nobilitie, a small territorie: here the stem and seede Royall, with the Honour and Hope of this whole Islands Gentry and Nobility.

But Slaughter none can I thinke of matchable therewith. Pharao slew the Males of Israel, but that was by Edict, and they were Children, and of his Vassalles. Herod massacred the infants, but that was to secure him of his State, shaken (as he thought) by a prediction, Math.2. Abimelech and Athaliah, killed all the allies of the bloud,, but their furie was stanched in the issue Royall. Of Achilles his furie, it is saide by the Poet, that he sent many worthy men to the grave: but that was in open warre, and in the compasse of many years.

And all these were Kinges and Tyrants, and so their mind the same with Polynices in the Tragady, *Imperia precio quomis constant ben/e*, that Kindomes are to bee bought at any rate but what should move this, a vermine of the basest sorte, a very *Tenebrio*, the slave of darknesse, like a Mole under the grounde, to subverte at one push as the Prophet speaketh, Esay. 9.14. *heade & tayle, braunch and roote*, all in one day. Caligula, was but a shadow, for he wished that all the Citizens of Rome, had but one necke, that at one blow hee might cut it off: but this Blood-sucker, not only wished it, but contrived it, prepared for it, and was ready to execute it. There was but one famous Nero, which for his crueltie got the name of Nero fro all the rest, him hath he matched in Affection for when one of Nero his dissolute company, had said *Me mortuo*, when I am deade, let heaven & earth goe together. Nay said Nero, *Me vivo*, while I am alive. So meant Guy Faulkes (the true name of a false traytor) to have beheld as (hee said) the houses and bodies flying up; he living & laughing at it. If hee had solde us for bond-slaves & hand maides, saith Hester of Haman, yet there had been life, and so hope of returne, but to make an utter dissolution of the whole State, had beene a misery incurable was a project most damnable.

Here was read the parties confession, so much as concerned the Plot.

And so much of the plot. Now for the Con-comitance what would have come to passe, even with that blow. The olde Greake Proverb is, that no great exploit can suddenly be effected, especially, alterations of States, doe aske a long time & must bee wrought by degrees: for *omnis subita mutatio est periculoa*, even to the Conquerors themselves, and therefore in their purpose to change a State, they will begin with one thing at once, as with weakening the force, or exhausting the wealth, or altering the Religion, or removing their Governors, but in this design *Uno flatu, uno ictu, uno nictu,* with one blast, at one blow, in one twinkling of an eye, should have been crushed together, the Government, the Councell, the wisedom, the Religion, the Learning, the strength, the justice of the whole land. The want of one of these is a blemish to a State, and brings a miserie with it. A realme without a Monarch as the skie without the Sunne is a clowde of darkeness, a darkeness of confusion

A Monarch without counsel, as a head without eyes, obnoxius of itselfe to danger, and a burden to the members and Counsell without Wisdome, as an arrow out of a childes bow, accidentally fortunate, but originally weake.

Wisedome without Religion, like Tullies Offices, politique but prophane.

Religion without Learning, like the Athenian Altar. Act. 17. superstiously devoute, but fundamentally unsound.

Learning not guarded with strength, as a rich Citie without wals, naked & unfenced.

Strength without Justice, as a Lyon broke from his Cage, furious and unsatiable. And yet this darkenes, this blindenes, this prophanes, this superstition, this weakness, this lawless fury, had with this blowing up, bin blown in & over this whole nation, a thing which neither the greatest Potentate of the world, with his strongest invasion, nor the most dangerous rebel, though most popular & powerfull, coulde have brought to passé after many repulses, & in many years, namely, to take away at once, the hope of succession, the Oracles of wisedome, the Chariots of Israel, the Beau-peeres of Learning, the buttresesses of strength, the guardians of justice, the glory of the Nobilitie, and in one word, the Flower of the whole Kngdome, not as Tarquinius, the poppy heades ,one after one, but with Sampsons crush, al in a moment. And which makes the fact more odious, in the sanctuary of the Kingdom. These would have gone with the blow, but what should the Issue have been?

If the light which is within thee be darkenesse, saith our Saviour, Mat. 6.23. how great is that darkeness? and yet such had beene ours, when all the lights together were extinguished. Begin first with the chiefest and brightest. *Lucerna Israel*, so is the King called, 2 Sam. 21. It is a wo to a land saith the Preacher, where the king is a child Ecce. 10.16. But *Write this man childless*, Jer. 23.30. is a more dreadfull case. For *ubi nullus gubernator*, neither in act, nor hope, *populus corruit* saith Salomon, Pro. 11.14. there followes a generall dissolution. Then come we to the inferiour lightes, 1. the lights politike, In the multitude of Counsellors there is health, Pro. 23.6. *Sed dissipantur cogitationes ubi non est consilium.* Pro. 15. 22. The joyntes of the whole State are loosened where there is no Counsel. 2. The Lightes Ecclesiasticall *The Priestes lips shall preserve knowledge, and at his mouth the Law must be learned.* Mal. 2. 7. for they are *Lux mundi*. Mat. 5. both for inlightening the mindes of men with knowledge and directing their lives by good example. Now these Priestes to be slain by the sword, Psa. 78.64 is a miserable calamitie, but to have no priest, no *Teraphim*, no *Ephod*, no Church-governor (as our case had bin) is that horrible desolation threatened by the prophet, Ose.3.1. Then the Lights Civil, Magistrates inferior, who bveing sub-ordinate to the greater, these being quenched, what light can the lesse give? What obedience could they have? Their authority (at the best) is but derived. When the fountaine therefore is stopped, the rivers are dried, the Chieftains removed, the Lieue-tenancie ceaseth. L:astly, *Lux morum*, Mat. 5.16. *Let your light so shine*, etc. These lights of good manners where had they bin in such a Cyclopicall Confusion, wherein as the poet saith

No-body heares nothing of No-body. As the Scripture speaketh wherein every man dooth what seemeth good in his own eyes, be it nevere so bad which Rapes, what Rapines, what risings, what slaughters had insued? A thing more miserable to the survivors then to them which were slaine wherein, what could be any mans? and yet what might not be every mans? wherein *optimum misericordiae genus esset occidere*, the best kind of pitty had bin to slay, and the happiest newes, to heare of death. The hedge lying open for the wild boare of the forrest to enter, a Forrener to invade, or the slie Foxe of the wood to clime, a domesticall usurper to intrude, this had bin the Cimmerian darkenesse of our nation, when these lights had bin extinguished. And blowne out should they have bin, unlesse the *father of lightes* had caused light to shine out of darkenesse, by discovering and revealing this worke of darkenesse: so that we may truly now conclude with David , Psal. 97. I1. *Lux orta est iusto*, Light is sprung up for the Righteous, and joy unto them that are true hearted.

Now doe as Assuerus did, cause the Records to be read & Chronicles to be searcht, ancient, moderne, divine, prophane, Greeke, Latin among the Turkes, in Paganism, yea if Hell keepe any Records, search there, and looke if yee can patterne this conspiracie, or match this daunger so desperate, so cruel, so insuitable and judge whether this Conclusion of Davids, do not well forthwith this escape of ours. [*Great deliverances giveth hee unto his king*] but this, perhaps you will say, was but one great indeed, even a riddance as the Prophet speaketh, from the *nethermost pit*. Psal. 30. What is this to the plural in the Text, [deliverances?] yes, because in this one there were many; for had our gracious Soveraigne only escaped, the deliverances had bin many, for that even in the very person of the King, there are many lines, *Thou art worth ten thousand of us said the people to David.* Sam. 18.3. So many lives preserved by the kings safetie, so many deliverances but that speech, I Reg. 22.17. *I saw all Israel* scattered as sheepe wandering a Shepherarde, argueth that the lives of the whole Nation, are contained in the Kings person. But this was not all, for withal was delivered both his fruitfull vine, and his Olive branches, as David calleth them. Psalm. 12.8. his Queene and Children, the Crowne of his Table, the Diademe of his Crowne; the glory of his Diademe, the hope of his glory, the assurance of his hope, and the pledges of his assurance. The slaughter of Zedekiah his sonnes, did more grieve him. Jerremy 52.10. then the losse of his Kingdome, or the Captivity of his owne person, and such being the affection of our loving King unto his deare Children, hee accountes their escape, no meane partr of his Deliverances. Neither was this all, because the best part of his people were withal delivered, besides the number which was very great. In the multitude of the people, is the Honour of the King, sayeth Salomen, but a Realme dispeopled is presently ruined. Proverb. 14. 28. Therefore it pleased his Maiestie to protesse (in his Royal, judicious, grave, and learned speech uttered yesterday in the Parliament) that the deliverance of the Estates and Commons, (which were aymed at) whose lives and welfare, hee vowed, were more deare unto him then his own safety, did more Comfort him then his Peersonall escape. But in this point of the Pluralitie If I woulde bee curious in an other Realme (as then it was) I might fill uppe the number of the King his Deliverances, and match them with Davids.

It seemeth by his Maiesties speech yesterday; that his case & race hath bin the same with the Prophet, being preserved in Utero, Psal. 139.13. *Ab utero*, Psal.22.10. *Ex utero*, Psal. 71.6. For no sooner was hee conceived in the wombe, but presentlie he was hazarded, no sooner delivered from the wombe, but invironed with daunger, and what perils he hath passed ever since he was borne, need not be related, they are so manifest: dismissed from those parts with a dreadfull farewell of a desperate Treacherie, and entertained among us with a Conspiracie unnatural & as dangerous: here Crowned with Thornes, before hee coulde get on the Crowne of Golde. Now therefore, as for these rescues hee and wee may truly say with David.[*Magnificasti salutes*, thou hast shewed great deliverances]: so, for the discovery of the danger; we must needs adde with the same Prophet, Psal.. 17.7. *Mirificasti misericordias*, thy mercies thou hast made marvelous; for surelie, there were wonders in the disclosing thereof: As first by a letter written without a name, in a disguised hand (for *mendax odit luce*) to a Noble Gentleman (affected that way in Religion) who hath threin discharged the part both of a loyal and honourable Subject: his duetie hee shewed, in revealing what was written * fearing some danger might be intended, his honour appeared in the detestation of such a horrible intention.

(Here was the Letter, read and varied upon with some mater.)

2, By his Maiesties apprehension, who though he walketh securely, in the sinceritie of his Concience, and innocency of his carriage (which makes him lesse jealous and suspitious of daunger) yet his heart gave him (by some wordes in that letter) that there might bee some fiery Engine, perhaps remembring his Fathers Case, who was blowne up with powder.

Here were such Papers read, as concerned the confession which was then knowne, and notes given upon them by the Preacher.

This solertia and ingeniositie of spirit (which in his Majestie I have before observed) makes mee to thinke that speech of the heathen man to be true, *Nullus vir magnus sine afflatu divino*, and that in Kinges there is a divine inspiration.3. In God almighty his judgement, both upon the Caitiffe of the Cave, who being not many houres before in the Celler (when some of the Lordes came together for some other occasions, as was thought) had not the power to suspect, or the grace to flie: but when the Privie watch came in the night, he was the first man that appeared at the dore, as if God himselfe had presented him unto their handes, and also upon the rest of the Cospirators. In who hee verified that speech of his sonne, Mat. 7 *In qua mensura*, etc. retaliating their purpose with the effect of their owne project, as if he would not suffer them to bee taken, till they were fired out of the house, who woulde have fired us within a house: striking some of their eyes out with Gunne-powder, (the instrument of our death) and some slaine with Musket. there also is Fire and Powder the Engines of their own Conspiracie. Now surely, *Mirificasti Misericordias*, O Lorde *thou hast made thy mercies wonderfull*. And thus much shall serve for the first generall, the intensive parte. The Conclusion and use whereof shall bee, that sithens GOD, hath been good to us in a double quantitie of Number and Dimention, for Many, for Great Deliverances, wee againe aunswere him in the like proportion, quantitie for quantitie, as David prescribeth, Psalm 150.2. *In multitudine magnitudinis*. Hath GOD done great things for us, Psalme, 126.3? Let us with the Prophet aunswere him in the same kinde, and say; *Wee wil give great thankes unto the Lorde*. Dooth hee *sundere beneficia*, powre out his benefites upon us, Psalm. 68.19? Let us againe *sundere Corda*, powre out our heartes before him, for GOD is our hope, psalme 62.8 Doth hee give us cause to triumph, it is our parts as David here to aunswere him with an and that in all sortes as the word hath been used, i. to declare this deliverance in triumphant speeches, 2. to give Triumphantly our Almse to the poore, our dole to the needy; for all shoulde have been taken from us, therefore wee the better may part with some to so good uses, 3. to sacrifice in triumph the Calves of our lippes, the prayers of our heartes, the praises of our tongues, and, to eate triumphingly, to feast extraordinarily, For so did the people of GOD among the Jewes upon any straunge deliverance. The Father at the returne of his Sonne, Luke 15. did so, and why not wee? Sithens that is verified of our most gratious King, which hee thre spake of his recovered Sonne, *Mortuus est & revixit*, hee was dead and is alive again. Dead in the Cabinet of the Conspirators, dead in the intention of the Villaine in the Vault, dead in the preparation of falsehearted rebels, but *revixit*, hee is alive again, 1. *vixit*, escaping manie daungers, Hee lived, *ut induceretur ad nos*, to bee brought in unto us, from Hebron unto Jerusalem, from the Northerne climat to these Southerne partes , now *revixit*, hee is alive afresh, *ut reduceretur ad nos*, to bee brought againe unto us, *Acherontis faucibus*, as his Majesty: yesterday said, from the very gates of death, from the Jawes of the devourer, from the lowest pit. And long may he live with us, and raigne over us, to the comfort of himselfe, to the joy of his Realmes, to the confusion of his enemies, to the maintenance of the Gospell, to the glory of the highest.

And now (but that the time is so farre spent) I should come to the seconde parte, which is the Extensive, vz. to whome God hath shewed these deliverances, namely, [to his King and his annointed] wherein I might truly have taken occasion, to have shewed how these titles doe agree to our dread Soveraigne, both that hee is a King, and that he is Gods King, as having in him all the partes that may concur either in a king, or in a good King, to whom that title, first attributed to David, (which once before I named) the light of Israel, principally appertaineth, as one from whose resplendent brightnesse, al the kingdoms of Christendome may receive their light. Whether wee looke unto the light of nature; of pregnant wit, of ready apprehension, of sound judgement, of present dispatch, of impregnable memory.

Or the light of Art, being an universall Scholer, acute in arguing subtle in distinguishing, Logical in discussing, plentifull in inventing, powerfull in perswading, admirable in discoursing,

Or the light of grace, whether intellectual, for speculative Theology, a perfect Textuar, a sound Expositor, a faithfull Christian, and a constant Professor, or affectuall, for Regeneration, an assiduous prayer, a chast husband, of sweete carriage, of humble deportment, of mortified lusts, of sanctified life.

Or the light of government, an upright arbitrator in cases of Justice, a loving father to his subjects, a carefull guardian of his kindomes, a wise manager of his State, an especiall favourer of this Citty, an absolute Monarch both for Regiment & judgment: And yet these lights thus gloriouslie shining this golden candlesticke, this *Nocturnus Ambulo*, this *diurnus Nebule*, this nightes gadder, this daies Pioner, would have at once blowne out.

So I also have handled this worde Annointed, which makes a King a sacred person and therein I purposed, to have shewed unto you, that this practice of murthering princes, is made an Axiom of Theologie among the Romanists: who so reads Parsons, Dolman, Alien and Parsons their cases of conscience, Stapleton his quodlibetical Oration at Doway, Rossaeus, Reynoldes, Gyfford, or the bitter expostulation of Ludovicus of Orleance, in the case of the Guyses faction against Henry of Navar now King of France, and lastly, the positions of the Jesuites of Salamanca, shall finde it a conclusion of positive Divinitie. Whereof, were there no other, this worde Annointeed, is an unanswerable confutation. *Touch not mine annointed*, saith the Prophet, Psal. 105. 15. For this David took as an inviolable restraint, both when Saule was given into his handes, *How should I lay handes upon the Lords annointed*, I. Sam, 23. and as a sufficient reason to execute Sauls murtherer, at least the messenger of his death, 2. Sam.1. Howe durst thou touch the Lords annointed? *Honoravit vivum, Vindicavit mortuum*, saith Saint Augustin, only for this reason, because he was anointed: and yet, those which make Religion the stawking-horse for Treasons, pretend the Catholike Cause, (as these Conspirators now did) to murther the lords Annointed. Against whome, I would (if the time had served) in this case have been more bitter, but that I remember there are some amongst us, who challenge unto themselves the quintessence of Annointing as He, Esay 65. *Come not neere mee for I am Holier than thow*, yet come very neare to the same dangerous position: not to speake of Knox and Buchanan, the two fiery spirites of that Church and Nation where they lived, what means that speech of some of our owne Countrie, extant in Print, in the late Queenes time of blessed memory? *that if their reformation shoulde not bee yielded unto there woulde bee shortly a bloody day in England* . But the time being so farre gone, I will cut off that whole part (being forced hereunto.) In the meane time I shall desire you to joyn with me in hearty prayer unto Almighty God for the continuance of our good King, our State, and our Religion amongst us, giving him thankes for his wonderfull mercie, in preserving us from this terrible blow (as they called it) from this desperate, dreadfull and damnable attempt, saying,

O Eternal God and our most mighty Protector, etc.

As it followeth in that prayer, beginning with those wordes, printed in the book of Thanksgiving for this discovery and delivery: But made by the Preacher.

And let all true Subjects say Amen. **FINIS.**

William Barlow

William Barlow was born in London into a family from Barlow Moor near Manchester. His father is unknown but in his will he listed Alice Field as his mother. Barlow attended St. John's College, Cambridge, from 1580 obtaining his BA in 1584, MA in 1587, becoming fellow of Trinity Hall and obtaining BTh in 1594, and DTh at Oxford in 1601. Barlow became chaplain to Archbishop Whitgift. Whitgift helped him to become rector of St. Dunstan in the East, London. He then became canon of Westminster shortly thereafter and then rector of Orpington in Kent. Barlow became a royal chaplain in 1601. He had the unique task of both praising and condemning the earl of Essex in sermons preached at St. Paul's Cross, praise for the victory at Cadiz and condemnation for the earl's rising. It is known that Robert Cecil drafted guidelines for the first sermon if not the second.

Whitgift several times proposed Barlow for a chaplaincy to the queen, and was disappointed to see others preferred whom he considered less worthy. It was thought that Barlow had turned on the Earl and had violated the seal of the confessional and he was shunned at court. The queen also turned against him as he reminded her of her lost favorite. However, Elizabeth as well as James admired his preaching style and this helped him to overcome all other obstacles. In 1601 he became prebend of Chiswick in St. Paul's Cathedral; shortly thereafter he became canon of Canterbury, then canon of Westminster Abbey and treasurer. Barlow held this position until 1605, becoming subdean from 1605 to 1607. He was known for his sermon to the convocation of 1601 which was called by his opponents the "Barley Loaf".

In 1602 he was made dean of Chester. This allowed him to attend the Hampton Court Conference in 1604 and write the proceedings which discussed the confrontation of the Puritans by the church hierarchy. Barlow took part in the translation of the Bible, being responsible for the translation of the epistles Romans through Jude. He became bishop of Rochester in 1606 and bishop of Lincoln in 1608. Barlow preached sermons promoting an Episcopal form of church government in Scotland. On behalf of the government he composed the response to Robert Persons and argued against lay involvement in enacting canons defending royal supremacy. He did not completely allign himself with Arminianism. Barlow died at his palace in Buckden, Huntingdonshire, September 7, 1613, and is buried in the parish church.

Some thoughts about this sermon

William Barlow preached this sermon only a few days after he would have been killed had the plot been successful. It was preached on November 10, 1605.

Prior to the plot Barlow had played an important role as servant of Cecil and the King. His sermons were not easy ones. One sermon based on notes given to him by Cecil found him praising Robert Devereux, Earl of Essex, for his heroism at the battle of Cadiz in 1596. Only a short time later Barlow had to represent the state condemning Essex for his ill-fated rebellion in 1601.

This sermon is interesting in that blame for the plot is given to those taking part in it, that is, the Jesuits and the plotters. Catholicism is not attacked broadly as a religion. Fawkes is singled out as the main villain. Barlow tells us that they pretended to be Catholics and discredited their religion by their evil deeds. He reflects on King James' speech to Parliament and tells us:

"the best part of his people...did more Comfort him then his Personal escape"

Barlow calls upon the auditory:

"I shall desire you to join with me in hearty prayer unto Almighty God for the continuance of our good King, our State, and our Religion amongst us, giving

him thanks for his wonderful mercy, in preserving us from this desperate and damnable attempt, saying O Eternal God and our most mighty Protector..."

The sense of this sermon is that the air had not yet cleared and the official state line had not yet been decided. He did not really want to mention or commemorate the villain.

"Of the Incendiary...those fire-brandes that would have set these maisterbrades on flame, not one word, either by way of invective or commemoration....let their names be forgotten, their houses forlorne, and their posteritie odious..."-
William Barlow, A Brand, Titio Ereptie., cited in: Nowak, 1992, p.52.

For a true cause Barlow wants us to look to Satan. The whole thing is part of the war between good and evil.

The deliverance is carefully examined and defined:

'In the part intensive, concur two parts; First, the double quantity, both that which they call discreta, the plurality of the number [Deliverances] as also that which they call continua, the magnitude thereof [great,] Secondly, the double quality, as well internal and essential [salutes, healths, wholesome Deliverances:] as outward and accidental, [magnificasti] deliverances, beseeming a Great God, whom Saint Basil calleth ;ξιωματικω τατον βασιλήα, a most magnificent King.

A Sermon Preached Before The Kings Maiestie At Whitehall On the Fifth of November Lancelot Andrewes, November 5, 1606

A Sermon Preached Before The Kings Maiestie

At WhitehallOn the Fifth of November, Lancelot Andrewes

Anno Dom. MDCVI, (1606)

Psal. CXVIII. Ver. XIII.XIV

A Domino factum est istud, & est mirabile in oculis nostris.

Haec est Dies quam fecit Dominus; exultemus& laetemur in ea.

This is the Lord *doing, and it is marvellous in our eyes.*

This is the day which the Lord *hath made, let us rejoyce and be glad in it.*

To entitle this time to this Text, or to shew it pertinent to the present occasion, will ask no long processe. This Day of ours, this *fifth* of November, a day of GOD's making; that which was done upon it, was the Lords doing. Christ's owne application (which is the best) may well be applied here: *This day, is this scripture fulfilled in our eares.* For, if ever (Luke 4.21) there was a *deed* done, or a *day* made by *God*, in our dayes; this *day*, and the *deed* of this *day* was it. If ever He gave cause of *marvelling* (as in the first) or *rejoycing* (as in the *second verse*) to any land; to us this day, He gave both: If ever *saved, prospered, blessed* any; *this day*, He *saved, prospered,* and (as we say) *fairely blessed* us.

Iiii (page 1)

Of the Gunpowder-treason. Sermon 1

The *day* (we all know) was meant to be the day of all our *deaths*; and many were appointed as *Sheepe* to the *Slaughter*, nay, worse than so. There was a thing *doing* on it, if it had been done, we all had been undone. And the very same day we (all know) the day wherin that appointment was disappointed by God, and we all saved, that we might *not die but live, and declare the praise of the Lord*: the Lord

Verse 17.

of whose doing, that *marvellous deed* was, of whose making , this *joyfull day* is, that we celebrate

This mercifull and gracious Lord (saith *David, Psalme* 1:15.) *hath so done His marvellous works, that they ought to be had, and kept in remembrance.* Of *keeping remembrance*, many wayes thre be: Among the rest, this is one, of *making dayes*;

Psl 1 11.f.

set solemne Dayes to preserve memorable Acts, that they be not eaten out, by them, but ever revived, with the returne of the Year, and kept still fresh in continual memory.

Exod. 12&c.

God himselfe taught us this way. In remembrance of the great delivery from the *destroying Angell*, He himselfe ordained the day of the *Passe-over* yearly to be kept. The *Church*, by Him taught, tooke the same way. In remembrance of the dissappointing of Hamans bloudy lots, they were like wise appointed the dayes of *Purim*, yearly to be kept. The like memorable mercy did He vouchsafe us. The destroyer passed over our dwelings, this day: It is our *Passe-over*. *Haman*, and his Fellowes had set the *dice* on us, and we by this time had been all in peeces: It is our *Purim* day.

We have therefore well done and upon good warrant, to tread in the same steps, and by law to provide, that this *Day* should not die, nor the memorial thereof perish, from our selfes or from our seed, but be consecrated to perpetual memory, by a yearly acknowledgement to be made of it through all generations. In accomplishment of which order, we are now here in the presence of God, on this day, that He first, by His Act of *doing*, hath made, and we secondly, by our act of *decreeing*, have *made* before Him, His holy *Angels*, and men, to confesse this His goodnesse, and our selves eternally bound to Him for it. And, being to cofesse it, with what words of Scripture can we better or fitter do it, that those we have read out of this *Psalme*? Sure, I could thinke of none fitter, but even thus to say, *A Domino Factum*, &c.

The treaty where of may well be comprised in three points: 1. The *Deed* or *doing*: 2. The *Day*, and 3. The *Duty*. The *Deed*, in these: *This is the Lord,s &c*. The *Day*, in these: *This is the day, &c.* The *Da,y* in the rest, *Let us, &c*. The other two reduced to the *Day*, which is the center of both. The *doing* is the cause; The *Duty* is the consequent: from the *day* groweth the *duty*.

To proceed orderly, we are to begin with the *day*. For though (in place) it stand after the *deed,* yet to us, it is first: our knowledge is *a posteriori*. The effect ever first, where it is the ground of the rest. Of the *day* then first.

1. That such *dayes* there be, and how they come to be such. 2. Then of the *doing*, that maketh them: wherein that this of *Davids* was; and that ours is no lesse, rather more. 3. Then of the duty, how to doe it, by *rejoycing*, and *being glad*, for so, *guadium erit plenum*, these two make it full. How to take order, that we may long and often do it, by saying our *Hosanna*, and *Benedictus*, for, *gaudium nostrum nemo tolles a nobis*, those will make, that our joy no man shall take from us.

Sermon 1. Of Gun-Powder-Treason 891

This is the day! This Why, are not all dayes *made* by Him? is there any dayes not made by Him? Why then say we, *This is the day the Lord hath made?* Divide the dayes into *naturall* and *civill*, the *naturall*, some are *cleare* and some are *cloudy*; the *civill*, some are *luckie dayes*, and some are *dismall*! Be they faire or foule, glad or sad; (as the Poet calleth him) the Great *Dies pater*, the *Father of dayes* hath made them both. How say we then of some one *day*, above his fellow, *This is the day*, &c.?

No difference at all, in the *dayes*, or in the monenths themselves: by nature, they are one. No more in *November* than another moneth, nor in the *fifth*, than in the *fifteenth*. All is, in God's *making*, For, as in the Creation, we see, all are the *workes*, and yet a plaine difference between them for all that, in the manner of making: Some are made   Six, Let there be light, a firmament, drie Land; Some, with *Faciamus* with more adoe, greater forecast, and framing, as *man*, that *master-peece* of His *workes*, of whom therefore in a different sense, it may be said: *This is the Creature which* God *hath made* (suppose, *after a more excellent manner*.) In the very same manner, it is with dayes; All are His making, all equal in that but, that letteth not, but He may bestow a *speciall Faciamus* upon some one day more than other; and so that day, by speciall perogative, said To be indeed a day, that God hath made.

Now, for God *making*, it fareth with *dayes*, as it doth with *yeares*. Some yeare (saith the *Psalme*) God *crowneth with His goodnesse*, maketh it more seasonable, healthful, fruitfull, than other. And so for *dayes*, God leaveth a more sensible impression of His favour, upon some one, more than many besides, by *doing* upon it some *marvellous work*. And, such a day on which God vouchsafeth some speciall *factum est*, some great and publike benefit, notable for the time present, memorable for the time to come, in that case, of that *Day* (as if God had said *Faciamus diem hunc*, shewed some workemanship, done some speciall cost on it) it may with an *accent*, with an *emphasis* be said, *This verily is a day which* God *hath made*, in comparison of which, the rest are as if they were not; or at least were not of *His making*.

As for *black* and *dismall dayes*, dayes of sorrow and sad accidents; they are and may be counted (saith Iob) for no *dayes*: *Nights* rather, as having the *shadow of death* upon them; or, if *dayes*, such as his were, which *Sathan* had *marr'd* than which *God* had *made*. And for common and ordinary *dayes*, wherein as there is no *harme*, so not any notable good, we rather say, they are gone forth from *God* in the course of nature (as it were) with a *fiat*, then made by Him; specially, with a *faciamus*. So, *evill dayes* no *dayes*, or *dayes marr'd*: and common *dayes*, *dayes*; but no *made dayes*: Onely those *made*, that *crowned* with some extraordinary great *Favour*, and thereby get a dignity, and exaltation above the rest: exempted out of the ordinary course of the *Calendar* with an *Hic est*. Such, in the *Law*, was the Day in the *Passe-over, made by God*, the head of the yeare. Such, in the *Gospell*, of CHRISTS *Resurrection, made* by *God, Dies Dominicus*; and to it, do all the Fathers apply this verse. And we had this day, our *Passe-over*, and we had a *Resurrection* or as *Isaac* had. But, I forbeare to goe further in the generall. By this that hath been said, we may see, there be dayes of which it may be safely said, This the day, &c. and in what sense, it may be said. Such there be then, that this of ours, one of them; that if it be, we may so hold it, and doe the duties that pertain to it.

Iiii2

David's day here, was one certainly, *dist (?) ante Spiritu*; and they, that are like it, to be holden for such: so that, if ours be as this was, it is certainly *dies a Deo factus*. Now then (to take our rule from the former verse) *Factum Domini facit diem Domini*. It is Gods *deed*, that maketh it God's *day*; and, the greater the *Deed*, the more God's *day*. There must be first, *Factum est*, some *doing*: and secondly, it must be *a Domino*, He the *doere*: and thirdly, that *somewhat* must be somewhat *marvellous*: and fourthly, not, in it selfe, so; but, *in our eyes*. These foure goe to it; these foure make any day a *day* of *God's making*. Let us see then these four; First,.in *David's* here, and then in our owne; and if we finde them all, boldly pronounce, *This is the day, &c.*

First, the *factum est*, in *David's;* what was *done*, set downe at large in the forepart of the *Psalme*. It was a *deliverance*: all the *Psalme* runneth on nothing else. Every *deliverance* is from a *danger*, and, by the *danger*, we take measure of the *deliverance*. The greater that, the greater the *Delivery* from it: and the greater the delivery, the greater the *day*, and the more likely to be of Gods owne *manufacture*. His *danger* first: what should have been done. He was in great distresse. Three several times, with great passion, he repeats it, that *his Enemies: came about him; compassed him round: compassed and kept him in on every side*: were, no swarm of *bees* so thicke: That they gave a terrible lift or *thrust* at him, to overthrow him, and very neare it they were. And at last, as if he were newly crept out of his grave, out of the very jawes of death and despaire, he breaks forth and saith, *I was very neare my death*, neare it I was, but *non moriar, die I will not* now, for this time, *but live* a little longer *to declare the works of the Lord*. This, was his *danger* and, a shrewd one (it seemeth) it was. From this *danger*, he was *delivered*. This, the *factum est*.

But, *man* might do all this; and so it be *man's* day, for any thing is said yet Though it were *great*, it maketh it not *God's* unlesse *God*, *God* (I say) and not man, but God Himselfe were the doer of it: and, if He the *Doer*, He denominates the *Day*. This then was not *any mans*, nor any *Princes* doing, but GODs alone, His *might*, His *mercy*, that brought it to passe: Not any *arme of flesh*, but Gods *might*, not of any *merit* of his, but of His owne *meere mercy*. This was *done* by His might: Thrice he tels us of it, *It was the right hand of the Lord, that brought this mighty thing to passe*. This was done by His *mercy*. His *ever-enduring mercy*: foure times he tels us, it was that, did it. With that he begins, and makes it the key of the *song*. Then, as we have *factum est*, so we have *A Domine*: The *deed* and the *doer* both.

Gods *doings* are many, and not all of one size. The Prophet * *Zachary* speaketh of a *day* of *Small things*, and, even in those small, must we learne to see *God*, or we shall never see Him in greater. Yet, so dimme is our sight, that unlesse they be great, commonly we see Him not: nay unlesse it be *greate usque ad miracalum*, so great, that *marvellous* withall, we count it not worth a *day*, nor worthy *God*: unlesse it be such. But, if it be such, then it is *God's*, *Qui facit mirabilis solus, Who only workes great marvells*: then, man is shut out, and *Gods* must the *Day* be. *A Domino factum, & mirabile*.

And yet this is not enough. The truth is, all that *God* doth, all His *workes* are *wonderful*: *Magna, sed ideo parva quia afitata. Great, wonders*, all: but, not *wonderfull*; seeme *small* to us, because they be *usuall*: His *miracles* are no more *marvellous*, than His *ordinary works*, but that, we see the one daily, and the other, not. Therefore he addeth [*in our eyes*] for a full period: His *doings*, all *marvellous* in themselves; but, not marvellous, *in our eyes,* unless they be rare, and the like not seene before: But then they be; and then we say, *Digitus Dei est*, it is *the finger of God*, nay, the *right hand of God*, that *brought this mighty thing to passe*. Then we give the *day* for *God's,* without more adoe. Now then, we have all that goeth to it: 1, A *Deliverance* wrought; 2, wrought, by *God*, 3, a *wonderfull deliverance,* 4, and that, even *in our eyes,* These make *David's day*, a *day* of *Gods making*.

Will *these* be *found in ours*, and then ours shall be so too? They will, all of them certainly; and that, in an higher degree, in a greater measure; match *David's day,* and overmatch it in all. 1. We were *delivered*, and from a *danger*, that is cleare. How great? (for, that makes the oddes.) Boldly, I dare say, from a *greater* than *Davids*. Thus I shew it, and go no further than the *Psalme* it selfe.

1. *David* called upon God in his danger; he knew of it, therefore, We did not: we imagined no such thing; but that all had been safe, and we might have gone to the *Parliament*, as secure as ever. The *danger* never dreamt of, that is the *danger*.

2. His was, by *compassing* and *hemming in*, that is *above ground*, and may be descried from a watch- tower. Ours was by *undermining,* digging deep *under ground*, that none could discerne.

3. One cannot be beset, but he may have hope to break through, at some part. But here, from this, no way, no meanes, no possibility of escaping. The *danger* not to be descried, not to be escaped, that is the danger.

4. His were a *swarme of bees* (He calleth them so) they *buzze* and make a *noise* when they come. Ours, a brood of *vipers, mordentes in silentio, still*, not so much as a *hisse*, till the deadly blow had been given.

5. His was but of *himselfe* alone, so he saith, *I was in trouble, They came about me, kept me in, thrust sore* at me. But one person, *Davids* alone. Ours of a farre greater extent; *David*, and his three Estates with him.

Now, though *David* himselfe were valued by them at *ten thousand* of themselves (and not over valued neither; for he is worth more; and all Kings like him, no lesse worth) yet he and they too, must needs be more, than He alone. Not onely *King David* had gone but *Queene Esthere* too: and not onely they, but *Salomon* the young *Prince*, and *Nathan* his *brother*. Nor these were not all. The Scriptures recount, *David* had *Jehosaphat* for his *Chancellour*, *Adoran* his *Treasurer*, *Seraja* his *Secretarie*, *Sadoc* and *Abiathar*, and twenty two more, the chiefe of the *Priests*, *Admo* his *judge*, *Joab* his *Generall*; all had gone. His *forty eight Worthies* or *Nobles*, all they too. The Principall of all the *Tribes* in the kingdome: all they too; and many more than these; no man knoweth how many. It is out of question, it had exceeded this of *Davids* here.

6. One more. His *danger* (he confesseth) was from *man*. He goeth no further, *I will not feare what* man *doth unto me*. This of ours was not: meerly mans, I deny it, it was the *devill* himselfe. The instruments (not as his, a *swarme of bees*, but) a swarme of *Locusts, out of the infernall pit*. Not *men*, no not *Heathen men*: Their *Stories*; nay their *Tragedies* can shew none neare it. Their *Poets* could never faine any so *prodigiously impious*. Not men; No, not *Savage wilde men*: the *Hunnes*, the *Heruli*, The *Turcilingi*, noted for *inhumanity*, never so inhumane: Even among those barbarous people, this fact would be accounted *barbarous*. How then? *Beasts*: There were at *Ephesus, beasts in shape of men*, and (Greek), *brutishness* is the worst, *Philosophie* could imagine of our *nature*. This is more than *brutish*, What *Tiger*, though never so inraged, would have made the like havock? Then, if the like, neither in the nature of *men*, nor *beasts* to be found (it is so unnaturall) we must not looke to patterne it upon earth, we must to *hell*, thence it was certainly, even from the *devill*. He was a *murderer from the beginning*, and will be so to the ending. In every sinne of bloud, he hath a *claw*, but, all his *clawes*, in such an one as this: wherein so much bloud as would have made it *raine bloud*, so many baskets of *heads*, so many peeces of rent bodies cast up and downe, and scattered all over the face of the earth. Never such a day; all *Joels* signes of a *fearfull day, bloud*, and *fire* and the *vapour of Smoake*. As he is a *murtherer*, so we see (in *Marke*) by his *renting* and *tearing* the poore *possessed childe*, he is *cruell*, and in this, all his cruelties should have met together. *Pharoahs* and *Herods* killing *innocent* and *harmless children*, yet, they spared the *Mother*: *Esau's* cruelty, smiting *mother*, *children* and all. *Nebuzaradens* (?) not sparing the *King*,

nor his *Lord*: *Hamans* not sparing *Hester*, nor her *Ladies*. *Edoms cruelty*, not sparing the *Sanctuary* nor the wals, *downe* with them to the *ground*. His owne *smiting* the *foure corners* and bringing downe the house upon the heads of *Jobs children*. Put to all the *cruelties*, in *Jeremies Lamentations*, the not *honouring the faces of Nobles, Priests, Judges*, the making so many *widowes* nd *orphans*; the voice in *Rama* of *Rachel* comfortlesse. Cruelty, more cruell to them, it spared and left behind, than to those, it took away. It yrketh me to stand repeating these; That every age, or land, but that our age, and this land should foster or breed such monsters!

That you may know it for that perfectly, consider but the wickedness of it, as it were in full opposition to God, and you must needs say, it could not be His doing: God *forbid* (saith *Abraham*) *thou shouldest destroy the righteous with the wicked. Kill not Dam and young ones both* (saith *Moses* in the *Law*.) *You shall not touch mine Annointed* (saith *God* in the *Psalmes*.) *You shall not pull up the good corne, rather let the tares stand* (saith CHRIST in the *Gospell*.) *You shall not doe evil that good may come of it.* (saith *Paul* in his *Epistles*.) But, here is *Satan* flat contrary, in despite of *Law, Prophets, Psalme, Epistle* and *Gospell*. *Hoc est Christum cum Paule conculare*, to throw downe *Abraham* and *Moses*, and *David*, and *Paul*, and CHRIST, and GOD, and all, and trample upon them all.

One more yet: That this *abominasien of desolation* (so calleth *Daniel*, so calleth our *Saviour*, the uttermost extremity of all that bad is. so may we this truly) that this *abomination of desolation* tooke up his *standing* in the *holy place*.

1. An *abomination*: so it is, abhorred of all flesh, hatred and detested of all, that but heare it named: yea, they themselves say, they should have abhorred it, if it had taken effect. It is an *abomination*.

2. Every *abomination* doth not forthwith make *desolate*. This had. If ever a *desolate kingdome* upon earth, such had this beene, after that terrible blow. Neither *root* nor *branch* left, all swept away. *Strangers* called in, *murtherers* exalted; the very *dissolution* and *desolation* of all ensued.

3. But this, that this so *abominable* and *desolatory* a plot, stood in the *holy place*, this is the pitch of all. For, there it stood, and thence it came abroad. Undertaken with an *holy oath*, bound with the *holy Sacrament* (that must needs be in a *holy place*) warranted for a *holy Act*, tending to the advancement of a *holy Religion*, and by *holy persons*, called by a most *holy name*, the *name of Jesus*. That these *holy religious persons*, even the *chiefe* of all *religious persons* (the *Jesuites*) gave not onely *absolution*, but *resolution*, that all this was well done; that it was by them *justified* as lawfull, *sanctified* as meritorious, and should have been *glorified* (but it wants *glorifying*, because the event failed, that is the griefe, if it had not *glorified*) long yer this, and *canonized*, as a very good and holy act, and we had

had orations out of the *Conclave* in commendation of it. (Now I think, we shall have no more of it.) These good *Fathers* they were *Davids bees* here, came hither, only to bring us *honey, right honey* they, not to *sting* anybody: or (as in the XXII. verse) they (as *builders*) came into the land, only for *edification*, not to *pull down*, or to destroy any thing. We see their practice, they begun with *rejecting* this *Stone*, as one that *favoured Hereticks* at least, and therefore excommunicate, and therefore deposed, and therefore exposed, to any that could handle a *spade* well, to make a mine to blow him up, *Him*, and all his *Estates* with him to attend him: (The corner *Stone* being gone, the *walls* must needs follow.) But then, this shrining it (such an *abomination*) setting it in the *holy place*, so ugly and odious, making such a treason as this a *religious, missal, sacramental treason*; hallowing it with orison, *oath* and *Eucharist*, this passeth all the rest. I say no more, but as our SAVIOUR concludeth, when you see such abominations so *standing, qui legit intelligat*, nay *qui videt*. God send them, that (not *read* of it, but) *see* it, and had like to have smelt of it, to learne that, they should by it: and so I leave it.

Tell me now if this were not *His doing*, and if it should not have beene a day of His *making*, the Devils owne *making*.

This should have beene done; this, the *danger*: what was done. This, the *factum fuisset*, what the *factum est*? All these were undone, and *blowen over*, all the undermining dissappointed; all this murder, and crueltie, and desolation defeated. The *mine* is discovered, *the snare is broken and we are delivered*. All these, the *King, Queene, Prince, Nobles, Bishops, Judges*, both Houses *alive*, all: *not a haire of any of their heads perished*; not so much as the *smell of fire on any their garments. Give thankes o Israel, unto the Lord thy God in the congregation from the bottome of their heart; here is little Benjamin thy ruler, the Princes of Juda &c.* that they are here and do see them here and that the *Stone* these *Builders* refused, is still the *Head-stone of the corner*. That, should have beene done; this, was done: and we all, that are here this day, are witness of it; Witness above all exception of this *factum est*.

But by whom, whose *doing*? Truly, not mans doing this; it was the *Lords*. *A Demone factum est illud*, or *fictum est il*lud. It was the *Devils doing*, or *devising*. (*the plot*) *A Domino factum est hoc,* This was *God's doing* (the *deliverance*.) The *blow* was the *Devils*. The *ward was Gods*. Not *man*, but the *Devill*, devised it: Not *man*, but God defeated it. He, that *sate in heaven* all this while, and from hence looked downe and saw all this doing of the *devill* and his *lims*, in that mercy of his, which is over *all his works*, to save the effusion of so much blood, to preserve the soules of so many innocents, to keep this Land from so foule a confusion, to shew still some token, some *sensible token upon us for good, that they which hate us may see it, and be ashamed*; but especially, that that, was so lately united, might not so soone be dissolved, He tooke the matter into his owne hand. And, if ever

God shewed, that He had a *hooke in the Leviathans nose*, that the *Devil* can go no further than his *chaine*, if ever that thre is in him more power to *help*, than in *Sathan to hurt*; in this, he did it. And , as the *devils* clawes to be seene in the former; so *God's right hand*, in this mighty thinkg (He brought to passe) and all the *fingers* of it.

1. To shew it was *He. He held his peace and kept silence,* sat still, and let it go on, till it came neere, even to the very period, to the day of the *lot*; so neere, that wee may trruly say (with *King David*) *as the Lord liveth, uno tantum gradu, nos morsque dividimur*, there was but a step between death and us. We were upon the point of going to the *hill*, all was prepared, the *traine*, the *match*, the *fire, wood*, and all, and we ready to be the *sacrifice*, and even then and there, *In monte providebat Dominus, God provided for our safety*, even in that very place, where we should have been the *burnt offering*; from heaven, *stayed the blow*. It was *the Lords doing.*

2. When treachery *hath his course like water*, and creepes along like a *snail* (it is the *fiftie eight Psalme*) then to make it *like the untimely birth of a woman*, never to see the sun (not, as in this, *arserunt sicut ignis in spinis*, but was *a blaze, as in a bush of thornes:*nay, if it come so far, it had gone wrong with us:) but, as in that, *priusquam intelligerent spinae*, or even the *thornes* gate *heat*, or the *powder, fire;*) then, saith he there, *dicit homo, Utique est Deus*, Men shal say, verily, there is a *God*, and this was His *doing*.

3. And not only, that it was bewrayed, but that he made them the bewrayers of it themselves, and even according to the place (*Eccl.* 10.) made *things with feathers* to disclose it: When (as in *Psalme* 64.) *their owne tongues* (or, which is all one, *their owne pens*) make *them to fall*: all that consider it, shall be amazed; and then all men shall say, *This hath God done*; *for they shall perceive it plaine, it is His worke*. They shall be changed in *confession*, they shall *sweare*, they shall take the *Sacrament* not to doe it, and yet, contrary to all this, it shall come out by themselves. Was not this Gods *doing*?

4. Yet further, to shew it was so: This which was written, was so written, as diverse of profound wisdome, knew not what to make of it. But then commeth *God* againe (God most certainly) and (as in the Prov. 1610.) puts (hebrew,) a very *divination*, a very *oracle*, in the Kings lips, and his mouth missed not the matter; made him, as *Joseph*, the revealer of secrets, to read the riddle: giving him wisdome to make both explication, what they would doe and application, where it was they would doe it. This was God certainly. This, *Pharaoh* would say, none could, unless he were *filled with the Spirit of the holy God*. It was *A domino factum*.

5. Lastly, as that, when it was come forth they were not reclaimed, not then when they saw, the hand of God was gone out against them, and that it was even God *they strove withall*: no, but even then, from hidden treacherie, fell to open rebellion and even perished in it (if God shewed not a *miracle* of his *mercie* on them) perished there, and perished eternally: as this I say did (that it was *factum a Demone*, who never left them, till he had brought them thither) So, that (before they came thither) *God* cast their owne *powder* in their *faces*, *poudered* them and disfigured them with it. and that their quarters stand now in pieces, as they meant, ours should: It is the case of the CIX. *Psalme, And hereby shall they know, that is in thy hand, and then the Lord hast done it*. How? in that, they are thus *cloathed with their owne shame*, and even *covered with their owne confusion*; that they fall as fast as they *rise*; are still *confounded*, and still *thy servants rejoyce*. These five (as prints) shew, it was *God's hand*. It was the *Lord*, that made the *day*, it was the *day*, that the *Lord made*. Be thou exalted Lord in thine own strength. It was thy *right hand*, that brought this mighty thing to passe.

This will not serve the turne. His *doing* makes it not the *Day*. His *doing* a miracle, that makes it, and that is too. I take no thought, to prove this point: by the *Law*, the *Prophets*, the *Gospell*. To put them to it; *Moses: enquire now of the dayes, that were before us, since the day that God created man upon the earth, and aaske from one end of heaven to the other, if there came to passe such a thing as this, whether any such like thing have been heard*, and, if we cannot suit it or for such another by it, we must needs yeeld it for one. By the *Prophets, Goe to the isles and behold, send to Kedar and take diligent heed, and see if you can possibly* finde the like: if not, confesse it for *mervailous. Come hither* (saith David*) and behold, how marvelous God is!* and what is that? that such, as are *rebellious*, are not able to *exalt themselves*. We need not goe so farre, we have it here to see. We may say to him, *Come ene strange things today*. We never *saw it on this fashion. The like was never seen in Israel*. Therefore *marvailous* certinly. It is now no *miracle*, no *strange thing*, to have a *King* delivered: every othere yeare, we see it, and therefore wonder not at it. But to see *King, Queene*, their *seede* and all their *estates* delivered, that is *mirabile*, that is *a new thing created on the earth*, I conclude: as, that was the *Divels doing*, and *was monstrous in our eyes*. so, this is *God's doing*, and it is *marvellous in our eyes*. And againe, upon all these markes, that, as this was a *day*, the *divell* would have marred, so this is a *day*, that the *Lord made*.

Mervailous then it is: yet hath it not (as we say) his *full Christendome*, unlesse it be so in our *eyes*. For the time it was, and that (of the *Psalme*) fits us well, *When God* (saith he) *turned away the captivitie* (say we, *the destruction*) *of his people; then were wee like to them that dreame*. No man, but stood in a maze, as if he knew not well, whether he saw it making or reams of it, it was so strange.

And let me goe further. Not, in *ours* only for (sure I am) that which followeth there, is true (*Then said they, inter Gentes*) of other *nations*; The *Lord hath done great things for them*: and we are too blame, if we answer them not, with the *Eccho* there following, *Yea indeed, the Lord hath done great things for us. for which wee have cause to rejoice.* If strangers think it strange, and say, and write, *A feculo inauditum,* The like was never heard before. If it were *marvellous in their eyes*, It were very *mervaileus* if it should not be so, *in our eyes too.*

I adde, they that were in (?) of it, *in their eyes*, it is so; and that of the Apostle, may aptly be applied to them. *Behold ye despisers, and wonder, and vanish, for God hath wrought a work in your dayes, a work which you yourselves that were the doers, shall scarce believe, when it shall be told* that even astonished themselves, to see it goe forward so long, and suddenly cast down. Nay, I goe further, to make it a *miracle* consummate. I doubt not, but it was strange news, even in *Hell* itself, insomuch as even that place had never hatched the like monster before. You see the welcome they in *Hell* gave him of *Assur*, (*Esay.* 1`4.) *What art thou come, that makest the earth to tremble, and dost shake whole kingdomes?* And yet it is well known all his shaking was but in a *metaphore*. He never made it *shake actually* as these would have done: and therefore this of greater admiration, and (I doubt not, but) *more wonderful in their eyes.* And *ours* are very dimme, if in all other it be, and be not so in *ours*.

Then if such *dayes* there be, if this of ours be one of them, if the fore-part of the verse doe, then must the latter also belong to us: If this, the *day, the Lord hath made* then, this, the *day*, wherein we to *rejoyce*. When He *makes*, we to *make*; and our *rejoycing* in it, is our *making* of it.

To *rejoyce*, no hard request, nor heavie yoke, let it not be grievous to us. We love to doe it, we seek all meanes to doe it in all cases else: then to assay to doe it here. This (sure) the *Prophet* would not require nor make it the office of the day, but that upon such dayes, God himselfe cals us to *joy*.

And even as, when God calleth us to mourning, by *black dayes*, of famine or warre, or the like; then to fall to *feasting* or revelling, is that that highly displeaseth God: so, when God, by good *dayes*, calleth us to joy; then to droope, and not to accommodate our selves to seasons of his sending, is that which pleases him never a whit.

What? (saith *Nehemias*, upon such a blessed day as this) *Droope you today? Nolite*, at no hand to doe it, *Dies enim festus est*, it is a *festival day*: what then? why it is essential, it is the nature of every *Feast* (saith *God* in His Law*) omniogaudere*, by any meanes in any wise therein to rejoyce. And *Nehemias* promise is to incourage us, that if the strength *of the Lord* bee our *joy*, the very joy of the *Lord* shall be our *strength*.

To conclude: Sure I am, that if the *plot* had prevailed, it would have beene an high Feast in *Gath* and a day of *Jubilee* in *Ascalon*; *The daughters of the uncircumcised would have made it a day in triumph*. Let us not be behind them then, but shew as much *joy* for our *saving*, as they would certainly have done, for our *perishing*.

Exultemus & Laetemur. God loveth our *joy* should be full; it is not full, except we have both these, the *body* (as it were) and the *soule* of *joy*: the *joy outward* of the *body*, and the *gladnesse inward of the soule*. (So much doe the two words signifie, in all the three tongues.) Both he will have: for; if one be wanting, it is but *semiplenum*; halfe full.

And he beginneth with *Exultemus*, the outward: not to ourselves within, which we call *gaudere in sinu, joy of the bosome* but such, so exuberant, as the streames of it may overflow, and the beames of it shine and shew forth, in an outward sensible *exultation*. It is a *day*, so would he have us *rejoyce*, that, as by day-light it might be seene in our face, habit and gesture: Seene and heard both: Therefore hee faith (at the 15, *verse*.) *the voice of joy is in the dwellings of the righteous*. And *in the dwelling* it doth well: But yet, that would not serve his turne; but, *open me* (saith he at the 19. *verse*) *the gates of righteousnesse*, that is, the *Church-doore* (his *house* would not hold him) *thither will I go in, and there, in the congregation, in the great congregation, give thanks to the Lord*. And that so *great a congregation*, that it may *constituere diem solemnem in condensis usque ad Cornua altaris,* that they may stand so thicke in the *Church*, as fill it from the entrie of the doore, to the very edge of the *Altar*.

This same joy that is neither seene nor heard, there is some *leven of malignitie* in it; he cannot skill of it. He will have it *seene* in the *countenance*, heard in the voice; not only *preaching*, but *singing* forth His *praise*. And that, not with *voices alone*, but with *instruments*, and not *instruments* of the *Quire* alone, but instrument of the steeple too, *bels* and all, that so it may be *Hosanna in altissimus* in the very *highest* key we have. This for *exultemus*.

But, many a close *Hypocrite* may do all this, and many a counterfeit *Schemei* and *Sheba* did all this, to *David*; got them a *fleering forced countenance*, taken-on *joy*. And there fore the other, that God will have his joy, not be the joy of the countenance alone, a cleere face and a cloudy overcast heart, he will have the *gladnesse* of the heart too, of the inner man: *Cor meum & caro mee;* the *heart,* as well as the *flesh,* to be joyfull. The joy of the *soule* is the *soul* of joy, not a *body* without a *soul*, which is but a *carcase*. *Strange children may* (and will) *dissemble with me* (saith the *Psalme* 18.44) *dissemble a gladnesse*, for feare of being noted and yet within, in *heart*, you wot what. But, God calleth for his *defontibus Israel*, which we read, *from the ground of the heart*. That is (indeed) the true fountaine of joy, that our *lips may be faire, when we sing unto Him, and so may our soule which he hath delivered.* Nay, he delivered both: and therefore, both the body to *rejoyce*, and the *soul* to be glad. This doth *Laetemur* adde, to *exaultemus*.

If then we be agreed that we will doe both, I come to the last, how to *order our joy*, that it may please Him, for whom it is undertaken. It is not every joy, that He liketh. Merry they were, and joyfull (they thought) that kept their Kings day (*Hos. 7.*) by taking in *boule* after *boule* till they were sick again. So they that *Malachi* speaks of, there came nothing of their *feasts* but *dung* (beare with it, it is the *Holy Ghost* his own terme) that is, all in the *bellie* and *bellie-cheere*. So they, that sate *downe to eat and drink and rose up to play,* and there was all, that is the *Calves feast*, a *Calfe* can do as much. *But with none of these was God pleased*, and as good no *joy*, as not to the purpose, as not to please him.

That it may be to the purpose, that God may take pleasure in it, it must begin at *Hosanna*, at *Aperite mihi porta Iusitia*, at the *Temple doore*, there must it goe in, it must *blesse*, and be *blessed* in *the house of the Lord. I will* first *make joyful in my house of Prayer (it is God by Esay:)* the streame of our *joy*, must come from the spring head of *Religion*.

Well then, to the *Church* we are come. So far onward. When we are there, what is to be done? Somewhat we must say, we must not stand mute. There to stand still, that, the *Prophet* cannot skill of. That then, we may (there) say something, hee here frames, he here endites a versicle, which after grew into such request, as no *feast* ever without it, without an *Hosanna*: it grew so familiar, as the very *children* were perfect in it. The summe and substance whereof (briefly) is no more, but (which we all desire) that God would still *save*, still *prosper*, still *bless* him that in His name, is come unto us (that is) *King David* himselfe, whom all in the house and all of the House of the *Lord* blesse in His name.

And to very good purpose doth he this for, *joy* hath no fault, but that it is too short, it will not last, it will be taken from us too soone. It is ever a *barre*, in all *joy*, *tolletur a vebis*, subject to the *worme*, that *Jonas gourd* was. It standeth us therefore in hand, to begin with *Hosanna*, so to *joy*, as that we may long joy to pray for the continuance, that it bee not taken from us: ever remembering, the true temper of *joy*, is (*exultate in tremere*) not without the mixture of some *feare*. For, this day, wee see what it is, a joyfull day: *we knew not* (saith *Salemon*) *what the next day will be* and if not what the *next day*, what the next *yeare* much lesse. What will come, we know not; what our sinnes call for to come, that wee know; even that God should call to judgement, if not by *fire*, by somewhat else. If it be but for this, it concerns us neerly, to say our *Hosanna*, that the next yeare be as this. It is our wisedome therefore, to make the meanes, for the continuance of it, that God would *still stablish the good worke, He this day wrought in us*; still bless us, with the continuance of the same *blessings*.

And this that we may doe, not faintly but cheerefully with the *lifting* up of our *soules* therefore, as far as art or spirit can doe it, he hath quickened his *Hosanna*, that he may put *spirit* and *life* in us to follow him in it, with all fervor and affection: foure times twice with Anna, and twice with No, either of them before, and after, but eightwords, and foure of them *interjections:* all to make it passionate, and that, so as (in the original) nothing can be devised more forcible, and so, as it is hard, in any other tongue, to expresse it; which made the *Evangelist* let it alone, and retaine the *Hebrew* word still. But, this, as neere as I can it soundeth. *Now good Lord save us yet still now good Lord prosper us yet still.* Be to us as last yeare, so this, and all the yeares to come, *Jesus a Saviour, yesterday and today and the same for ever.*

And three things doth he thus earnestly pray for, and teacheth us to do the like.

1. to *save*, 2. *prosper*, and 3. *blesse*

1 To *save*: that should be first with us; it is commonly last. We have least sense of our *soules*. To save us, with the *true saving health*; (it is a word whereof our *Saviour Jesus* hath His name) it importeth the salvation of the *Soule*; properly to that it belongeth, and hath joyned to it *Hosanna* in the *Gospell* (*Hosanna in excelsis*) to shew it is an high and heavenly salvation.

2. Then, to *prosper*, If He but grant us the former alone, to have our *soules* saved though without prosperitie, though with the dayes of adversity, it is *sors sanctorum*, the lot of many a *Saint* of his, of farre more worth than we: Even so, we are bound, to thanke Him, if even so, we may be but saved. But, if he adde also *prosperitie* of the outward, to the *saving* of the inward man, that not so much *as a leafe of us shall wither, but looke what we doe shall prosper,* and that, whasoever men of evil counsels do, shall not prosper against us,. if He not onely vouchsafe us *Hosanna in excelsis*, but *Hosanna de profundis* too, from *deepe cellers, deepe vaults,* those that dig deepe to undermine our prosperitie, If he adde the *shadow of his wings,* to shelter us from perils, to the *light of his countenance* to save us from our sins, then have we great cause to rejoyce yet more and, both with *exultemus* from without, and *laetemur* from within, to magnifie his mercie, and to say with the *Prophet, Praised be the Lord*, that (not only *taketh care for the safetie,* but *taketh pleasure in the prosperitie of his servants.*

3. Lastly, because both these and one and the other, our future *salvation*, by the continuance of His *Religion* and *truth* among us, and our present *prosperitie* (like two wals) meet upon *the head-stone of the corner,* depend both, first, *upon the name of the Lord*, and next upon him, that in his *name*, and with *his name*, is *come unto us* (that is) the *King*. (So, do both the *Evangelists* S. *Luke* and S. *John* supply, and, where we read, *Blessed be he,* there they read *Blessed be the King that commeth,* so that neither of them sure, unlesse he be safe, that he would blesse

him, and make him blest, that in His blessed name, is come amongst us. The building will be as *mount Sion*, so the corner stone be *fast;* so the two walls, that meet, never fall asunder. If otherwise: but I will not so much as put the case but as we pray, so trust, it *shall never be removed, but stand tall for ever*

This then we all with that are now in *House of the Lord*, and *we that are of the house of the Lord*, do now and ever, in the *Temple* and out of it, morning and evening, night and day, wish and pray both, that he would continue forth his goodnesse, and blesse with length of dayes, with strength of health, with increase of all honour, and happinesse, with terror in the eyes of his enemies, with grace in the eyes of his subjects, with whatsoever *David*, or *Salomon* or any *King*, that ever was happie, was blessed with; Him, that in the *Name of the Lord* is come to us, and hath now these foure years stayed with us, that he may be blessed in that name, wherein he is come, and by the Lord, in whose Name he is come, many and many yeares yet to come.

And, when we have put this *incense* in our phials, and bound *this sacrifice with cords to the altar* fast, we blesse you and dismisse you, to eat your *bread* with *joy*, and to drink your *wine* with a *cheerfull heart*: for God accepteth your work, your *joy* shall please Him: this *Hosanna* shall sanctifie all the *joy*, shall follow it.

To end then. This *Day*, which the Lord hath thus *made* so *marvellously*, so *marvillously*, and *mercifully*, let us rejoyce in the Maker, for the making of it, by His doing on it that deed, that is so marvellous in our eyes, in all *eyes* returning to the beginning of the *Psalme*, and saying with the *Prophet*: *O give thanks to the Lord, for he is gracious, &c Let Israel, let the house of Aron, yea, let all that feare the Lord, cofesses that His mercie endureth for ever.*

Who only doth great wonders. Who remembered us when we were in danger, and hath delivered us from our enemies, with a mightie hand and stretched out arme. And, as for them, hath turned their device upon their owne head. And hath made this day, to us a day of joy and gladnesse. To this God of Gods, the Lord of heaven, glorious in holinesse, fearefull in power, doing wonders, be, &c.

Lancelot Andrewes

Lancelot Andrewes was born in 1555 and died in 1626. He was an English minister, preacher and scholar. He served the Church of England in the reigns of Queen Elizabeth I and King James I. Under James I, Andrews was Bishop of Chichester. He directed the committee that created the Authorized Version or

King James Version of the Bible. The Church of England commemorates Andrewes with a lesser Festival each September 25.

Andrewes was born in Barking, London. His family came from Suffolk. Thomas Andrewes, his father, was master of Trinity House. Lancelot went to Cooper's Free School in Ratcliff and later the Merchant Taylors' School where he studied under Richard Mulcaster. He began his university education in 1571 at Pembroke Hall, Cambridge, graduating with a a B.A., and then obtained an M.A. in 1578. Andrewes was named as one of the Foundation Fellows of Jesus College, Oxford in 1571. He took orders in 1580. Andrews became vicar of St. Gile's, Cripplegate in 1588 where he delivered memorable sermons. In 1588 he vindicated the Church of England against the Romanists. Francis Walsingham helped Andrewes to to become prebendary of St. Pancras in St. Pauls, London in 1589. Soon thereafter he became master of his own college of Pembroke and chaplain for Archbishop John Whitgift. He was prebendary of Southwell from 1589 to 1609. Andrewes became chaplain to Queen Elizabeth I in 1590. Andrewes turned down appointment of the bishoprics of Ely and Salisbury because he opposed the alienation of ecclesiastical revenues. He was appointed dean of Westminster in 1601, assisted in the coronation of James I, and took part in the Hampton court conference of 1604. In 1605 he became Bishop of Chichester and Lord High Almoner.

Andrewes was known for his debates with Cardinal Bellarmine. On behalf of James I he argued in Scotland in 1617 that Episcopacy was preferable to Presbyterianism. He was well known for his lectures on the Decalogue published in 1630. Soon after his attendance at that synod of Dort he became dean of Chapel Royal and then was translated to Winchester. Andrews died in Southwark and is buried by the high altar at Southwark Cathedral.

Some Thoughts About this Sermon And Lancelot Andrewes' other Gunpowder Treason Sermons

Andrewes would have been killed in the blast. The deliverance of the government, the people, the clergy, a large section of the city of London from an horrific, high-tech blast of gunpowder was truly a wondrous miracle. Despitee deliverance the terrible nature of the threat called for an equally strong and furious commemorative response. For Andrewes the event was even more terrible than those documented in the Old Testment.

For Andrewes it was a Passover and resurrection.

He was charged with determining how and why the government and the people should commemorate the event and he founded his response in the thanksgivings and commemorations of the Old Testament.

The people clearly had to do their part. If they did not do so, all might lose their covenant or conversation with God. Unlike the covenant, God was not bound to respond; however, if the state and church and people maintained the conversation In a polite, righteous way while continually serving God, the chances of a favorable outcome would grow. In no way did Andrewes ever proclaim the English Church or People as the chosen ones. The best that could be said of the church was that it was reformed. The monarchy could proclaim that it was just. The people struggled to stay on the right path.

English men and women had only to look across the channel at France to see what that disfavored nation was forced to endure. All must pull together, pray, fast and celebrate this their day through the generations, or else.

God made the day, he performed the deliverance, but the people must keep it blessed.

The maintenance of the commemoration of the day in "continual memory" would have to continue from this sermon onwards.

Prayer would also be important. But, importantly, not just prayer alone. The people must also rejoice.

Andrewes sets another precedent here. You have to pray but you have to also rejoice, have fun, have joy and seek all means of celebration possible. The people must do everything in their power to make sure that God knows that we celebrate our day. Not to do so would be to have little chance of future deliverance.

Church attendance is a must but note also as with the marking of houses for Passover it is something to be celebrated at home. The individual residence is important.

Andrews recommends the use of one important artifact of celebration: Bells. This shall go on for centuries. Note also his references to singing and music. The use of instruments throughout the centuries following is well documented.

Celebration should be from the heart and soul, from the bowel and centers of the bones.

Feasting and celebration need to be sanctified by visits to church. It should have serious meaning . A feast should be much more than just the creation of "dung."

Andrewes firmly condemns the enemies of the bonfire or those who do not celebrate willingly.

It was not until that tenth and last of Andrews' Gunpowder Plot sermons that he takes time to carefully justify feasting.

These sermons launched the celebration into the future. One can propose that this strong introduction helped the celebration to survive. No other commemoration or calendar custom received such powerful official support. In fact, Gunpowder Treason Day became the only day of thanksgiving to ever be included in the Book of Common Prayer where it remained until the last part of the 19th century.

It is helpful to review the important details of all of Andrews' Gunpowder Treason Sermons in order to re-discover in his theological paradigm at last one sense of purpose for celebrations of the deliverance.

Sermons by Lancelot Andrewes on the Gunpowder Treason: Excerpts Prescribing Means and Nature of Celebration and Thanksgiving

An Outline of SERMONS OF THE GUNPOWDER TREASON, by Lancelot Andrewes
(1555 – 25 September 1626)

Sermon I
(Page 203)
Preached before the King's majesty at Whitehall, on the fifth of November, A.D. 1606

Psalm cxviii, 23,23.

This is the Lord's doing and it is marvelous in our eyes.
This is the day which the Lord hath made; let us rejoice and be glad in it.

"If ever He gave us cause of marveling, as in the first, of rejoicing, as in the cause of marveling, as in the first, of rejoicing, as in the second verse to any land, to us this day He gave both."

"Of keeping in remembrance, many ways there be: among the rest this is one of making days, set solemn days, to preserve memorable acts that they be not eaten out by them, but ever revived with the return of the year, and kept still fresh in continual memory. God Himself taught us this way."

"We have therefore well done and upon good warrant, to tread in the same steps and by law to provide that this day should not die, nor the memorial thereof perish, from ourselves or from our seed; but be consecrated to a perpetual memory, by a yearly acknowledgment to be made of it throughout all generations. in accomplishment of which order, we are all now here in the presence of God on this day that He first, by His act of doing, hath made; of and we secondly, by our act of decreeing have made before Him, His holy Angels and men, to confess this His goodness and ourselves eternally bound to Him for it. And being to confess it with what words of Scripture can we better or fitter do it than those we have read out of this Psalm?"

"3. Then of the duty, how to do it? By rejoicing and being glad, for so *gaudium errit plenum*, these two make it full. How to take order that we may long and often do it? By saying our Hosanna, and *Benedictus;* for *gaudium nostrum nemo tollet nobis* those will make that "our joy no man shall take from us."

"Yea, indeed, the Lord hath done great things for us, for which we have a cause to rejoice."

-p. 216

"if " this the day the Lord hath made," then this the day wherein we are to "rejoice." When He makes, we to make; and our rejoicing in it, is our making of it.
To "rejoice" no hard request nor heavy yoke, let it not be grievous to us. We love to do it, we seek all means to do it in all cases else; then to essay to do it here. This sure the Prophet would not require, nor make it the office of the day, but that upon such days God Himself calls us to joy.
And even as, when God calleth us to mourning by black days of famine or war, or the like, then to fall to feasting or reveling is that that highly displeaseth God; so when God by good days calleth to joy, then to droop and not to accommodate ourselves to seasons of His sending is that which pleases Him never a whit."

"What, saith Nehemiah upon such a blessed day as this, "Droop you to-day?" *Nolite,* at no hand to do it, *dies enim, festus est,* "it is a festival day." What then? why it is essential, it is of the very nature of every feast, saith God in His law, *omnio gaudere,* by any means, in any wise, therein to "rejoice." And Nehemiah's promise is to encourage us, that if the strength of the Lord be our joy, the very "joy of the Lord" shall be our "strength."

"To conclude. Sure I am that if the plot had prevailed, it would have been a high feast in Gath, and a day of jubilee in Askelon, "The daughters of the uncircumcised" would have made it a day in triumph. Let us not be behind them then, but shew as much joy for our saving as they would certainly have done for our perishing."

"*Exultemus et latemur*. God loveth our joy should be full: *Exultimus* it is not full except we have both these, the body, as it were, *mur* both. and the soul of joy; the joy outward of the body, and gladness inward of the soul. So much do the two words signify in all the three tongues. Both He will have; for if one be wanting, it is but *semiplenum,* 'half full."

"And he beginneth with *exultemus,* the outward; not to *Exulte* ourselves within, which we call *gaudere in sinu,* 'joy of the the outbosom, but such, so exuberant, as the streams of it may over-ward joy flow, and the beams of it shine and shew forth in an outward sensible exultation. It is a "day;" so would he have us rejoice, that as by day-light it might be seen in our face, habit, and gesture, seen and heard both. Therefore he saith, at the fifteenth verse, "The voice of joy is in the dwellings of the righteous." And "in the dwelling" it doeth well; but yet that would not serve his turn, but " Open me," saith he at the nineteenth verse, "the gates of righteousness," that is, the church door—his house would not hold him—thither will "I go in," and there in the congregation, in the great congregation, "give thanks to the Lord." And that so great a congregation, that it may *constituere diem solennem in condensis usque ad cornua altaris,* 'that they may stand so thick in the church, as fill it from the entry of the door to the very edge of the altar.' This same joy, that is neither seen nor heard, there is some leaven of malignity in it, He cannot skill of it. He will have it seen in the countenance, heard in the voice; not only preaching, but singing forth His praise. And that - not with voices alone but with instruments, and not instruments of the choir alone but instruments of the steeple too, bells and all, that so it may be *Hosanna in altissimis,* in the "'very "highest" key we have. This for *exultemus Latemur,* But many a close hypocrite may do all this, and many a counterfeit Shimei and Sheba did all this to David, got them a fleering forced countenance, taken-on joy; and therefore the other, that God will have His joy not be the joy of the countenance alone, a clear face and a cloudy overcast heart, He will have the gladness of the heart too, of the inner man;. *cor meum et caro mea,* "the heart" as well as the "flesh," to be joyful. The joy of the soul is the soul of joy; not a body without a soul, which is but a carcass. "Strange children" may, and "will, dissemble with me," saith the Psalm; "dissemble" a gladness, for fear of being noted; and yet within, in heart, you wot what . But God calleth for His *de fontibus Israel,* which we read, "from the ground of the heart." That is, indeed, the true fountain of joy, that "our lips may be fain when we sing unto Him, and so may our soul which He hath delivered." Nay, He delivered both; and therefore, both the body to rejoice, and the soul to be glad. This doth *latemur* add to *exultemus.*

If then we be agreed that we will do both, I come to the Last how to order our joy, that it may please Him for Whom it is undertaken. It is not every joy that He liketh. Merry they were, and joyful they thought, that kept their "King's day," by taking in bowl after bowl, till they were "sick" again.

So they that Malachi speaks of, there came nothing of their feasts but "dung"—bear with it, it is the Holy Ghost's own term—that is, all in the belly and belly-cheer. So they that "sat down to eat and drink, and rose up to play," and there was all; that is the calf's feast, a calf can do as much.

"But with none of these was God pleased;" and as good no joy as not to the purpose, as not to please Him.

That it may be to the purpose, that God may take pleasure in it, it must begin at Hosanna, at *Aperite mihi portas justitice,* at the temple-door; there must it go in, it must bless and be blessed in the house of the Lord. I will first make joyful in my house of prayer"—it is God by Esay; the stream of our joy must come from the spring-head of religion.

Well then, to the Church we are come; so far onward. When we are there, what is to be done? Somewhat we must say, we must not stand mute. There to stand still, that the Prophet cannot skill of. That then we may there say something, he here frames, he here indites us a versicle, which after grew into such request, as no feast ever without it, without an Hosanna; it grew so familiar as the very children were perfect in it. The sum and substance whereof briefly is no more, but, which we all desire, that God would still "save," still prosper, still bless him, that in His name is come unto us, that is King David himself, whom all the house and all of the house of the Lord, bless in His name.

And to very good purpose doth he this; for joy hath no fault, but that it is too short, it will not last, it will be taken from us too soon. It is ever a bar in all joy, *tolletur a vobis,* subject to the worm that Jonah's gourd was. It standeth us therefore in hand, to begin with Hosanna, so to joy as that we may long joy to pray for the continuance, that it be not taken from us; ever remembering, the true temper of joy is *(exultate in tremore)* not without the mixture of some fear. For this day, we see what it is, a joyful day; "we know not," saith Solomon, "what the next day will be;" and if not what the next day, what the next year much less. What will come we know not; what our sins call for to come, that we know, even that God should call to judgment, if not by fire, by somewhat else. If it be but for this, it concerns us nearly to say our Hosanna, that the next year be as this. It is our wisdom therefore to make the means for the continuance of it, that God would still establish the good work He this day wrought in us, still bless us with the continuance of the same blessings.

And this that we may do, not faintly but cheerfully with the lifting up of our souls therefore, as far as art or spirit can do it, he hath quickened his Hosanna, that he may put spirit and life in us to follow him in it, with all fervour of affection: four times, twice with *Anna,* and twice with *Na;* either of them before, and after; but eight words, and four of them interjections; all to make it passionate, and that so as in the original nothing can be devised more forcible; and so as it is hard in any other tongue to express it; which made the Evangelists let it alone, and retain the Hebrew word still But this, as near as I can, it soundeth: "Now, good Lord, save us yet still; now, good Lord, prosper us yet still." Be to us, as last year, so this, and all the years to come, "Jesus" a Saviour, "yesterday and to-day and the same for ever."

And three things doth he thus earnestly pray for, and teacheth us to do the like. 1. To save, 2. prosper, 3. and bless.

To save: that should be first with us, it is commonly last, we have least sense of our souls. To save us with the true saving health—it is a word whereof our Saviour Jesus hath His name—it importeth the salvation of the soul; properly to that it belongeth, and hath joined to it Hosanna in the Gospel, *Hosanna in excelsis,* to shew it is a high and heavenly salvation.

2. Then to prosper. If He but grant us the former alone, to have our souls saved, though without prosperity, though with the days of adversity, it is *sors sanctorum,* 'the lot of many a saint of His,' of far more worth than we; even so we are bound to thank Him, if even so we may be but saved. But if He add also prosperity of the outward to the saving of the inward man, that not so much as a "leaf" of us shall "wither," but look what we do shall "prosper," and that whatsoever men of evil counsels do, shall not prosper against us; if He not only

vouchsafe us *Hosanna in excelsis,* but *Hosanna de profundis* too, from deep cellars, deep vaults, those that dig deep to undermine our prosperity; if He add the shadow of His wings to shelter us from perils, to the light of His countenance to save us from our sins, then have we great cause to rejoice yet more; and, both with *exultemus* from without, and *Letemur* from within, to magnify His mercy, and to say with the Prophet, "Praised be the Lord, That" not only taketh care for the safety, but "taketh pleasure in the prosperity of His servants."

3. Lastly, because both these, the one and the other, our future salvation by the continuance of His religion and truth among us, and our present prosperity, like two walls, meet upon "the Head-stone of the corner;" depend both, first, upon "the Name of the Lord," and next upon him that in His Name, and with His Name, is come unto us, that is, "the King," (so do both the Evangelists, St. Luke and St. John supply; and where we read, "Blessed be He," there they read "Blessed be the King that cometh") so that neither of them sure, unless he be safe; that He would bless him, and make him blest, that in His blessed name is come amongst us. The building will be "as mount Sion," so the corner-stone be fast; so the two walls that meet, never fall asunder. If otherwise—but I will not so much as put the case; but as we pray, so trust, it "shall never be removed, but stand fast for ever."

This then we all wish that are now in the "House of the Lord," and we that are of "the House of the Lord," do now and ever, in the temple and out of it, morning and evening, night and day, wish and pray both, that He would continue forth His goodness, and bless with length of days, with strength of health, with increase of all honour and happiness, with terror in the eyes of his enemies, with grace in the eyes of his subjects, with whatsoever David or Solomon, or any King that ever was happy, was blessed with, him that in the Name of the Lord is come to us, and hath now these four years stayed with us, that he may be blessed, in that Name wherein he is come, and by the Lord in Whose Name he is come, many and many years yet to come.

And, when we have put this incense in our phials, and bound this "sacrifice with cords, to the altar" fast, we bless you and dismiss you, to eat your bread with joy, and to drink your wine with a cheerful heart; for God accepteth your work, your joy shall please Him, this Hosanna shall sanctify all the joy shall follow it.

To end then. "This day, which the Lord hath" thus "made" so marvellously, so marvellously and mercifully, let us rejoice in the Maker, for the making of it, by His doing on it that deed that is so "marvellous in our eyes," in all eyes; returning to the beginning of the Psalm, and saying with the Prophet, "O give thanks to the Lord, for He is gracious." "Let Israel, let the house of Aaron, yea let all that fear the Lord, confess that His mercy endureth for ever."

"Who only doeth great wonders." "Who remembered us when we were in danger." "And hath delivered us from our enemies," "with a mighty hand and stretched-out arm." And, as for them, hath turned their device upon their own head. And hath made this day, to us, a day of joy and gladness. To this God of Gods, the Lord of Heaven, "glorious in holiness, fearful in power, doing wonders," be &c."

-pp. 216-222

SERMON II.

(Page 223.)

Preached before the King's Majesty at Whitehall, on the Fifth of November,

A.D.1607.

Psalm cxxvi. 1

When the Lord brought again the captivity of Sion, we were like them that dream.
Then was our mouth filled with laughter, and our tongue with joy; then said they among the heathen, The Lord hath done great things for them.
The Lord hath done great things for us, whereof we rejoice.
O Lord, bring again our captivity, as the rivers in the South.

"Now to alter the property of all this, and to convert it to our own and shew first both this Hallelujah, and then that this Hosanna will no less agree to us, and our choir— if not more, but certainly more—a review must needs be granted of all the former points. And in them there is no remedy but we must fall to measuring, that it may appear there is great odds between this of ours and that of theirs. Consequently, that we are bound to give thanks with another manner of Hallelujah than ever did they. And that whether we look to that which was turned away, ours was worse; to the manner of turning itself, ours was better; to the means of this turning, ours to be preferred; to the likeness of a dream, to the *Dicebant inter gentes,* to the *Facti sumus latantes,* in all and every point we are still beyond them."

-p.234-5

"He was the doer; He the doer of these great things, and we the people for whom these great things were done; and so a people highly magnified by Him in His mercy; and so a people deeply bound to magnify Him for all His mercies, but for this above all, that all the world speaks of. And though we cannot with other words than they, yet can, and will, I trust, with far other affections. God forbid but *facere nobiscum* should be sounded in a higher key than *facere cum Mis.* In dangers, I am sure it is; never any men's dangers touch us as our own; never they from the shore cry so heartily, Lord save them, that they see in danger of drowning upon the sea, as they in the ship themselves cry, "Lord save us." God forbid but we that felt it should take up our Hallelujah in a higher strain than they that were but lookers-on; heard of it, and spake of it, but were not partakers as we were of it .

Let this be the difference: that we say the same that they say; but they say, *Magnificavit Dominus facere cum Mis,* and *facti sunt gementes;* and we, *Magnificavit Dominus facere nobiscum, et facti sumus latantes.*

And since our case doth so many ways surpass this of the Jews, in all the points along, our Hallelujah must needs do so too. It is but reason I will require. Theirs, here, went no further than their "mouth" and their "tongue," *os et lingua;* more they mention not. But in a certain place the Psalmist, when he would express a far greater joy, thus he saith, " All my bones shall say, Lord who is like Thee?" This I think reason, that seeing our "bones" should have been " scattered" in every corner like as chips, "when one heweth wood on the earth "—should have but were not—not only our "mouth" and "tongue," as theirs, but our very "bones should say," Hallelujah, Lord who is like Thee," Who hast rid us from a danger the like whereof never was? I add further, that if we and our "bones" would hold our peace, "the stones should cry it." For timber-work and stone-work and all had flown in pieces, we know, then; even, as Habakkuk speaketh, "that the beam out of the timber-work, and the stone out of the walk may cry one to another;" the beam to the stone, Hallelujah, and the stone to the beam again, Hallelujah, to Him That hath kept them fast, and not made Jerusalem as a heap of stones. Even they to cry; every bone to have a tongue, and every stone and beam to have a tongue to put down theirs, and to make our *Dicebant,* our Hallelujah, our *Magnificavit* the louder.

And now, shall we stay here and end with Hallelujah, and Our cut off Hosanna quite? I dare not; I seldom see Hallelujah hold long, if Hosanna forsake it and second it not. For I ask, What, are they all dead that sought our lives? Say they are; is the devil dead too? If he be not, it not if they were. His powder-mill will still be going; he will still be as busy as ever in turning over all his devices, in turning himself into as many shapes as Proteus, and all to turn us to some mischief. The more it concerns us not to be too long at our Hallelujah, but when we have done it, before we stir, to take up our Hosanna; not to forget it in any wise. After we have praised Him for *In convertendo,* that so it is, to return to our *Converte Domine,* that so it may long be. The wheel will stand, it will not turn on still, without it.

Then, in the person of humble supplicants cry we all, Hosanna to the Highest, and *Converte Domine* to Him That is Lord of Ezekiel's "wheels," and of all their conversions. The rather, for that there is no one design hath more laid open and let us see the defects and weakness of all human wisdom and watchfulness than this. There wanted neither, but it went beyond both. No, nor any design hath let us see, how dangerous and undiscoverable plots the devil is able to possess his limbs withal. All to let us see what need we have to turn to Him with our *Converte,* That can see what they do at midnight in the vault, as well as what is done at noonday on the house-top; can see and discover, discover it and turn it away. That He would, as many as are coming this way, turn them all away.

And turn them all away by the way of prevention; not suffering them to light on us as theirs did and then after remove it, but averting it before it come lest after it be too late.

And, that we forget not *sicut,* that He turn it by such and no other means than the "streams in the south," that is, with no great ado; not in boisterous or rigorous means, as that of Egypt, but in mild and calm manner, as this of Babel, and our own. By the same means still; even by the turning of the heart, which is in His hands, which as the "streams in the south" He now did turn, and so still and ever may. That from that fountain still may flow the streams that may give us refreshing in time of our need. That if it be His blessed will, that may ever be the *sicut,* as now it was.

And now, "Turn our captivity O Lord," past and to come, turn both; that as the "streams of the south" they may melt, fall away, and come to nothing; that our future dangers may still be *sicut somnia,* ever 'as dreams,' but never visions; that, as we have been now matter of praise to the nations for our former delivery, so we never become a by-word to them for any after calamity, but that our conclusion may be ever *Facti sumus latantes,* still in joy, and this joy may never be taken from us; that we still may laud and magnify Thy glorious Name, evermore praising Thee and saying, *Magnificetur Dominus.* The Lord hath magnified His power and goodness toward us this day, for which His holy Name be magnified this day, and for ever!"

-p. 238-240

SERMON III.

(Page 241.)

Preached before the King's Majesty at Whitehall, on the Fifth of November,

A.D.1609.

Luke ix. 54—56.

And when His disciples James and John saw it, they said,
Lord, wilt Thou that we command that fire come down from
Heaven, and consume them, even as Elias did?
But Jesus turned about and rebuked them, and said, Ye know
not of what spirit ye are.
For the Son of man is not come to destroy men's lives, but to
save them.

"This we learn. But we come not only for that, but to congratulate this poor town that escaped the fire, and ourselves no less, that should have perished by the same element, though not from Heaven, yet another way; though not by

Dicimus, yet by another means; and in public manner to render our yearly solemn thanksgiving, that we also by the Son of man were delivered from the powder laid ready to consume, and from the match-light to give it fire; that they were rebuked, yea more than that destroyed themselves, that sought our destruction. Every way our case hath the advantage, and therefore bindeth us to greater duty."

-p. 257

"And shall I then, upon all this, make a motion? Master, wilt Thou we speak to these whom Thou hast delivered, that seeing Thou tookest order the fire should not ascend to consume them, they would take order their prayers may ascend up, and as the odours of the Saints' phials burn before Thee still and never consume, but be this day ever a sweet smell in Thy presence? Their fire, they came to put under the earth, Christ would not have burn; another "fire" He came to put upon earth and His desire is that it should burn, even that fire whereon the incense of our devotion and the sacrifice of our praise burn before God, and be *in odorem suavitatis*. We were appointed to be made a sacrifice: if Isaac be saved, shall nothing be offered in his stead? Shall we not thank God that He was better to them than James and John; and to us better than those were, that will needs thrust themselves to be of His society? That when this *Dicimus* was said of us too, stayed it at *Dicimus,* and never let it come to *Perficimus,* miraculously made known these unknown spirits; that He turned and rebuked the motion, and the spirits that made it; that He came once and twice, to save us, and destroy them.

If we shall, let us then do it, Let our souls magnify the Lord, and our spirits rejoice in God our Saviour; that the beginning of the text and of our case was "fire" to "consume them," in the first verse; that the end was, *non perdere sed salvare*, in the last. Such may ever be the end of all attempts to destroy us. So may He come still, and still as here He came; never to destroy, ever to save us. And as oft as He to save us, so oft we to praise Him.

And God grant that this answer here of Christ may serve for a determination of this case for ever; and every Christian be so resolved by it, as the like never come in speech more by any *Dicimus*. But if—as we know not what spirits are abroad, that every destroying spirit may be rebuked, and every state preserved, as this town here was, and as we all were this day. And ever, as He doth save still, we may praise still; and ever magnify His "mercy, that endureth for ever." Amen."

-pp. 259-260

SERMON IV.

(Page 261.)

Preached before the King's Majesty at Whitehall, on the Fifth of November,

A.D. 1612
Lamentations iii. 22.

It is the Lord's mercies that we are not consumed, because His compassions fail not.

"And shall we not allow one day to the magnifying of Him and His mercies, That was the cause of all? It should have had the first day by right, and we were pointed to it by *Misericordia Domini super omnia opera Ejus.* Well at last, now in this seventh year, this *annus Sabbaticus,* let us make it our Sabbath, rest upon it, and put it off no longer. Be this day dedicated to the celebrating of them."

-p. 262

"Then last our recognition. That seeing His mercies fail not us, that we fail not them; seeing they consume not, nor we by their means, that our thankfulness do not neither, that it fall not into a consumption. But that in imitation of the three we render Him 1. plural thanks; 2. and these from the bowels; and 3. that incessantly, without failing. And this not in words only, but in some reality, some work of mercy, tending to preserve those that are near *consumpti,* pining away."

-p. 263

"And now to our recognition. To perform it to the full, as it deserveth, that I know we cannot. Worthily to celebrate and set forth His mercies therein, according to their merit, what tongue of men or Angels can do it? But shall we not therefore do it as we can? We were not consumed ": shall our thankfulness fall into a consumption? His compassion failed us not, shall our recognition fail then? Shall we not find our tongues as well to praise His mercies as to pray for them? Can we pour out petitions in time of need, and can we not drop forth a few thanks when we have what we would? No, let this be the first, that we answer *Misericordia non consumpta* with *gratia inconsumpto?;* that our thanks fall not into an hectic.

Then, that we imitate the three properties of this virtue that saved us, and to whom we owe ourselves, no other than those that be expressed in the text.

   1. That we keep the number, do it plurally. Not single thanks for plural mercies—that agrees not. Iterate them over and over, as much as we may. In the weight we shall surely fall short, let us make amends with the number. Do it oft, and many times, in hope that *sape cadendo* they shall effect that which *vi,* by any force in them, they are not able.

This, to give as many as we may, make them many. Now, as many as we are many. As we should have gone all together, as we should have gone; so and no otherwise let us together here all acknowledge His mercies, this day shewed us, and praise Him all of us for them: Praise Him King and Queen, &c.

Yea, not only *Dicat nunc Israel,* but *Dicat nunc paries,* Praise Him walls and windows, praise Him lime and stone, praise Him roof and foundation, "let them praise the Name of the Lord:" for "He said but a word," and they stood fast; He "commanded," *non,* and they were not stirred. Jeremy speaks to a wall to weep, (Lamentations, the second chapter and eighteenth verse); we may, with as good reason, to rejoice and give thanks. All that should have perished together, praise Him together.

2. Next, that we put Him not off with certain, I know not what, hollow thanks, that have no bowels at all in them. But do it *do visceribus, de intimis fibris,* 'from the very bowels, from the innermost veins, and the smallest threads of them; with Him, "Praise the Lord O my soul," and "all my bowels, all that is within me, all my bones shall say," &c.

When the bones, the bones that should have been shivered in sunder; when the bowels, the bowels that should have been scattered abroad, speak, that is the right speaking. If every one of us, to himself, would but say the very words of this verse only as they stand, "It was," &c. "It was," &c.

Even this onward were worth the while, if it be not for form, but feelingly spoken. *Die, die, sed intus die,* 'say it, but say it from within,' let the bowels speak it; though our words fail us, they do not. And, indeed, the consumption should have been with fire; shall our recognition be frozen? No spark, no *vigor igneus,* no fervour at all in it? How agree these, a fiery destruction and a frozen confession? It standeth us upon to be delivered no less from cold thanks than from a hot fire.

3. And that we never fail to do it. No year to intermit it, no week, and I would I might add, no day neither. Answer *Misericordia Ejus manet in aternum,* with *Misericor-dias Domini cantabo in aternum;* and not mercies that never' fail with short thanks and soon done, specially seeing their not failing lieth upon our not failing them.

Now it would do well to seal up all with a recognition real, that is, the praise of mercy with some work of mercy. What was done upon us this day? Our preserving. A work of mercy it was. This work can no way so lively be expressed, as by a work of like nature; nothing so well, saith St. James, by jas. 2.16. warm breath as by warm clothes. *Erga consumendos,* such as are in danger of it, not by fire, but by cold and nakedness.

This, as it is a most kindly way to resemble it, so withal it is a most effectual means to procure the continuance and not-failing of it. *Magnes est misericordia Dei erga nos misericordia nostra in fratres;* 'of God's mercy to us, keeping us from consuming, our mercy toward our poor brethren is the loadstone to keep them from the like. So, under one, shall we both set it forth and procure it; procure that we so much stand in need of, and set forth that virtue to which we were so much this day beholden. Now to God, to Him and to His mercy, the bowels of His mercy, and the fresh fountain of them; that suffered us not to be consumed but delivered us, and that from that fire, and that universal, utter, sudden, unnatural consuming by it, the decree whereof was so certainly gone forth against us, come so near us, and we not aware of it; that suffered us not to be consumed, but gave them to be consumed in our steads, and hath this day presented us all alive to give Him praise for it; to Him, for the multitude of His mercies, for the *paterna viscera miserationum suarum,* that never fail, nor consume themselves, nor suffer us to fail, and be consumed; to Him I say, &c"

-pp. 274-276

SERMON V.

(Page 277.)

Preached before the King's Majesty at Whitehall, on the Fifth of November,

A.D.1613.

Proverbs viii. 15.

By Me Kings reign.

"But if a good, for to that case I return, never to look upon Him, but to lift up our eyes withal to this *Per Quem.* As to thank Him that He hath preserved him many other times, but especially and above other this day—him and his, that is, him and us all; so duly to pray to Him, that he which reigneth thus by Him, that is, by His appointment, may safe and well and long reign by Him, that is, by His protection. To thank Him for *Per Me regnat,* and to be suitors to Him for *Per Me regnabit;* that He would draw out this *Per,* and make it a long *Per, Per multos annos.* That it may ever be, as in the text it is, *regnabit* still, still, in the future, "shall reign." "Shall reign" out his own age himself, in person: there is one *regnabit.* "Shall reign" in his issue and offspring, and that many ages: there is another *regnabit. "*Shall reign" in the life of memory, and a blessed remembrance of his time and reign, and that through all ages: there is a third *regnabit.*

"Shall reign" all these. And beyond all these there is another yet, as the last, so the best of all: "shall reign" all these, *per* Deum, 'by God;' and, after all these, shall reign *cum Deo,* 'with God,' in the glory, joy, and bliss of His heavenly kingdom, and that perpetually; which kingdom shall have none end, be in *sacula saculorum.* To which kingdom, I &c."

-p. 294

SERMON VI.

(Page 296.)

Preached before the King's Majesty at Whitehall, on the Fifth of November,

A.D. 1614

Proverbs xxiv. 21—23.

My son, fear thou the Lord, and the King; and meddle not with them that are given to change.
For their destruction shall rise suddenly; and who knoweth the destruction of them both?
These things also belong to the wise.

"But let them take this from Solomon, that *toties quoties,* so oft as they seek to "build Sion in blood," so oft shall their building end in destruction; and so oft as they rise to that end, they shall rise to their ruin—fathers and sons, and sons' sons, to the end of the world.

But we, beloved, who have better learned to fear God, I trust, if Solomon shall acknowledge us for his sons, or God for His servants; if we will be the children of Wisdom, let Wisdom be justified of her children. Let us do Solomon the honour to think him wise enough to give us counsel. And since we see he is proved a prophet, and not a word of all this text is fallen to the ground, that strange examples there have been of it, and that many, and this day one *exemplum sine exemplo,* an example *per se,* a matchless one in this kind; having these before our eyes, and having in remembrance the four *novissima* in the text, 1. destruction, 2. ruin, 3. *repente,* and 4. *Quis scit?* let us fear those four, and fearing them persist as we have done hitherto, in the fear of God and the King, and ever fear to have to do or to deal with them that fear neither. So I pray God we may, and that this may be the fruit, even our fruit; and His blessing upon that hath been spoken, that we may live and die *timentes Deum et* Regem, ever pure from this mixture. And so God make us all."

-p. 316

SERMON VII.

(Page 318.)

Preached before the King's Majesty at Whitehall, on the Fifth of November,

A.D.1615.

Psalm cxlv. 9.

The Lord is good to all, and His mercies are over all his works.

"TEN years it is now since our memorable delivery as upon this day: and we here to celebrate not the anniversary only, but the *decennalia* of it. Now in numbering it is well known that at ten we begin anew at the figure of one, we return again ever to the first. So do we now. For this was the first, *misisericordio Domini super opera Ejus*.

We shall never forget it so many of us as then heard it, that it was the first, that it was thought (and that *authore magno*) to be the fittest theme of all wherewith to begin the first solemn thanksgiving of all for the great mercy of God, and for the great work of that mercy this day shewed upon us all."

-p 318.

"And it is the tenth year, this; and naturally, *decumana sunt grandiora. Aluctus decumanus,* a deep flood it was had like to have "gone over our souls;" and a *misericordia decumana,* a mercy of a large size it was, that made it went not then. That we perform then *laudes decumanas,* great praise and large thanks, now this *anno decimo,* some way answerable to the greatness of our peril, and to the greatness of the mercy that made us so well pass it. The numbers of seven and ten are not without their weight. The seventh the Sabbath, the tenth God's part. Both ways, as the Sabbath day, as the tenth year, sacred to God is this day and our duty upon it."

-p. 321

"Many ways might this be made appear, and many days brought to give us light to it; but let all else pass in silence, this day, this fifth of November, is *instar omnium.* Nay, is *super omnes,* 'before, beyond, above them all;' to elevate to us this point of "the tender mercies of our God, whereby this Lu. 1. 78. day sprung from on high did visit us." This day, I say, enough and enough to bring from all our mouths that it brought from his Majesty's, and that with admiration, *Misericordia Dei super omnia opera Ejus!* And the *Confiteantur* and the Benedicant of right belonging to it."

-p. 332

"The *super* upon all God's works follows in the words From His next ensuing, *Confiteantur*. Are "His mercies over all His works?" Why then, O all ye works of the Lord, all flesh, "every thing that hath breath," but chiefly His chief work, "the sons of men," the nations and the kindreds of the earth, come all to confession; all owe this, to confess, at least. Confess? what? Nothing but mercy, and the *super* of the mercy. Nothing, but that it is as it is: do but as God doth, exalt it, place it where He sets it. Let the deep say, It is over me; and the dry land say, It is over me: and so of the rest every one; so many works, so many confessions.

There is a further *super,* "upon" His "saints;" they owe from Him more to Him than His ordinary works. His works but to confess; His saints, to confess and "bless" both. They are double works, "needle-work on both sides;" more becomes them. *Te decet hymnus in Sion;* both to confess it is above all, and to bless and praise it above all. For if it be above all, it follows more praise is to come to Him for it than for all. If mercy above all, the praise of His mercy above the praises of all."

-p. 337

"For if ever mercy were over work of His, if ever work of His under it directly, it was so over us, and we so under it, this day. If ever of any it might be avowed, or to any applied; if ever any might rightly and truly, upon good and just cause, say or sing this verse; we of this land may do both, it will fit our mouths best, best become us."

"To set off the *super* of this day then, and to conclude. If the generality of His works confess Him for theirs, and the speciality of His saints bless Him for theirs; what are we to do, how to confess, how to bless for the singular mercy of this day, and let all others go? Sure our "mouths to be filled with praise" as the sea, and our voice in sounding it out, as the noise of His waves, and we to cover the heavens with praise, as with clouds for it."

-pp. 338-339

"Wherefore the powers Thou hast distributed in our souls, the breath of life Thou hast breathed into our nostrils, the tongues Thou hast put into our mouths, behold, all these shall break forth and confess, and bless and thank, and praise and magnify, and exalt Thee and Thy mercy for ever. Yea every mouth shall acknowledge Thee, every tongue be a trumpet of Thy praise, every eye look up, every knee bow, every stature stoop to Thee, and all hearts shall fear Thee. And all that within us, even our bowels, those our bowels that but for Thee had flown we know not whither; even our bones, those bones that but for it had been shivered bone from bone, one from another, all shall say, "Who is like unto Thee, O Lord," in mercy? Who is like unto Thee, glorious in holiness, fearful in praise, doing wonders," wonders of mercy, as this day, upon us all, to be held by us and our posterity in an everlasting remembrance?

Glory be to Thee, O Lord, glory be to Thee; glory be to Thee, and glory be to Thy mercy, the *super omnia,* the most glorious of all Thy great and high perfections. Glory be to Thee, and glory be to it—to it in Thee, and to Thee for it; and that by all Thy works, in all places and at all times. And of all Thy works, and above them all, by us here; by the hearts and lungs of us all, in this place, this day, for this day, for the mercy of this day; for the mercy of it above all mercies, and for the work of this day above all the works of it. And not this day only, but all the days of our life, even as long as Thy mercy endureth, and that "endureth for ever"—for ever in this world, for ever in the world to come; *per,* 'through' the cistern and conduit of all Thy mercies, Jesus Christ."

-pp. 339-340

SERMON VIII.

(Page 341.)

Preached before the King's Majesty at Whitehall, on the Fifth of November,

A.D. 1616.

Isaiah xxxvii. 3.

The children are come to the birth, and there is not strength to bring forth.

"HAVE taken this piece, and no more. More I could not, you see. It will not fit our turn, or this day—the fore-end of the verse: "This is a day of trouble, rebuke, blasphemy," cannot we say. We must say, This is a day, not of trouble, but of joy; not of rebuke, but of praise; not of blasphemy, but of thanksgiving, with us. And so may we say too, and yet keep these words for our ground still. Nothing lets, but that one and the same day may be, both a day of joy, and of sorrow. They that have the day, and they that lose the day, the day is but one; but to the winner a joyful day, to the loser not so, but a day of sorrow and of blasphemy otherwhile. And so was this day a day of sorrow to some, they might have taken up the whole verse as it stands; those I mean that, do what they can, must be fain to father the children that this day were coming but came not forth. That they came not forth, the want of strength to be delivered, made it to them a day of sorrow, some say of blasphemy too—not so to us. To us a day of praise and thanks, that they lost their so looked for and longed for children; that they were not born, who if they had been born, would have been the bane of us all. To us then, as this day a day, so this a verse of joy. The words are in Hebrew of the nature of a proverb; and used by them, as a by-word, upon the defeating of any plot . Not every defeating, but then when a plot is cunningly contrived and closely followed, and is near brought to the very point to be done yet not done though, but defeated even then: then take they up this proverb and say, *Venerunt, Sic.* "

-pp. 341-342

"And this, lo, is our very case this day. For why are we here met but that, as the text is, a birth there should this day, the fifth of November, this very Tuesday, have been with us? should have been, but was not—that it was not; this day should have been a dismal day—that it was not so. A birth was in bearing, and *Venerunt ad partum,* I promise you: that it was not born, that it was *partus* non *partus,* 'a birthless birth,' it is with us a day of joy; and as this a day, so this a text of joy, and thanks be to God it is so. And we say these very words of Hezekiah, not as here he did, but as after he might have, and as we this day may speak them, with a cheerful accent, *Venerunt ad partum,* &c/"

"No more there was. And that there was not, it is holiday with us to-day. Applying all to our case, I am to tell you first: 1. these children, who they were; 2. and secondly, how near to the birth they came; 3. thirdly, of the strength to bring them forth, the failing of it, and how it came to fail. Upon these two questions, 1. one, why they were not suffered to come forth? 2. Why they were suffered to come so far? 3. And last of all, of the *Tu ergo,* or inference upon all this; which is not that which Hezekiah infers, the next verse, *Tu ergo leva orationem;* but another *ergo,* as it were a new birth of ours, *Tu ergo leva gratiarum* actionem. Yes, yes, that and *leva orationem* too; and so let us lift up our prayer, and for nothing more than that we may raise a good levy of thanks indeed, to send up to God that there was no strength to bring it forth, when it was so near brought."

-p. 344

"What is that? The text will lead us to it, if we look but over to the next verse. For there, when any evil travail threatens us, we find by Hezekiah, the kindly birth then on our parts is *Tu ergo leva orationem,* "a levy of prayers." Now that being turned away, and turned away in a manner so miraculous, the natural kind issue then is another *Tu ergo, Tu ergo leva gratiarum actionem,* a new levy of thanks; a new *Leva quia levatus,* for His easing of us of so heavy a chance like to light so heavy on us.

At the present, sure, while it was fresh, we were ravished with it; for the time we seemed to be even with child, as if we would bring forth somewhat, and somewhat we did bring forth, even an Act that we would from year to year, as upon this day, bring forth and be delivered of thanks and praise for this delivery for ever. And here we are now to act that we then enacted, even to travail with this new birth. God send us strength well to be delivered of it!

For so shall we double our joy: 1. one joy, for the turning away of that miscreant birth of theirs; 2. another, for the welcoming this of our own.

This birth we now travail with, is a good and a blessed birth. Blessing and glory, and praise and thanks, are *in bonis,* all; all good in us, if any thing be good in us; the best fruits of our nature, when it is at the very best. And if they be brought forth, it is as it should be, and as God would have it.

But if, which God forbid, they should either not come, or when they be come, our strength fail and they not brought forth, then are we at an after-deal again; then would not this day be so joyful for the misgoing of the other, as sorrowful for the abortion of this. Our joy at least not so entire, but mixed with sorrow; for there is sorrow even to death, if we go with so good a fruit, and it come to the birth and there perish, if we shall but make an Act and do not act upon it.

We seem to sorrow at nothing more than that many a good purpose there is, and many a vow made in time of need, sickness, or adversity—so many, as it is by divines held there be more good purposes, and that by odds, in hell than there be in Heaven—but abortive purposes and vows all. For, O that we were but the one half of that we then promise to be, when we want and would have somewhat! O then how thankful we would be! How never forget! How fast the children come to the birth then! And when we have what we would, our vigour quails presently, our strength is gone from us; *et non sunt vires pariendi.* For all the world seeth nothing we bring forth. Alas, how many aborcements are there daily of these children! Nowhere may this verse be taken up, nowhere so oft, so fitly applied; nowhere so used upon better cause than this, upon the failing of good desires and intents.

That this we may do, to take us to *Leva orationem;* let this be our last. To lift up our prayer first against such unnatural births as that was, the Prophet Osee's prayer: "Give them, O Lord—what wilt Thou give them? a barren womb and dry breasts." There was no strength for that birth of theirs, it was well there was not; thanks be to God there was not, thanks be to God for *Non erant vires.* And *ne sint vires,* say I, 'never let there be strength' for any like this birth; never strength, but weak hands and feeble knees for any such enterprise. *Ne vires pariendi;* nay, *ne veniant ad partum;* not neither, not so far; nay, *ne ad conceptionem;* nay then, *ne ad generationem,* if it may be. If it may not, but they escape thither to the birth, then lift up your last prayer, and let this be it, and let it come up to Heaven, into God's presence, and enter in even to His ears, for the equity of it; in all such designs that *pariens* may be *sine viribus,* and *partus, sine vita;* the mothers no strength, and the children no life, but child and mother perish both, as this day they did. And better so they perish than such a number, than a whole country, perish by their means. This a *Ne veniant* and a *Ne sint vires* against theirs.

But for ours, for our praise and thanks, *veniant,* 'let them come;' and *sint, O sint vires,* 'and let there be strength' when they come, for such, for so good a birth. Ever be there strength to kindness, to thankfulness, to the accomplishment thereof whereto we are in duty so deeply bound. Strength ever to all honest and good resolutions. Pity but they should be so, pity there should want strength for them. Well may they be conceived, come well to the birth; when they be come thither, vigour enough to deliver them, and never when they be come so far, to miscarry.

We may take our light from that. It is *Venerunt filii;* and *filii* is the plural number. So more than one, many there would be. And *filii* falls well with the word *gratia,* which lacks the singular. No such phrase as *agere gratiam.* A single thank was never heard of. And both falls well likewise, to quit the birth we were quit of; for the barrels were many and full, and so would our thanks be.

Again, they would be *filii,* that is, such as children be, and children be flesh, blood, and bone; I mean, some real, some substantial thanks. Not to travail as it were with wind, with a few words only, which are but air, and into the air they vanish again. *Partus opus,* ye remember, we said before; some work there would be, *actio gratiarum,* somewhat actually done, leave some reality behind it, as in a child there is.

Thus far like; but then a difference. Come it would, not as did theirs, *ad partum exclusive,* thither and no farther, but *inclusive,* to the birth, and from the birth; have the blessing of the womb and of the breasts, of the womb to bring it forth, of the breasts to bring it up, till it proved somewhat worth the while.

That so we may rejoice as much in the affirmative of this birth of ours, *Venerunt et sunt vires,* as we did in the negative of that of theirs, *Venerunt et non erant vires.* So doing, God shall again and again turn away those births, if any be in breeding; take away all strength from them being bred, as today He did, and give us new occasions daily to bring Him forth praise and thanks, for His daily continued mercies, in delivering our King, our land, us and ours all."

-pp. 357-360.

SERMON IX.

(Page Ml.)

Preached before the King's Majesty at Whitehall, on the Fifth of November, A.D. 1617

Luke i. 74, 75.—7th and 8th verses of Benedictus.

That we being delivered from the hands of our enemies might serve Him, without fear, In holiness and righteousness before Him, all the days of our life.

"THE children were come to the birth, and there was no strength to deliver them." There we left last. Their not being delivered was the cause of our being delivered. And before- now I go on.

And our being delivered was to this end, "that we being The end, delivered from the hands of our enemies, might serve this day's Him," &c. For I demand: Delivered we were, as this day; why was it? Was it that we might stand and cry out of the foulness of the fact? or stand and inveigh against those monsters that were the actors in it? Was it that we might bless ourselves for so fair an escape? or bestow a piece of a holyday on God for it? And all these may we do, and all these we have done; and upon good ground all. Yet none of these the very *ut;* nor we delivered that we might do these.

But when all is said that can be said, hither we must come, to this *ut* here, and pitch upon it; for this is indeed the *ut finalis,* the right, the true, the proper "that;" "that," for our deliverance, we bethink ourselves how to do Him service.

Take the whole tract along, from the first word *Benedictus:* there is "visited and redeemed" in the first verse; "a horn," or a mighty salvation, in the next; after, we "saved from them that did hate us;" but you shall see that all these suspend still, no perfect period till you come to this. But at this there is. "Visited," "redeemed," "saved," mightily saved: why all? For no other end but that being so "visited," "redeemed" and "saved," we might wholly addict and give over ourselves to the service of Him Who was author of them all.

I wot well, that principally and properly, the whole song referreth to the deliverance of deliverances, our final deliverance from our ghostly enemies, and from their fire, the fire of hell, by our blessed Saviour, which was so great as it was able to open the mouth and loose the tongue of a dumb man, and make him break forth into a *Benedictus*."

-pp.361-362

"And now to the *finis ad quem*. For we are as easily and no less dangerously mistaken in that By mercy's means, The same without all merit of ours, we were not consumed, but delivered to. from so great a misery so near us: why were we so? Were we *liberati* to become libertines, to set us down and to eat, and to drink healths, and rise up and see a play? was there no *ut* in it? Yes; what was that? *ut serviamus Illi*.

"The "covenant" on our parts rests, that then "we should serve Him" for it . His part is kept, *liberati* shews that; then may we put in suit for ours, that is, for *serviamus*."

-p.363

"On ours I reckon these: our service, the matter and the manner of it. The matter wherein: "serve Him in holiness," The con- "serve Him in righteousness ;" not "holiness" or "righteousness" alone, but serve Him in both. The manner how, often no less acceptable than the service The manner.itself. 1. *Ut sine timore;* that our service be freely and cheerfully done, now we are out of fear. 2. *Ut coram Ipso,* that unfeignedly, as " before Him," not before men, before whom 3. we may and do often halt . 3. And for the time of it, *ut omnibus diebus,* that we faint not, or give over, but continue in it "all our life long." Three qualities of ours, and indeed of every true and faithful service. That these be done, and that they may be done; and that that which shall be spoken may tend to this, that they may be done, &c. I- *Ut liberati,* "That we being delivered." To shew the great equity of God's equity on God's part of the covenant, we say first, that we were to serve Him, though *liberati* were left out, being or not being "delivered." This to be our first point."

-p.364

"But then *ut* with *liberati*. If God take us as He finds us, 2. *Ut* with and say with the Apostle, *Parco autem vobis,* "Go to, I bear with you;" and "by way of indulgence" condescend to condition with us, if He come to *ut liberati,* shall not that hold us? Our duty being absolute, depending upon no *ut,* if upon special favour God will come in bonds, and let it run in this tenor, That being delivered we shall serve Him, else not, shall we not then do it? This being done, I marvel what we can allege to decline our duty, unless we mean it should be fast with

God and loose with us; He bound to do all for us, and we free to do nothing for Him.

And yet a third—to magnify His mercy yet more, and to tie us the harder to our covenant—*ut* is not only with *liberati,* but with *liberati* first; God is bound, and first bound to do for us, before we do aught for Him. It is not, that we should serve Him first, and then He deliver us after; but that He should first deliver us, and after, when we are delivered, then and not before we should do our service. It is not *liberandi,* shall be or may be hereafter, it is *liberati,* are already. So we are aforehand with Him. He hath done His, before we begin ours. *Liberati,* you see, precedes *serviamus; liberati* the tense past, *serviamus* but the present (and I would it were the present) I doubt, for a great part it is yet to come.

And the reason why He will have it so to precede is, He would have our service grow out of His favours, our duty out of His bounty. That is the right, and, indeed, the evangelical service. If He have us at the advantage, on the hip as we say, it is no great matter then to get service at our hands. None more servile than we then. But that is the legal, for fear. And that sometimes He hath, but likes it not; He would have it out of love, out of the sense of His goodness, have our hearts broken with that. That is the only acceptable service to Him, that grows out of that root, the *serviamus* that grows out of *liberati,* delivered and serve; first delivered, and then serve. This for the equity of the covenant on God's part..."

"Now come I to plead, that on God's part this covenant was performed, that *liberati* we were. Heaven and earth would rise against us and condemn us, if we should not confess covenant *liberati,* this day. Heaven saw it, and was astonished; and it is gone over all the earth, the fame of it. But that we do. The keeping of this day, the meeting of this assembly, are both to acknowledge and profess that a *liberati* there hath been."

-p. 365-366

"But we may well reconcile them both, if we say, which truly we may say, "that without fear we were delivered, to serve Him in a state without, or void of, fear."

-p. 369

"Now to our part, which we may be put in suit for. *Liberati* then is clear. But how? absolutely? at large? *absque aliquo* condition. *inde?* No condition annexed? No *ut?* Yes; take the *ut* " with you. *Liberati ut,* "Delivered that we should;" should that we do somewhat; for *naturaliter obligamur ad dantem.* This *ut* is natural, there groweth a natural obligation between him that doth and them that receive a good turn; and a deliverance, specially such an one, is a good turn. The fields we till, the trees we plant, shew it. They return their fruit to them that bestow labour or cost upon them. That, I know not how, but so it falls out in matter of benefits, we be not so soon loosed, but we be tied again; nor eased, but loaden afresh; nor freed, but bound anew. It is the law, the bond of nature this, *Liberati ut.* "

" And that *ut* is *ut serviamus*. And this particular *ut* groweth out of the law of nations. There the law is *ut victus sit in potestate victoris,* the conquered ever in the power of the conqueror, to take his life or to save it at his pleasure. But if he will save it, then comes the voluntary *ut* or covenant. He that hath his life saved, to vow to bestow it in his service that did save it. *Servi,* the very name, came of *servati*. They that should have died and were saved, did willingly covenant, *Serva et serviam,* to serve him by whom their lives were preserved. This being the law of nature and nations, why should not the God of nature, the King of nations, be allowed it? that if our lives have been by Him saved, we should from thenceforth come to this *ut, ut serviamus Illi*.

Well, well, it is past now, if it were to come—it is, "that We would we being delivered;" if it were, that we being to be delivered, we would tell another tale then, we would be glad and fain so to covenant, O deliver us then but for this once, and we would serve Him, that we would, and be holy and righteous and what He would besides. Put any *ut* to *liberati* then. We would then seek it of Him that now is offered by Him, to be delivered, if being so delivered we will covenant but to do that which we were bound to do, delivered or no.

And why should we think much of this *serviamus?* All the world knows if the plot had gone on and the powder served, if gone off, the whole land should not have escaped *ut serviamus;* but should have served *duram servitutem,* been not in service, but in servitude. Their servitude is changed into this service, A blessed exchange for us. Great odds between those two;, nay no comparison at all between God's service and their servitude; their bondage, thraldom, slavery, tyranny—I cannot heap too many names. God's service is freedom in respect of that, nay without any respect at all His service is perfect freedom; we say it, we pray it, every day.

And if no comparison in *serviamus,* none in *Illi,* I am sure. Nay, if there were any thing to mislike in *serviamus,* amends is made for it in *Illi.* For the service is much thereafter as the *Illi,* the party is, Whom we serve. *Dignitate Domini honorata fit conditio servi;* 'He may be so great a state we serve, as it is an honour to serve Him. Now, how great a Lord His Lord of lords is, what shall I need tell you? "There is no end of His greatness." How great, and how good withal, *res* goodness *ipsa loquitur;* that appears by our delivery in part, and more shall by His eternal reward laid up for them that serve Him.

There is in all the world no more honourable nor beneficial service than this *serviamus Illi.*

But say we have no mind to serve Him; if we serve not Him, yet serve we must, and serve we will, if not Him some other. It is the condition of our life, one or other serve we do. We must hold of some lord: if free from one, another we serve; and who is that other? When we are "free" from God, "from righteousness," we serve sin and Satan, a worse service I dare say; better then be free from them, and "serve God in righteousness."

"But if we will not serve Him, I ask what will we do then? will we serve His enemies? for so are these. We were not "delivered from our enemies" to serve His enemies, I am sure. That were a foul shame for us, that were against all reason. But if we serve not Him, we serve them. Resolve then to serve Him That hath saved us; not His enemies, in a profane and unrighteous, but Him, in a holy and righteous course of life. And so am I now come to that wherein our service lieth."In holiness and righteousness." In which two, in a sort, are recapitulate the two tables of the law; holy to God, righteous to men. *Quod quis reverenter se habeat ad divina, quod quis laudabiliter cum hominibus conversetur,* saith Chrysostom; reverently to perform holy duties, laudably to have our conversation among men. Both these, first; not either of them. To spend our service but in one is but to serve Him by halves; in both then to serve Him. Neither in an unrighteous holiness, nor in a holy kind of unrighteousness. Neither with the Pharisee, to have all our holiness in our "phylacteries" and fringes, and frequenting the lectures of the law, no matter how we live; nor with the Sadducee, live indifferently honestly, but neither believe "spirit" nor look for "resurrection;" be Christians like Agrippa, *in modico,* a little religion upon a knife's point will serve us. Neither in "holiness" then only, nor in "righteousness" only, but in both."

-p. 370-372

"But then you will mark, it is to "serve Him in holiness." "Holiness" is one thing, to "serve" God "in holiness" is another; "holiness" we have, at least think ourselves to have, but a stately, surly kind of "holiness" it is, so as in our "holiness" we "serve Him" not. But it is not enough to be holy, a service "in holiness" is required at our hands; that we acknowledge a service "in holiness," and as servants carry ourselves, and serve Him in it.

Our service "in holiness" I divide, as the Psalm doth, either *in secreto sanctorum,* when we are alone by ourselves, as there holiness" "in secret" good folks fail not to serve Him; or *in synagogd,* "'in the open assembly "with the congregation.

Our secret "holiness" I meddle not with. *Abscondita Deo nostro,* I leave it to God. I hope it is better and more service-like than our outward is. As *abscondita Deo,* so *revelata nobis.* Our Church-service, our service in *synagogd,* the outside of it so, that is no secret; all men see what it is, that full homely it is, nay full rude it is, and lightly the meaner the persons, the more faulty in it. Our "holiness" is grown too familiar and fellow-like, our carriage there can hardly be termed service, there is so very little of a servant in it."

-p. 373-374

"Thus we have laid forth our covenant, both for matter and done to manner. Wherein if we deal as just men we must keep it, and if we deal with it as wise men we will keep it. For who knows but we may, perhaps, stand in need of a delivery again? If we behave ourselves frowardly in His covenant, what shall become of us then? How shall we hope for such another at His hands? And if He do not, who can deliver us from such another?"

-p. 382

SERMON X.

(Page 385.)

Preached before the King's Majesty at Whitehall, on the Fifth of November,

A.D.1618.

Esther ix. 31.

To confirm these days of Purim according to their seasons;
as Mordecai the Jew, and Esther the Queen had appointed
them, and as they had promised for themselves, and for their
seed, with fasting and prayer.

"HERE have we the making of a new holyday, over and above those of God's in the Law. And the making it by royal authority and the people's assent, and so of the nature of an act or statute, a good precedent for us that have made the like. Here is a joint concurrence, of Mordecai's advising, Queen Esther authorizing, they, that is the people, undertaking for them and "their seed" to confirm—what? "Purim:" there is the day. When? at the appointed times: that makes it a set day. How? with "fasting" and crying, that is, "prayer:" that makes it a holyday. Upon what ground all this? That is in the word Purim, the name of the day. It is called Purim; Purim, that is, lots, as much to say as, The lotholyday."

-p. 385

"This God hath drawn for us; shall we now draw for Him again, and for this so fair a lot allot Him somewhat of our part" *Afemaito* is set before the great, and so before all holydays. All He would draw from us is, but that the lot of this day or the day of this lot may never be forgotten. A benefit would not be forgotten, not man's; God's much less. Such a benefit especially. For even in God's there is a difference; God hath His daily benefits, and those to be remembered of course. But some other He hath so rare as the like never seen; those would have a more than ordinary regard. For where God is extraordinary, we to be so too. If He make it a memorable day by some strange delivery, we to make it memorable by some rare acknowledgment. They seem willing so to do here. *Illi sunt dies quos,* say they. *Ille est dies quem,* may we say, *nulla unquam delebit oblivio;* and so let us say, and so said and so done is as much as God requireth. But our thankfulness is not to fly away like a flash of powder. To fix it then, *fiat volatile fixum;* that would be done. And fix it in any thing else but time, time will eat it out. Best then fix it in time itself, and that hath been ever thought a wise way; so shall it roll about with the time, and renew as it doth. And so time which defaceth all things and bringeth them to forgetfulness, shall be made to preserve the memory of it, whether it will or no. Fix it in time: what part of time? A day: *Memento diem,* saith God in His law, and so points us to the proportion of it. Set some day, and let there, then on that day, be some special commemoration of it.

But that day or time is to be a set day. Fix it in time, but fix the time too. The word of the text, is an appointed time, or day, that comes once a year; as *solenne* is *quod solum in anno."* Now this some will not hear of; no set days, no appointed times they, but keep them in memory all the year long. I like not that. For so, when time was, it was said by some, they would not have this day nor that day to fast on, but keep a continual fast, they; and it seemed a pretty speculation at first, but proved nothing but a speculation: what their fast is come to, by this time we see. It is to be doubted, if other set times were likewise taken away, their continual feast would prove to no better pass than their fast is; better be as it is, and we do as God and good people have done before us.

Provided that it shall be lawful for them to keep the memory of this day every day, if they be so disposed. So yet as they be content to allow some such day as this for them that are not of so happy memories, for fear lest if it be left at large to every man's daily devotion, it may fall to be forgotten, and where it now hath one day, then to have none at all.

And if a set time, what day can we set so fit as the day itself it fell on? With them the fourteenth of Adar, with us the fifth of November. It cannot but be the best way, this, that God took Himself; and God took this. The same days He did His noble acts upon, those very days did He order once a-year solemnly to be kept. The fourteenth of Nisan did the destroyer pass over them; that day, from year to year, did He ordain the Passover to be holden. Fifty days after He granted them His law: in memory of this gift they to keep yearly the day of Pentecost. Can we go by a better example than this of God's own?

These two were not all; but God did as great acts after, as these were, for the same people. They then, setting before them this way scored them out by God, for every famous benefit, a solemn day; for those other benefits after vouchsafed them, they did appoint like solemn days of themselves."

- p. 398-400

"Now a word of the manner of the keeping them, and so an end. They enacted to keep the Purim-days. How to keep of them? It will lead us, this, to the nature of them, whether as holydays or no. For at this there be that stick too. A *feria* they will allow them, a play-day, or ceasing from work; or a *festus dies,* if you will, a day of feasting, or increase of fare; but not *dies sanctus,* no holyday, not at any hand; for then may Esther make holydays, they see it follows. What should one say to such men as these?

For 1. first, it is plain by this verse, they took it *in animas,* "upon their souls;" a soul-matter they made of it. There needs no soul for *feria* or festum, play or feasting. 2. Secondly, the bond of it reacheth to all that *religioni eorum voluerunt copulari* (verse the twenty-seventh) "to all that should join themselves to their religion." Then a matter of religion it was, had reference to that: what need any joining in religion for a matter of good-fellowship? 3. Thirdly, it is expressly termed a rite and a ceremony, at the twenty-third and twenty-eighth verses, as the Fathers read them: rites, I trust, and ceremonies, as holydays are no more, pertain to the Church, and to the service of God, not to merry meetings; that is not their place. 4. Fourthly, they fast and pray here, in this verse; fast the eve, the fourteenth, and so then the day following to be holyday, of course. 5. Fifthly, with fasting and prayer here; alms also is enjoined, at the twenty-second verse. These three will make it past a day of revels or mirth. 6. Lastly, as a holyday the Jews ever kept it, have a peculiar set service for it, in their seders; set psalms to sing, set lessons to read, set prayers to say—and that at four several times as, out of Nehemiah the ninth chapter, and the third verse, their manner is on holydays—good and godly all. None but as they have used from all antiquity. 1. Being then taken on their souls; 2. restrained to the same religion; 3. directly termed a ceremony; 4. being to be held with fasting, prayers, and 5. alms—works of piety all; 6. the practice of the Church concurring; theirs was a holyday clear, and so ought ours to be. Thus have we a precedent upon record to draw up ours by; the superiors to enjoin such a day, the inferiors to observe it.

And as a warrant to do it, so a rule how to do it; with fasting and with crying, that is, prayer, earnest prayer, the last word. What, and must we fast then? That were no good lot in the end of a text. No, if we will pray, well; I dare take upon me to excuse us from fasting. Their fasting was to put them in mind of the fast their fathers used, by means whereof they turned God, and God turned the King's heart, and so all turned to their good. But for us, we have no such means to remember in ours; we used not any, and so hold ours without any. They had two days, their holyday had a fasting day. Our lot is to have but one, and that no fasting day; an immunity from that. So much the better is our lot; a feast without any fast at all.

But though without fasting, not without earnest prayer— meant here by crying— nor without earnest thanks and praise neither. For joy also hath her cry, as well as affliction: "The voice of joy and health is in the dwellings of the righteous." But prayer, sure, will do well at all hands, that a worse thing happen not to us. But prayer is but one wing; with alms it will do better, make a pair of wings, which is before prescribed, at the two-and-twentieth verse. "So to eat the fat and drink the sweet ourselves, as we send a part to them for whom nothing is provided: *Dies enim sanctus est,"* saith Nehemiah; for, by his rule, that makes it a right holyday.

But prayer is the last word here, ends the verse; and with that let us end. Even that all that shall ever attempt the like, let Haman's lot be their lot, and let never any other light on them but *sors funiculus*. Let Queen Esther's prayer, and King Ahasuerus' sentence ever take place: *Malum quod cogitavit, convertatur in caput ipsius—ipsius* or *ipsorum,* one or many. "Let not the rod of the ungodly light on the lot of the righteous." Let God, in Whose hand our lots are, ever maintain this day's lot to us; never give forth other but as in this text, and as on this day, on the fourteenth of Adar, and on the fifth of November. And praised be God, this day, and all our days, That this day shewed that He taketh "pleasure in the prosperity of His servants," and from all lots and plots doth ever deliver them."

--p. 403

-Andrewes, Lancelot, Works: Ninety-Six Sermons, Vol.IV, 1841, (MDCVI.-MDCXVIII).

-See also:

Robertson, Diana, The Gunpowder Treason Sermons of Bishop Lancelot Andrewes, 1606-1618, University of Melbourne, 1987.

1

James, Anne Marie Ph.D, Reading, Writing, Remembering: Gunpowder Plot Literature in Early Modern England, 1605—1688, 2011.

Nowak, Thomas Stephen Ph.D, Remember, remember, the fifth of November": Anglocentrism and anti-Catholicism in the English gunpowder sermons, 1605-1651, 1992.

Johnston, Neil Barclay Ph.D, Pulpit Rhetoric and the Conscience: The Gunpowder Plot Sermons of Lancelot Andrewes, 2011.

William Leigh Preaches

November 5 1606

William Leigh, in Standish, Lancashire preached the sermon Great Britaines, Great Deliverance from the Great Danger of Popish Powder by way of Meditation upon the Late Intended Treason against the King's Most Excellent Majestie, the Queene, the Prince, and all their Royall Issue, 1606.

It was dedicated to Prince Henry (heir apparent)

"Pardon me (my gratious good Lord, and deare Prince , *(Ed. Note: Prince Henry*) if out of a loyall heart I present unto your Princely viewe, what I conceived upon these late intended Treasons in solace of my soule, after the Lord had made the land so glorious by deliverance: I say *Deliverance* out of the hands of cruell enemies, who stroke at our fairest tree, to have cut it down both roots, bole, and branches, if the Lord had not been propitious, and because your excellency is the highest straine in all experience, and Heire apparent to that Crowne and dignitie, whose undoubted right, they have so wrongly by sinister thought. word and worke, as in former ages the like was never devised in any Nation, nor (by the grace of God) ever shall, I have made bold in these fewe leaves, and lines, to lay open the danger, with the deliverance and the rather to your Highnesse……

…But of all lhat ever were, this last devise of Gunpowder to blowe up all, was most detestable, divelish and damnable, as wherein hel was shake, and with all it furies, to have effected their thrice bloudy practice, with this firy resolution, of their angry Goddesse *Juno*…..

…O unnatural and degenerate Englishmen, how could you ever endure, to thirst after the destruction of so sacred a Senate, and sweeete an assembly: How could you finde in your hearts to seeke the destruction of so benigne a Prince and so Royal an issue, with the utter subversion of so glorious a state by bringing into the bowels thereof that Romish *Apolion*, mentioned in the Revelation, who where he is victorious, staineth the earth with bloud, the aire with blasphemy, and the heavens with his abominable, and luxurious incontinences…..

…Surely, surely, for this you entended mischief, and your former murthers, the worme that never dieth, will gnaw your rebellious hearts and the furies of hell which never give rest, will haunt you in your habitations: where ever ye goe, they will speak in the voice of those Kings, Queenes, and Princes, with whose bloud you have embrewed your trayterous hearts, and hands, as it is said Caesars ghost did to Brutus and Cassius, whom in the Senate they murdered with such crueltie…

…emptie your praises, pipe by pipe, from the highest Maiestie, even to the lowest of the people and give God the glory….

…Thus endangered, and yet thus delivered; endangered by men but delivered by God. Now let us jointly give him the glorie…

…Thou high Court off Parliament, dissolve for a time, and say, O Angell of the great Councell, We will consult with thee. And lastly, Thou Lord God of Gods, and preserver of men, let there be silence in heaven, for the space of halfe an houre, till these Saints praises and praiers be offered up….

…Take heed of Poperie, take heed of Papists, and tolerate neither their cause nor person: if you tolerate the cause, it will infect the person: if you tolerate the person, it will credit the cause: therefore to tolerate neither of both, in a state so sanctified as ours is, I hold it safest. What then is to be done, will some say, away with both head , and taile: for Popereie kept under, will practice treason: if it get aloft, it will play the tyrant: therefore no way to have it, is safest, and with least danger…

…And surely so it is, for to be of two religions, is to be of no religion: and to tolerate both, is to confound all, either in a kingdome, or in a conscience…..

…The worme is spred undere thee and the wormes cover thee, while England is at rest and queit, o sing for joy, and sing to the praise of God in all your flockes and families, the Psalme 124…..Sing it with David's Passion…and it will be …honie to the mouth, musicke to the eare, and joy to the heart….

William Leigh 1550-1639

Born in Lancashire. He took holy orders and preached at Oxford. He became justice of the peace and chaplain to Henry Stanley 4th Earl of Derby. He was appointed tutor to Henry Frederick Prince of Wales. He became master of Ewelme Hospital Oxfordshire in 1608

Literature Was Created

Thomas Dekker Published on December 9, 1605

Introductory Riddle from :THE DOUBLE PP.,Thomas Dekker, 1605.

A Riddle on the double PP.

UPon the double P.P. badder fruits grow
Tha on al letters in the *Christ-Crojfe-Row*;

It sets (by reason of the *Badge* it weares)
The *Christ-Crojfe Row,* together by the eares:
The reason is, this haughtie double PP.
Would clyme aboue both A. B. C. and D.
And trample on the necks of E. F. G.
H. I. {Royall K.) L. M. N. O. and Q.
Threatning the fall of R. S. T. and V.

The Resolution.
PP. = Pa Pa. = the PoPe.
Christ-Croje-Row,—Christendome.
A. B. C. D. E. &c. the States of the land: As
Archbishop, Bishops, Councellors, Dukes, Earles, &c.
K. the King.

Q. the Queene.
R. Religion.
S. State.
T. Truth.
V. You all.

-<u>The Mon-dramatic Works of Thomas Dekker: In five volumes</u>, Volume 2, 1885, 16.. p.161. (December 9, 1605)

<u>Songs Were Written</u>

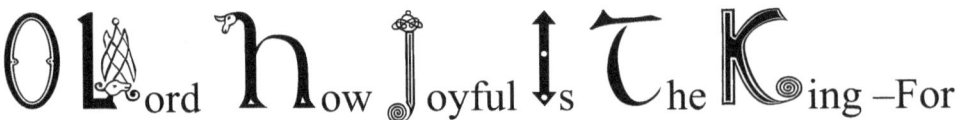

O Lord how Joyful Is The King —For the Fifth of November, Thomas Weelkes, c.1605

O Lord how joyful is the King in Thy strength and power:
how vehemently doth he rejoice in Thee his saviour.
For Thou hast given unto him his godly heart's desire:
to him nothing hast Thou denied that he did require.
Thou didst prevent him with Thy gifts and blessings manifold:
and Thou hast set upon his head a crown of perfect gold.
And when he asked life of Thee, thereof Thou mad'st him sure:
to have long life, yea, such a life as ever should endure.
Great is his glory by Thy help, Thy benefits and aid:
great worship and great honour both Thou hast upon him laid.
Thou wilt give him felicity that never shall decay:
and with Thy cheerful countenance wilt comfort him alway.
For why, the King doth strongly trust in God for to prevail:
therefore his goodness and his grace will not that he shall quail.
But let Thine enemies feel Thy force and those that Thee withstand:
find out Thy foes and let them feel Thy power, the power of Thy right hand.
And like an oven burn them Lord in fiery flame and fume:
Thine anger shall destroy them all, and fire shall them consume.
And Thou wilt root out of the earth their fruit that should increase:
and from the number of Thy folk their seed shall end and cease.
For why, such mischief did they muse against Thine holy name:
yet did they fail, and had no power for to perform the same.
But as a mark Thou shalt them set in a most open place:
and charge Thy bow strings readily against Thine enemies' face.
Be Thou exalted, Lord, therefore in Thy strength ev'ry hour:
so shall we sing right solemnly praising Thy might and power.
So shall we sing right solemnly, praising Thy might and power.

Amen.

- Notes for: 1605: Treason and Dischord., William Byrd and the Gunpowder Plot, The King's Singers, C.D., Signum, 2005.

Gun-Powder Plot: Or, A Brief Account of that bloudy and subtle design laid against the King, his Lords and Commons in Parliament, and of a Happy Deliverance by Divine Power, 1605

To the Tune of Aim not too high licensed according to Order.

True Protestants I pray you do draw near,
Unto this Dity lend attentive Ear;
The Lines are New although the Subject's Old,
Likewise it is as true as e'er was told.

When James the First in England Reigned King,
Under his Royal Gracious Princely Wing
Religion flourished both in Court and Town,
Which wretched Romans strove to trample down.

To their old plotting Trade they strait did go
To move Their Kingdom's final Overthrow
A Plot contriv'd by Catholics alone;
The like before or since was never known.

Rome's counsel did together often meet,
For to contrive which way they might compleat
This bloudy Treason which they took in hand
Against the King, and Heads of all the Land

At length, these wretched Romans all agreed
Which way to make the King and Nation bleed,
By Powder, all agreed with joint Consent,
To Blow up both the King and Parliament.

For to keep secret this their Villany,
By solemn Oaths they one another tye:
Nay farther, being void of Grace and Shame,
Each took the Sacrament upon the same.

Their Treason wrapt in this black Mantle then,
Secure and safe from all the Eyes of Men,
They did not fear, but by one fatal Blow,
To prove the Church and Kingdom's Overthrow.

Catesby, with all the other Romish Crew,
The Powder Plot did eagerly pursue;
Yet after all their mighty cost and care,
Their own Feet soon was taken in the Snare.

Under the House of the Great Parliament
This Romish Den, and Devils by consent,
The Hellish Powder-Plot they formed there,
In hopes to send all flying in the Air.

Barrels of Powder privately convey'd,
Billets, and Bars of Iron too was laid,
To tear up all before them as they flew,
A black Invention by this dismal Crew,

And with the fatal Blow all must have blown,
The gracious King upon his Royal Throne,
His gracious Queen, likewise their Princely Heir
All must have dy'd and perish'd that was there.

The House of Noble Lords of high Degree,
By this unheard of bloudy Tragedy,
Their Limbs in thunder strait would have been tore
And fill'd the Air with noble bloudy gore.

The worthy learned Judges Grave and Sage,
The Commons too, all must have felt Rome's rage
Had not the Lord of Love stept in between
Oh! what a dismal Slaughter had there been.

The King, the Queen, and Barons of the Land,
The Judges, Gentry, did together stand
On Ruine's brink, while Rome the Blow should give
They'd but the burning of a Match to live.

But that Great God that sits in Heaven high
He did behold their bloudy Treachery,
He made their own Hand-writing soon betray

The Work which they had Plotted many a day.

The Lord in Mercy did his Wisedom send
Unto the King, his People to Defend,
Which did reveal the hidden Powder-Plot,
A gracious Mercy ne'er to be forgot.

And brought Rome's Faction unto Parliament
Which did the Powder Treason first invent,
And all that ever Plots, I hope God will,
That the true Christian Church may flourish still

-Pepys Ballad Collection, 2.370 <u>GUN-POWDER Plot:/ OR,/ A Brief Account of that bloudy and subtle Design laid against the King, his Lords/ and Commons in Parliament, and of a Happy Deliverance by Divine Power.</u> Printed for P. Brooksby, I. Deacon,/ I. Blare, I. Back. Wing G2238[A].

A Forme of True Repentance, fit for Traytors to Sing and use now, and at all times while life is in them: made in part by one of Babingtons Conspiracy. And may be sung to the tune of the 25. Psal. John Rhodes, minister of Enborne: From A Briefe Summe, 1606

1 My prime of youthfull yeares,
2 but a frost of cares,
3 My croppe of Corne is turned now,
4 a field of tares.
5 The day is fled and gone,
6 saw I not the Sunne,
7 I seeme to live, yea live I doe,
8 yet my life is done.

9 The spring for me is past,
10 yet it hath not sprung:

11 My aged dayes are growing on,
12 yet I am but young.
13 My thrid is cut in two:
14 yet it is not spurne,
15 I seeme to live, yea live I doe,
16 yet my life is done.

17 I sought for mirth and ioy,
18 found I nought but paine:
19 My tree is dead, though leaves be greene,
20 losse is all my gaine.
21 My glasse was set but late,
22 yet the same is runne:
23 I seeme to live, yea liue I doe,
24 yet my life is done.

25 If subiect I had bin,
26 nought else could I be:
27 Then had I never heard or seene,
28 sorrowes now I see.
29 But I a kingdome sought,
30 else a State-mans roome:
31 Wherefore I am moste iustly brought,
32 unto my Tombe.

33 All men be rul'd my be,
34 not to *Papistry*:
35 For sure the same can not indure,
36 workes such treachery.
37 Ah woe to all that sleepe,
38 will be blinde at noone:
39 They seeme to liue, yea liue they doe,
40 yet their life is done.

41 Lord Iesus saue my soule,
42 mercy be my merrit:

43 Forgive the sinne that I am in,
44 heau'n I may inherrit.
45 O let me not beleeue,
46 purgatory doome:
47 For then I shall but seeme to live,
48 this my life is done.

49 The Commons euery one,
50 whome wee ment to destroy:
51 And with Gun-powder to blow vp,
52 secret suddainely:

53 Your Prayers we doe craue,
54 From Popes pardon we runne,
55 In which a man may seeme to live,
56 yet his life is done.

57 Thus you shall show yourselves,
58 Christian men indeede:
59 Though we have prou'd our selves to be,
60 *Cayne* and *Iudas* seede.
61 O Lord for Christ his sake,
62 us to thy kingdome:
63 Save us from hell, which wee deserve.
64 this short life is done.

65 Our King, our Queene, and Prince,
66 royall Progeny:
67 The counsell grave, God blesse, & saue,
68 the Nobilitie.
69 The clergy of this land,
70 all Iesuites soone,
71 Who seeme to live, and make us liue,
72 yet our liues are done.

FINIS

Guy Fawkes, Ink Blot Print, Dante Gabriel Rossetti, c. 1835

A Real Blast

No matter the view taken of the nature and importance of the plot, it is now certain that in material terms the blast would have been quite real.

In 2003 scientists at the University of Wales in Aberystwyth studied the impact that the gunpowder placed by the plotters in the cellar would have had if it had been ignited. The university's Centre for Explosion Studies found that the blast would have severely damaged buildings at a distance of 500 meters from the blast site. Westminster Hall and Abbey would have been totally destroyed. Windows would have been shattered up to a kilometer from the blast site. This is based upon a quantity of 2500 kg. of gunpowder which is the quantity which government records say was found in the cellar. This was 25 times the quantity needed to demolish the Parliament buildings. The true extent of the terror created by this threat can only be realized if one considers that gunpowder was the most terrible weapon in its day.

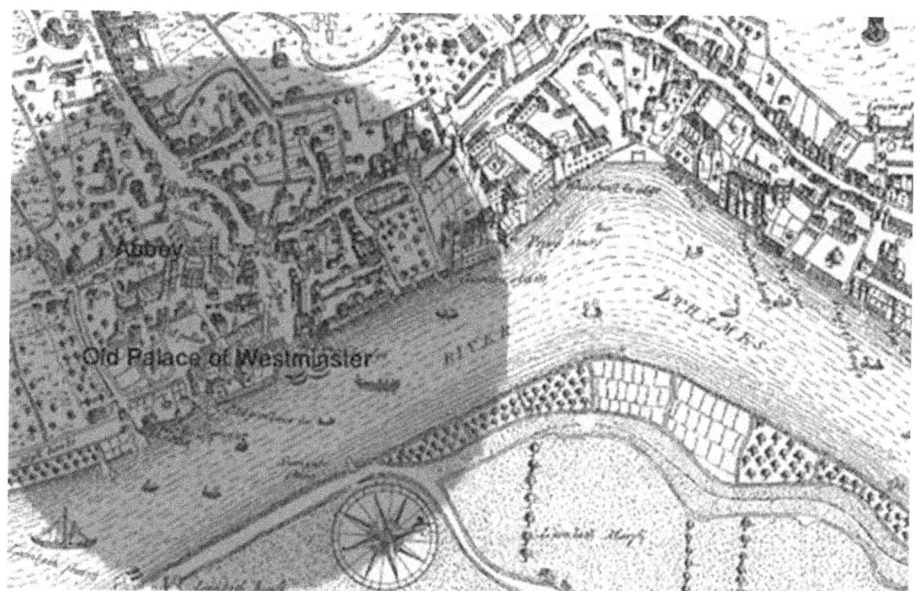

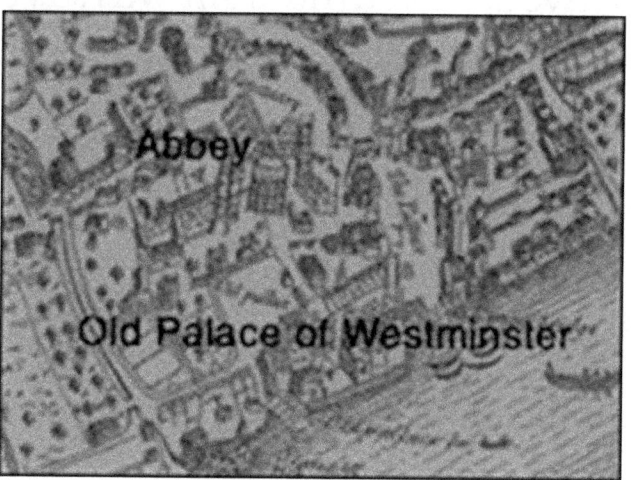

The event was the equivalent of the planting of an atomic weapon in a city center today.

-Kettlewell, Julianna, BBC News Online, <u>The New Civil Engineer</u>, Dr Alford, "Guy Fawkes plot 'was devastating.'"

So ends the first part of the creation of content, structure and purpose of the celebration. The people have been delivered once again by the hand of God from certain death and destruction, the King was saved, the Parliament was saved, the Catholics were once again found guilty and untrustworthy. The threat of the Counter-Reformation prompted a new warning, a rush to more provisions and the extension of homeland security measures. The Great Deliverance was immediately celebrated with bonfires and the ringing of church bells.

Lancelot Andrewes officially demonstrated that this deliverance deserves celebration. This was indeed a multi-faceted deliverance which saved everyone and every institution of the country. It preserved the culture and demonstrated once again divine protection and the ever present need to disclose eternal mysteries with complex artifacts of celebration.

King James instructed his people that the day must be celebrated.

We shall now see how the people and the state constructed artifacts of celebration, cultural productions which will serve as vehicles for this content, however, we must pause to consider another deliverance which provides even more content for the celebrations of the 5th of November. It has to do with a seaside port known as Torbay on the coast of South Devon in England in the year 1688.

Comes William

The Second Deliverance, 5th of November 1688

William of Orange Lands at Torbay

William III : Manner of Willem Wissing (c, 1656)

Mary II, After WISSING Willem, 1653-1687

One fifth of November, a gunpowder plot
Went off'eer its sting it had pow'r to display;
Our fifth of November will ne'er be forgot,
When freedom her ensign unfurl'd in Torbay;
"Nolumus mutari,"
Our laws ne'er shall vary,
Cried Britons, when welcoming William and Mary,
Who landed the Olive and Myrtle to twine...

-- Dibdin, Thomas, "With Emblems of Union Round Liberty's Shrine", <u>William and Mary. (From a Metrical History of England (1813) Vol.II Part the Eleventh, From the Revolution in 1688, to the Accession of the House of Brunswick ,</u> Air To "Anacreon in Heaven.

The Glorious Revolution freed the chosen people from the tyranny of the Catholic monarch James II. This was a major victory for Parliament in that it delivered England from absolutism as practiced by Louis XIV of France. Time itself was now firmly ordered by the important date.

Proclimation Two Additional Prayers to be Added to the Fifth of November Litany, William and Mary, October 30, 1689

Whitehall, October 30, 1689

It is His Majesty's Pleasure, That on the Fifth of November, in the Morning Prayer and in the Litany, these Two Additional Prayers be Used together with those Appointed in the Service for that Day; And that instead of the Collect and the Gospel in the Communion Serivice these here Appointed be used.

Shrewsbury

London

Printed by Charles Bull and Thomas Newcomb, Printers to the King and Queen's most Excellent Majesties. 1689

Additional Prayers to be used together with those Appointed in the Service for the Fifth of November

The Collect for Morning Service, to be added into the other.

O God, whose name is excellent in all the earth, and the glory above the heavens who on this day didst miracuously preserve our church and state from the secret contrivance, and hellish malice of popish conspirators and on this day also didst bring to give us a mighty deliverance from the open tyranny and oppression of the same cruel and bloud-thirsty enemies: We bless and adore thy glorious majesty, as for the former, so for this thy late marvelous loving kindness to our church and nation in the preservation of our religion and liberties. And we humbly pray, that the devout sense of this thy repeated mercy may renew and increase in us a spirit of love and thankfulness to thee its only author; a spirit of peaceable submission and obedience to our church and soverign, whom you madest the blessed judgement of it, and a spirit of fervent zeal for our holy religion which now again, thou hast to wonderful _____(?) and established a blessing to us, and our Posterity ____? we beg for Jesus Christ his sake. Amen

After the Collect for the Day in the Litany.

Accept also, most gracious God, of our unfeigned thanks for filling our hearts again with joy and gladness, after the time that thou hast assisted us, and putting a new song into our mouths, by bringing his majesty who now reigns over us, upon this day for the deliverance of our church and nation from popish tyranny and arbitrary power. We adore the wisdom and justice of thy providence, which so timely interposed in our extreme danger, and disappointed all the designes of our enemies. We beseech thee give us such a lively and lasting sense of what thou didst then, and hast, since that time, done for us, that we may not grow secure and careless in our obedience, by presuming upon thy great and undeserved goodness; but that it may lead us to repentance, and move us to be the more diligent and zealous in all the duties of our religion, which thou hast, in a marvelous manner preserved to us: Let truth and justice, brotherly kindness and charity, devotion and piety, concord and unity, with all other virtues, to flourish among us, that they may be the stability of our times, and make this church a praise in the earth. All which we humbly beg, together with thy continued blessing upon all orders and degrees of men amongst us, and the perfect deliverance of men amongst us, and the perfect deliverance of our brethern in Ireland, that they may rejoice together with us, and triumph in thy praise, for the sake of our blessed lord and saviour Christ Jesus; To whom with thee, O Father of Mercies, and the Holy Ghost be eternal praise. Amen

Into the Communion Service instead of the Collect for the Day

Eternal God, and our most mighty protector, we thy unworthy servants do humbly present our selves before thy majesty, acknowledging thy power, wisdom and goodness in preserving the king, and three estates of this realm assembled in Parliament, from the destruction this day intended against them. Make us, we beseech thee, truly thankful for this, and for all other thy great mercies twards us; particularly for the making this day again memorable, by a fresh influence of thy loving kindness towards us. We bless thee for giving his majesty, that now is, a safe arrival here, and for making all opposition fall before him, till he became our king and governour. Continue we beseech thee to protect and defend him, the queen, and all the royal family, from all treasons and conspiracies; preserve them in thy faith, fear and love; prosper their reign with long happiness here on earth, and crown them with everlasting glory hereafter, through Jesus Christ our only savior and redeemer. Amen

The Gospel. St. Luke 9.51

And it came to pass, when the time was come that he should be received up, he steadfastly let his face go to Jerusalem, and sent messengers before his face: and they went and entered into a village of the Samaritanes, to make ready for him. And they did not receive him, because his face was as though he would go to Jerusalem. And when his disciples James and John saw this, they said, Lord, wilt thou that we command fire to come down from heaven, and consume them even as Silas did? But he turned and rebuked them, and said. Ye know not what manner of spirit ye are of. For the son of man is not come to destroy mens lives, but to save them. And they went to another village.

Protestant Day, 1885, Douglas B. W. Sladen, 1885

Note that the victory at the battle of Inkerman, November 5, 1854 was added as another layer of significance.

1885

PROTESTANT DAY, 1885

The Anniversary of the Gunpowder Plot, of William III.'s landing in Torbay, and the Battle of Inkerman.

from A Poetry of Exiles

By Douglas B. W. Sladen: An Australian colonist: Second edition, revised 1885

Douglas Brooke Wheelton Sladen 1856-1947

  1 Protestant Day---and England's Church in danger!
  2 Tory and Liberal beside her stand!
  3 Are infidels to plunder Her and change Her---
  4 The mother of Church-freedom for our land?

  5 Outside Canossa's gate the German shivered,
  6 Humbled and impotent amid the snow;
  7 And France's mightiest King before It quivered---
  8 The Power unbroken till our Church's blow.

  9 The mother of Church-freedom, our great charter
 10 Of English freedom from the realm of Rome,
 11 Sealed with the blood of patriot and martyr,
 12 Bound up, from birth to death, with life of Home.

 13 Guy Fawkes! Torbay! This fifth day of November

14 Who can forget the Papists' famous plot?
15 Who but our Revolution must remember?
16 Who hath the Seven Bishops' tale forgot?

17 The Church of England! aye---and England's glory!
18 If Inkerman's shall come to us again,
19 'Twill be through those who love our Church and Story,
20 And not through godless, unremembering men.

21 From royal Westminster whose Abbey gathers
22 The bones of those who built up England's fame,
23 To little country-churches, where our fathers,
24 For centuries, to font and altar came,

25 From where at Canterbury, yet unminished,
26 Stands that same church, in which Augustine preached,
27 To mission-room, in mining-town just finished---
28 A mark how far Truth's last high springtide reached,

29 Ring out wild peals of peril, then the voices
30 Of strong men stern to guard their hearths and homes,
31 With fierce thoughts for the foeman who rejoices
32 That ruin runs behind where'er he roams.

33 Up Peer! Up Peasant! Children of the City,
34 From whose stout hands our English commerce rose,
35 Show them, that if they show your Church no pity,
36 You can be pitiless against Her foes!

The Evolution of the Celebration

In the volumes that follow I will trace the evolution of the artifacts of celebration that have been brought together to celebrate the Great Deliverance. Although the celebration was mandated by law and by the Book of Common Prayer, the conclusion that the celebration evolved in a top-down, purely imperialist manner as described by Brendan McConville (McConville, Brendan, "Pope's Day Revisited, "Popular" Culture Reconsidered", 1999) would fail to recognize the considerable autonomy exercised by municipalities, parishes, organizations and the public at large which was tolerated by the government. The celebration was only at its core nationalistic and patriotic . On one level it projected these values on behalf of the monarch, church and state. However, it was interpreted in many ways by celebrants. With time, communities exercised their autonomy to accept, reject and transform the celebration as they saw fit. Eventually the government would loose its monopoly. Pope's Day celebratrions in the Colonies energized the American Revolution. After protests and riots in places like Guilford and Lewes the government was forced to downgrade the celebration, removing it from the Book of Common Prayer in 1859, so as to enable prosecution of celebrants. (See Appendix VIV The Official End of Celebration).

The history of the celebration defies any simple explanation.

Conclusion

I leave you with the famous Amphibrach

Remember, Remember the Fifth of November

Remember, the Fifth of November,

Gunpowder, Treason and Plot,

I see no reason why Gunpowder Treason

Should Ever be Forgot!

Notation:

Origins Of the Chant-

1681-Roger L'Estrange. "Remember the Fifth November"

-L'Estrange, Roger, Notes upon Stephen College grounded principally upon his own declarations and confessions, and freely submitted to publique censure, 1681.

1699- Good Protestants will be very careful to remember the *Fifth* of *November*, and adorn their Windows with lighted Candles, in memory of *Guido Vaux*'s Dark Lanthorn, except such who had rather promote the Interest of the *Woodmonger*, than the Good of the *Tallow-Chaundler*, and they perhaps may give a Faggot to the Burning of the *Pope*, and Scorching of the Devil.
-Ward, Edward, The world bewitch'd ….,1699.

These and other examples support the conclusion that the rhyme was created some time during the last half of the 17th century or early in the 18th.

Amphibrach- A metrical foot consisting of three syllables in the order unstressed-stressed-unstressed, or, in quantitative metre, short-long-short, as in the word consider or the verse *Remember, remember the fifth of November*….

-- Trask, Robert,Lawrence, A Dictionary of Phonetics and Phonology.,p. 21., Routledge 1996

You will find more examples in our volume on Music and Chants.

Now that you know know why and how to celebrate, put all of this work to practical use. Go out and celebrate the Great Deliverance with Bonfires, Bells and revelry. Disclose the mysteries.

Apendix I Cast of Characters

The Plotters

Robert Catesby:

31 years old. Robert Catesby came from an old Midlands family. He was the originator of plot. His mother's 1st cousin (Elizabeth) was the wife of Sir Walter Raleigh. His ancestors had been famous as politicians. Due to his father's strong Catholic loyalties the family suffered greatly. Robert was born in 1573 and it seems conformed to the state religion. He studied at Gloucester Hall, Oxford in 1586 and married Catherine Leigh- a wealthy Protestant girl (related to the important Spenser family)when he was nineteen (1593). His wife Catherine Leigh and their oldest son (William) died a few years after their marriage in 1598. His second son Robert survived. Catesby's house, Morecrofts, in Uxbridge became a haven for priests. His father also died in 1598. It is believed that his grief turned him into a stronger supporter of the Catholic faith, Catesby already suspect by the government, was imprisoned in 1596 as a possible suspect in action leading to the illness of the queen. Involvement in the Essex rebellion (Feb. 8 1601) cost him a fine of 3,000 pounds. Later Catesby joined other Catholics such as Henry Garnet in the Spanish Treason. Catesby possessed a wild and reckless nature and was a popular man. He was known as a good swordsman and was a part of elite court circles. Father Tesimond described him as being over six feet tall with noble and expressive countenance and manners and with an impressive dignity. He traveled the countryside as did many Catholics, protecting priests as they traveled from safe house to safe house. Catesby's house in Lambeth was first headquarters of the plot and was used for the initial storage of powder. Robert Catesby was killed at the shoot-out at Holbeach House, Nov. 8, 1605, along with Thomas Percy (with the same bullet). While professing dedication to God and Church to the end, Catesby was primarily a leader of a Catholic political elite which was equally dedicated to obtaining wealth and power through the defeat of the King, the Government and the State Church. His body was buried at Holbeach but was later dug up and his head brought to Westminster for display.

Guy Fawkes

Also known as John Johnson, or as Guido Fawkes (this shows up in a possibly translated engraving text) When arrested he was known as "Percy's man". 34 years old. Son of Edward Fawkes, proctor and advocate in the consistory court of York, Guido was born in the Stonegate district of York. Baptized at St. Michael-le-Belfry in 1570, Fawkes entered St. Peter's School in 1578. He had two younger sisters, Elizabeth and Anne. His schoolmates included John and Christopher Wright. His father died in 1579. His mother Edith remarried into the Catholic Bainbridge family of Scotton. It is thought that his stepfather influenced him to become a Catholic. Perhaps he was influenced by the headmaster of St. Peters, John Pullen, a man later named as a suspected Jesuit. By the time he was 21 Guy had sold his inheritance and had joined the Catholic forces fighting in the Low Countries. For twelve years he served as a military man in the Netherlands. He was trained as a miner, skilled with gunpowder and in the arts of tunneling. He was at the siege of Calais. In 1603 Fawkes went to Spain to discuss the plight of English Catholics with King Philip II. There he met Christopher Wright with whom he tried to get Spanish support for an invasion of England. He arrived in England with Thomas Winter on April 25,1604 and in May 1604 he joined the plot at a meeting with Catesby at an inn, The Duck and Drake. Fawkes was captured at around midnight Nov.4 and was brought before the privy council on Nov.5. On November 7, after several sessions of torture, Fawkes admitted that the conspirators had planned to free Sir Walter Raleigh and other Tower Prisoners. Fawkes then said, "yt was past,and he is nowe sorry for yt, for that he nowe perceyveth that God did not concur with yt." Fawkes did not reveal the identity of the other conspirators until severely tortured on Nov.9 and only after he was told that some had been arrested. He was executed on January 31, 1606. To this day Guy is remembered for his bravery on November 5. Young children make scarecrows of Guy Fawkes which they exhibit while collecting money, "a penny for the Guy," to be spent on their fireworks. By the way the word "guy" pre-dates Fawkes in its origins. It comes from French Guy, then from Gui then from Late Latin-Uitus and then from Middle Latin Vitus as in the saint of epileptics.

Robert Keyes gentleman / Guydo Faux gentleman [Guy Fawkes]

Sir Everard Digby

(Image; Drawing by Athow, from : Edwards, Francis, The Gunpowder Plot, 1973, p. 96.)

24 years old. Wealthy, he was a Catholic convert, a swordsman, and a horseman. His role was to lead the Midlands Rebellion. Digby possessed wide estates in Rutland. If his parents were Catholic they avoided detection and did not attract the persecution of the state. Digby married Mary Mulsho and had two sons, Kenelm and John. Mary brought the wealth of the estate of William Mulsho as she was his only daughter and heiress. Once at court Digby became a gentleman pensioner. He was very popular at court. Mary, upon her introduction to the very fashionable and worldly Jesuit John Gerard, became a convert to Catholicism following the death of her parents. The

Digbys remarked as to the secular ways of the Jesuits and were much impressed by them. Sir Everard was also converted by Gerard after an illness in London. Working with Gerard, Digby set up a model Catholic household which combined card-playing with Ave Marias. He was knighted after welcoming King James at Belvoir castle on April 23 1603. Digby entered the plot via an introduction by Robert Catesby on a pilgrimage to St. Winifred's Well at the end of August 1605. He brought money and management skills to the plot. It is interesting to note that Digby only entered the plot once he was convinced that the Jesuits had given it their approval. This is of interest as Digby was very close to the leading Jesuits of the day and would have been in touch with them. Digby contributed the huge sum of 1500 pounds to the plot and would move to Coughton Court to be able to assist with the direction of the rising in the Midlands and assistance with the kidnapping of Princess Elizabeth. The headquarters for this operation would be the Red Lion Inn at Dunchurch where a group of 100 supporters had gathered on Monday November 4. After re-uniting with Catesby after the failure of the explosion in London Digby assisted Catesby in writing the letter to Father Garnet which explainined the plot, and broke the seal of the confessional. Digby fled the plot after the explosion of Holbeache but was arrested shortly thereafter near Dudly. Sir Everard was executed on Jan. 30 1606. The execution was dramatic as he was in high spirits and maintained courtly civility. He is said to have contradicted the executioner who holding his heart up for the crowd to see said: "this is the heart of a traitor." Digby is said to have replied:"thou liest. "

Thomas Percy

Crispijn van de Passe the Elder.

Thomas Percy: 44 years old. He received James I's promise of toleration, later to be broken. He was a Catholic with court contacts through his cousin, the Earl of Northumberland. Northumberland used Thomas Percy as a messenger to assist James I in his communications with the court in London prior to the death of Elizabeth I. He was described as "a tall gent." Thomas Percy attended Peterhouse, Cambridge from 1579 and may have gone to the Azores with George Clifford in 1589. From 1595 he served as estate officer for Northumberland. A fervent Catholic, Percy hated Scots and all things Scottish. He was experienced in violent political actions in and around the wild border areas of the Western

March. Percy was married to the sister of John(Jack) and Christopher (Kit) Wright. Because of his court contacts, it is he that rented the house for tunnel.

Thomas Winter (Wintour)

34 years old. A young man of considerable ability and great courage. Son of George Winter of Huddington Court, Worcesteshire and his wife Jane. He was the brother of Robert Winter. Their sister Dorothy married the conspirator, John Grant. He was fluent in several languages. Robert studied law, then became a soldier serving in the Low countries. By 1600 he had converted to Catholicism. He inherited the family home of Huddington Court. He became involved in the plot late February 1604. A Catholic and cousin of Catesby, he went to visit the Constable of Castile to ask that James I be pressured to end persecution. Thomas Winter took part in Essex's rising and was closely tied to Mounteagle, having served as his secretary. He located Guy Fawkes and returned with him to England. Thomas was shot in the shoulder and captured at the shoot-out at Holbeche House, Staffordshire, following the failed rising in the Midlands. Following the trial of January 27, 1606, he was executed for his role in the plot.

Robert Winter (Wintour)

Robert Winter was born in 1565 or 1657 and died on January 30, 1606. Robert was the oldest son of George Wintour whose house was Huddington Court. His mother was Jane Ingleby. Robert had interited most of his father's estate. The estate was supported by salt-evaporating and hops-farming. Through his first wife, Gertrude Talbot, Robert built ties to a very strong Catholic family. Robert used his house as a refuge for priests. Robert was described by Gerard as one of the smartest and strongest and wealthiest men in Worcestershire. The warrant for his arrest described him as meane stature, rather low, square made somewhat stooping forty years old with brown beard and hair. Robert came into the plot because of his money and influence. He gave money to the plotters and helped to gather weapons and horses for the planned uprising. Robert was reluctant to join the plot but joined with John Grant when they met at the Catherine Wheel inn, Oxford in February of 1605. He remained a less than enthusiastic member. He wanted to turn back during the march from Dunchurch to Holbeach House. He refused to ask John Talbot of Grafton to help with the plot. Robert escaped Holbeach House with Stephen Littleton on November 7 and managed to escape arrest for two months. They were betrayed and captured at Hagley Park, home of Humphrey Littleton on the 9th of January. Robert along with Stephen Littleton, was were sent to the Tower. While at the tower Robert admitted that the fleeing conspirators had made confessions to Father Hammond, a.k.a. Father Hart who was a the Jesuit Chaplain of Huddington Court. He was executed January 30, 1606, St. Paul's Churchyard. He did not say much on the scaffold but prayed to himself.

John (Jack) Wright

(Image-John and Christopher Wright)

37 years old. The Wrights were the Wrights of Plowland Hall in Holderness, Yorkshire (sons of Robert Wright and Ursula Rudston). The Wrights were staunch Catholics who suffered the full force of the law for their illegal activities. John took part in the Essex rebellion of 1601 along with his friend Robert Catesby. John spent time in solitary confinement for this offense. After the plot and prison, John moved the family to Twigmore Hall in northern Lincolnshire. an area which was known as a haven for priests. Camden described the Wrights as hunger-starved for innovation. Fr. John Gerard described John as being a "strong stout man...of very good wit...slow of speech." John Wright was an excellent swordsman, a taciturn man loyal to his close friends. His conversion to Catholicism was said to have calmed his quarreling nature. As yet another Catholic and a distant cousin of Catesby, he went to school with Guy Fawkes in York. His mother died in prison for religious belief. John and his wife Dorothy suffered greatly for their illegal acts related to their Catholic religious practices. John was the third to enter the plot around May 1604. Along with Thomas Wintour he introduced Guy Fawkes to the plot. John Wright left London on November 4 to join Everard Digby and the hunting party at Dunchurch, Warwickshire. He reached Holbeche House on the evening of Nov. 7. John was mortally wounded during the Holbeche shoot-out. His head was taken for display to Westminster as was the custom for criminals.

Christopher (Kit) Wright

(Image-John and Christopher Wright)

He was the brother of John (Jack) Wright. His wife was Margaret Ward, a relative of Thomas Ward who conveyed news of the discovery of the letter to the plotters) He was a schoolmate of Fawkes. A reluctant conformist and Catholic, he went into the plot to help his brother some time after Christmas 1605. Before March 25, he was recruited to help with the tunnel. He had studied with Tesimond, Oldcorne and Robert Middleton at St. Peter's school in York. Christopher Wright took part in the failed Essex rebellion in 1601 and was not punished severely for this action. He was a convert to Catholicism. This quality possible brought him to the attention of Father Garnet who assisted him in meeting with Philip III in order to arrange for a full-blown military action in support of the English Counter reformation against the English State. He was unsuccessful. His main ability was that of maintaining secrecy. Christopher Wright has been suggested as a possible source for the famous letter. He was killed in the shoot-out at Holbeche where he had fled with Thomas Percy.

John Grant

(Image: by Adam from: Caulfield, James, 1794.)

Born c.1570. 30 years old. Grant was a Warwickshire gentleman, the owner of Norbrooks, a strategic Warwickshire mansion. Grant had also taken part in the Essex rebellion. He was married to Thomas and John Winter's sister. A wealthy Catholic, he had resisted persecution. At the shoot-out at Holbeach House Grant was blinded by an explosion of gunpowder was later tried and executed on January 30, 1606. He was known for being melancholy and an intellectual.

Thomas Bates (Bate)

(A.K.A. Thomas Bate) As Robert Catesby's servant, he was ranked as a yeoman. His evidence was used to falsely implicate the Jesuits. Part of this evidence came after the death of Father Garnet and the rest is confused. It is said that Bates implicated Father Garnet, Father Tesimond and Father Gerard as knowing of the plot as early as mid-November when they learned of it at a meeting at Harrowden. This evidence is denied by Gerard. Bate's main role in the plot was as a runner and messenger who due to his low rank would go unnoticed. It was Bates who took the letter from Digby and Catesby to Garnet which after the failure of the plot broke the seal of the confessional. Bates abandoned the plot following the explosion of gunpowder at Holbeache House. He was Captured on Nov. 12 in Staffordshire. At his execution Bates claimed that it was his loyalty to his master which kept him from obeying God, his Country and the King. Bates was survived by his wife Martha who managed to meet him as he was being dragged off to his execution on Jan. 30, 1606.

Robert Keyes

40 years old (est.in 1604). He joined the plot on October 9, 1604. He was the son of a Protestant rector, Edward Keyes, of Stavely in North Derbyshire. His wife Christiana was of a well-known recusant family, the Tyrwhitts of Kettleby, Linconshire. Robert's mother, however, was of a strongly Catholic family. the Babthorpes of Osgodby. Keyes is described as being tall with a red beard. He was poor and dependent on the Catholic peer Lord Mordaunt for whom he worked as a property manager. He had one servant, William Johnson. Keyes' main function in the plot was to tend to Robert Catesby's Lambeth home which was used for storage of supplies. A Jesuit convert, Keyes complained at his trial that as a result of his illegal recusancy he had lost goods. He stated that he would rather die than obey the laws of England which he considered tyrannical. Keyes looked to the success of the plot as a path to riches which would come to him

after the installation of a Catholic state. In addition to managing the Lambeth house, Keyes probably also helped with the excavation of the mine. Keyes was concerned about the fate of his employer Lord Moundaunt and together with Francis Tresham approached Catesby with the hope of helping him to escape. It was Keys who presented Fawkes the watch for the timing of the fuse on behalf of Thomas Percy. Keyes left the plot early on the road to Dunchurch. He was captured in Warwickshire on Nov. 9. At his trial Keys drew attention to the goal of Counter Reformation. At his execution Keyes broke the rope but was swiftly taken to the block

Ambrose Rookwood

(Image, by Adam from Caulfield, James, 1794)

26 years old. Rookwood came from an old recusant family of Coldham Hall, Stanningfield, Suffolk. He was around 26, well-built, handsome, somewhat short, well-lettered and genial, his clothing- a bit wild. He studied the humanities in Flanders before inheriting the rich Stanningfield estate in 1600. He was well known for his fine horses and had married into the recusant family, the Tyrwhitts of Lincolnshire. Wealthy, he is related to Robert Keyes. Rookwood as a member of the Catholic elite used his house Coldham as a safe house for Priests. He was convicted in February, 1605 for his Catholic activities. At about the same time he joined the plot, either in March or September 1605. Rookwood was to use his fine and well-known horses to inform Catesby and the other plotters (waiting in Dunchurch) of the explosion in London. He also provided Catesby with gunpowder. Rookwood carried a special sword with its hilt engraved with the Passion of Christ which he seems to have specifically commissioned for the plot. Ambrose Rookwood, a reluctant plotter convinced only by Catesby's logic of the religious justification for the murder of innocents, paid dearly for his role. He was first injured by the explosion of the gunpowder at Holbeach House, then later was injured by John Street in the attack on the house. At trial he defended the Catholic cause as a champion of violent counter-reformation which sought to restore the control of the Pope to England and was executed Jan 31,1606 after a complete confession on the scaffold and a prayer for the king to be made Catholic.

The Popes and Priests
Priests
Father Henry Garnett (Garnet)

Henry Garnet By Jan Wierix, Early 1600's

Henry Garnet was born in Nottingham in 1555. His father was a schoolmaster and he received his education in Winchester. In the 1570's Garnet worked for the law printer Richard Tottel. He joined the Society of Jesus in 1575 and studied under Bellarmine in Rome. In 1586 Robert Persons proposed that Garnet join the English mission. After only a few year,s service. he was promoted following the imprisonment of the Superior of the Jesuits. As Superior Garnet worked politically to extend tolerance. While linked to the treasons of 1602 and 1603, Garnet had worked with Father Blackwell to inform the Government of the Bye plot. It was his belief that further treason could only set back the case of English Catholics for tolerance. Along these lines Garnet to important steps to bring as much of the information of the plot as he was free to disclose to the attention of the Pope. The seal of the confessional prevented him from disclosing information concerning the confession of Catesby given to him by Father Tesimond. Garnet was also visited by Robert Catesby concerning issues of conscience relating to murder. This consultation encouraged Catesby to undertake the plot. It was said that Garnet's execution blood spattered from his wounds

Image above-Princes Pretorium 1606

onto a grain of wheat painting his image.

Claudio Aquaviva 1543-1615

Jesuit priest often considered the second founder of the Jesuit Order. He joined the order in 1567 and became Superior General in 1581. Despite his reputation as a hard-liner, Aquaviva cautioned Father Henry Garnet, Chief Jesuit in England, to exercise prudence. Garnet, applying through him to the Pope Paul V for direction as to how to deal with his knowledge of the plot obtained through the confessional was unsuccessful in obtaining a response.

-Image: Galerie illustreé de la Compagnie de Jésus; volume 1; plate 14, Alfred Hamy, 1893.

John Gerard

A Jesuit Priest who wrote extensively concerning the plot (see bibliography). Due to the prohibition of Catholics from Universities in England, Gerard was sent to study at the Catholic school of Douai, Rheims, and then with the political arm of the papacy the Jesuits or Society of Jesus at Cleremont. As was the fate of so many Jesuits who often returned to England with foreign clothing and accents, Gerard was arrested soon after he landed to begin his political mission at Dover. He was sent to the prison of Marshalsea where there were already many illegal priests housed. (Catholics could freely practice their religion in prison and could meet and confer with others of the Jesuit counter reformation network still at large in England. Anthony Babington, who was later executed for treason being involved in a plot to free the Catholic Mary Queen of Scots, posted bond to secure Gerard's release. He then went to Rome and was eventually given another mission on behalf of the Jesuits to England. Eventually Gerard met up with the leader of the Jesuits in England, Father Henry Garnet. Father Gerard was soon a very popular figure in the illegal Catholic underworld. He impressed many as a very secular gentleman and was skilled in gambling and wore fashionable dressm, a clever disguise but a very necessary one for such a figure in the political war which was the Counter Reformation. Gerard wrote of many escapes from the law and of his attempts to evade due process by using priest-hides. He was eventually tracked down in London, was tried, found guilty and sent to the Counter in the Poultry. Later he was moved to the Clink prison where he was able to continue his Jesuit mission and meet regularly with other proponents of the counter reformation in England. Due to his continuation of this work he was sent to the Salt tower in the Tower of London where he was further questioned concerning his illegal activities by the authorities. After failing to provide the authorities with anything but further equivocation Gerard was tortured. He escaped along with John Arden with the help of other members of the Counter-Reformation. The escape was dramatic, upon a rope across the moat. Immediately following his escape he joined the other kingpins of the Counter Reformation: Henry Garnet and Robert Catesby. Later Gerard moved to the house of Elizabeth, Vaux a Counter Reformation Patriot. From this base of operations Gerard continued in his mission, illegally converting many including Sir Everard Digby (one of the plotters). He later suspected Digby of plotting but did not act upon his observations, thus allowing the plot to proceed undetected. When the plot was discovered he was a wanted man being linked to the main leaders. He was implicated by Robert Catesby's servant Thomas Bates. Staying a while at Harrowden, then escaping from there to London, he left the country with financial aid from Elizabeth Vaux and the Ambassadors of Flanders and Spain (supporters of the Counter Reformation in England) on the very day of Henry Garnet's execution. Gerard went on to continue the work of the Jesuits in Europe where he wrote his major works. He died in 1637, aged 73 in Rome.

Father Oswald Tesimond

A Catholic priest friend who heard Catesby's original confession and was given permission to tell Father Henry Garnet. Father Tesimond survived to write about the plot. Born c. 1563 he was a classmate of plotters Christopher and John Wright and Guy Fawkes at the Royal School of William and Mary in the Horse Fayre in York. He became a Jesuit in 1584. Tesimond concealed knowledge obtained via confessions of the plotters about the plot but was not a conspirator. His arrest warrant of January 15, 1606 described him as: "of a reasonable stature, black hair, a brown beard cut close on the cheeks and left broad on the chin, somewhat long-visaged, lean in the face but of a good red complexion, his nose somewhat long and sharp at the end, his hands slender and long fingers, his body slender, his legs of a good proportion, his feet somewhat long and slender." Tesimond was able to escape arrest fleeing to France and eventually to Naples.

Blessed Edward Oldcorne or Oldcorn alias *Hall*

Born 1561; executed 7 April 1606. Oldcorne was thought to have known of the preparations for the Gunpowder Plot due to his close relationships to the plotters. Oldcorne was born in York which was also the home town of Guy Fawkes and other plotters. He became a Jesuit in 1588. Oldcorne may have obtained knowledge of the plot while joining Nicholas Owen, John Gerard, Henry Garnet and others on a pilgrimage to St. Winefrid's Well at Holywell, North Wales. Oldcorne was at Hindlip Hall when the plot was discovered. In

December 1605 he joined Nicholas Owen, Father Henry Garnet and Ashley in hiding at Hindlip. They were eventually discovered, arrested and taken to the Tower of London. Torture of Oldcorn did not lead to evidence implicating him in the plot. Found guilty of protecting criminals, Oldcorn was executed for this crime..

Citizens
Anne Vaux

Born c. 1562 died c. 1637. A wealthy Catholic recusant. She was the third daughter of William Vaux of Harrowden. She supported Catholic priests, renting them houses. The most famous of these houses was White Webbs, Enfield Chase, used by the plotters. Vaux was linked to Father Henry Garnet. She was also related to the plotter Francis Tresham. Vaux played no active role in the plot. In 1605 she was arrested but released on bond. She later arranged for the hiding of Father Garnet at Hindlip House, Worcestershire, the home of Thomas Abington. After the discovery of Garnet she was taken to the Tower of London. After it was discovered that she had corresponded with Garnet in the Tower she was arrested in March 1606. She was freed in August. Later in 1625 she was convicted of recusancy and later founded a Catholic boys school at Stanley Grange.

Jer close friendship with Father Garnett was exploited during the trial to defame him.

Popes
Pope Pius V

Pope Pius V by El Greco

1504-1572

Issued the bull Regnans in Excelsis April 27, 1570, which excommunicated Queen Elizabeth I and justified the rebellion of Catholics against the state. He supported Mary Queen of Scots in her attempts to take over England. Elizabeth I was forced in response to the Pope's acts of Counter Reformation to end the tolerance of Catholics which had prevailed prior to issuance of the papal bull. On the Catholic side the bull was instrumental in the genesis of the Ridolfi Plot wherein the Duke of Norfolk plotted to kidnap or murder Elizabeth I and install Mary, Queen of Scots. It also inspired the second Desmond Rebellion in Ireland.

Clement VIII

Pope from January 30, 1592 to March 3, 1605

Clement worked to further the Counter Reformation. He rejected the plan to pay English Catholics to remain loyal but believed in rumors that James I was planning to convert to Catholicism.

Clement VIII,
Contemporary Portrait
artist unknown

Pope Paul V

Pope from May 16, 1605 to September 17, 1552

His effigy is still burned by celebrants in Lewes Sussex each November.

Despite congratulating James I on his accession, Pope Paul V failed to respond decisively to communicatons from the chief Jesuit of England Henry Garnet asking for direction as to the use of knowledge obtained through the confession to intervene to stop the plot.

Pope Paul V by
Ludovico Leoni

The Government Officials

James I of England and VI of Scotland

James I, VI by John de Critz, c.1606.

James became King of England on March 24,1603 at about eleven o'clock A.M. He was the son of Mary, Queen of Scots, but was a Protestant. He was tolerant by nature but a firm believer in the Divine Right of Kings. He has been characterized as "unpopular, filthy of person, homosexual, devious and a Scot." He supported the Essex rebellion which involved many members of the Gunpowder Plot, yet he praised Elizabeth for the execution of his mother. James promised tolerance to win the favor of important Catholics at court but he did not follow through. His father, Lord Darnley, was killed by a gunpowder explosion years before at Kirk o' Field and the memory of this event conditioned his response to the plot. James believed strongly in horoscopes and was interested in religion. He had three children: Elizabeth, age 10 during plot whom Fawkes revealed was to be proclaimed queen by the plotters; Charles, Duke of York, too well guarded in London for the plotters to seize; and Henry, Prince of Wales, the oldest of the three who was intended to be killed with his father in the blast. James spoke English perfectly and also knew Latin, French and Italian. James was hardened to politics by his violent upbringing in Scotland.

Queen Anne

Anne of Denmark by John de Critz

Born Oct. 14, 1574.
From Denmark. Her Mother was Sophia of Mecklenburg. Her father was King Frederick II of Denmark. Graceful, blonde, beautiful. When James came to the throne she had already borne five children- three had survived and she was pregnant again. Anne would have a total of 8 children. In a poem James called her his Juno, "the sweet doctor who could heal his heavy heart." She had a slight giddyness of character but was well loved by the people and was skilled in the role of queen. Brought up a Lutheran, she converted to Catholicism in her 20s. This event occured between 1600 and March 1603 in a secret room in the palace. She corresponded with Pope Clement VIII as early as 1601. Her confessor was the Jesuit Father Robert Abercromby. Anne's best friend was the Countess of Bedford. Anne enjoyed dancing in masques and patronized the architect Indigo Jones who designed a palace for her at Greenwich. She commissioned works by Ben Johnson and Robert Spencer. Anne personified the genuine tolerance of James I.
Anne attended the trial of the plotters but not the trial of the Jesuit Henry Garnet. Anne died March 4 1619.

Henry Frederick, Prince of Wales, February 19, 1594- November 6, 1612

Henery Frederick, By Isaac Oliver Contemporary

Eldest son of King James I and Anne of Denmark. Bright and promising, Henry died of typhoid fever at age 18. The plotters were going to blow Henry up with the explosion.

Charles I

19 November 1600 – 30 January 1649)

Second son of King James I of England and Anne of Denmark. Charles became King of England on 27 March 1625 and reigned until his execution in 1649. Charles was to have been blown up by the plotters along with Parliament. Image: By Robert Peake 1611

Charles I by Robert Peake, 1611

Elizabeth of Bohemia

(19 August 1596 – 13 February 1662)

By Robert Peake the Elder, 1606

Daughter of James I, King England, and Anne of Denmark. The Plotters intended to capture Elizabeth and make her a child queen. She became the wife of Frederick V, Elector Palatine, She was known as Electress Palatine and for a short time Queen of Bohemia. Elizabeth is often referred to as the Winter Queen.

With the end of the Stuart dynasty in 1714, her descendants, the Hanoverian rulers, succeeded to the British throne.

Robert Cecil

Robert Cecil by John De Critz the Elder

He was James I's Secretary of State. He was also titled as the Earl Of Salisbury. A king-maker, he was a hunchback, and chronically ill. As a landowner whose land was stolen from English Catholics, he lead a diabolical crusade against Jesuits. Cecil's philosophy of toleration stressed the distinction between the practice of religion and the practice of politics. Those who practiced religion only could be tolerated-and were. He was an enigmatic politician. It is thought that he tolerated the gupowder plot as a test to determine the loyalties of Catholic subjects. They failed the test. Had the plot been dropped or discouraged by the Jesuits with the influence of the Pope, the role of Catholics in English society might have been improved.

Sir Edward Coke

Image: Thomas Athow, after Unknown artist, after Cornelius Johnson, c. early 19th century)

Born 1552, died 1634. Coke was a famous English jurist and Member of Parliament. His work with the common law was definitive. Coke was Attorney General and while in that position prosecuted the Gunpowder Plot Conspirators. He was considered the greatest jurist of his age.

William Parker

William Parker by: John de Critz

Fourth Lord Mounteagle: It was he that received letter which exposed the plot. As a member of the House of Lords, he was secretly a friend of James I and Robert Cecil. He was Catholic but converted to Protestantism. He had taken part in the Essex Rebellion and was related to most of the conspirators. His main home was Great Hallingbury, near Bishop Stortford in Essex. He did take part in the Essex rebellion. Parker extended his assistance to Catesby to fund travel of his representatives to Spain. Parker was a close friend of Catesby and was present during key meetings related to the plot although he never became a plotter. Parker owed his power and prosperity to James who had promoted him at court. Mounteagle went with Thomas Howard on the investegation which discovered the gunpowder. Some believe that Parker served as a government spy following his confession and pardon for his role in the Essex rebellion. He is also credited with causing the murder of Tresham in the tower.

Henry Percy

Henry Percy by: Anthony van Dyck

Ninth Earl of Northumberland: An important Catholic at the court of Elizabeth, the Earl became an enemy of Cecil and was closely linked to the conspirator Thomas Percy. Northumberland had appointed Thomas Percy to the position of Gentleman Pensioner without administering the oath given to all Catholics. When Thomas Percy was observed to have fled after the plot, Northumberland sent word to him in Scotland demanding rents which Thomas had collected. This was viewed as a tip-off. Additionally, immediately prior to November 5, Northumberland met with Thomas Percy. It is speculated that Northumberland was to have become Regent on behalf of the conspirators to take charge of the heirs to the throne who survived the plot. Northumberland had also been involved in prior failed plots against the government.

(see: Nicholls, Mark, Investigating Gunpowder Plot, Manchester University Press,1991.)

Sir John Popham

Sir John was Speaker of he House of Commons from 1580 to 1583. He became Attorney General on June 1, 1581 serving in that position till 1592. He became Lord Chief Justice of England serving from June 2, 1592 to June of 1607. Popham was responsible for the investigation of the Gunpowder Plot. He presided over the trial of the Gunpowder Plotters.

Sir john Popham, Artist Unknown

Thomas James Knyvet, 1st Baron Knyvet (or Knevytt, Knyvett, Knevett, Knevitt), 1558 – 27 July 1622.

Second son of Sir Henry Knyvet of Charlton, Wiltshire and Anne Pickering, daughter of Sir Christopher Pickering of Killington, Westmoreland. In 1579 he became High Sheriff of Norfolk. He was a Gentleman of the Privy Chamber to Queen Elizabeth I, and in 1592, he was made Master at Arms; and Member of Parliament for Thetford in 1601. Tasked by James I to search Parliament Knyvet discovered Guy Fawkes and foiled the Gunpowder Plot. He was appointed a Privy Councillor, Member of the Council to Queen Anne, and Warden of the Mint. He served in Parliament as Baron Knyvet of Escrick, Yorkshire, in 1607. Lord Knyvet was the first resident of the site of 10 Downing Street, the residence of the British Prime Minister, in a building called Knyvett House. It was leased to him by Queen Elizabeth I. The house later went to his niece, Elizabeth Hampden. At the end of the lease in 1682, George Downing developed the site.

Sir William Wade (or Waad, or Wadd), 1546 – 21 October 1623

Statesman, diplomat, Lieutenant of the Tower of London. Wade interrogated Guy Fawkes at the tower. Wade worked closely with English intelligence officials.(See: Bengtsen, Fiona, Sir William Waad, Lieutenant of the Tower and the Gunpowder Plot, 2005.

Sir William Wade. Artist unknown. Published by W. Richardson

Legendary

John Dee (13 July 1527–1608 or 1609) a.k.a. Dr. Dee.

A 17th century portrait, artist unknown.

Mathematician, astronomer, astrologer, occultist. While Dee was an important figure of the time of the plot, and despite the fact that his image often appears in praryer books, Dee did not play a historical role in the plot or in its discovery. Dee was an important scholar of the period and put together one of the most impressive libraries of the period. It is said that Dr. Dee's mirror captured an image of Fawkes on his way to blow up Parliament. The image on the right is from a prayer book and depicts his mirror.

Apendix II Chronology of The Gunpowder Plot

Gunpowder Plot Chronology

1603 March 24- James VI of Scotland became James I of England.

1603, June 17- James informed Rosny of his intention to remit the Recusancy fies.

1603- James assured a deputation of Catholics that the fines will be remitted.

1603-- Robert Catesby helped to organize a mission to the King of Spain, Philip III, to convince Philip to launch an invasion attempt on England. English Catholic support was promised. Thomas Wintour (1571–1606) led the mission. Christopher Wright and Guy Fawkes took part. The king refused, being already dedicated to making peace with Spain.

Pope Clement VIII, hopeful that the rumors of the conversion of James I to Catholicism were true, responded that any rebellion would harm the Catholic community.

1604- February 22, Royal Proclamation banishing priests.

1604, February-- Robert Catesby called Thomas Wintour to his home in Lambeth, where they discussed Catesby's plan to reestablish Catholicism in England by blowing up the House of Lords during the State Opening of Parliament. Wintour agreed to join the plot.

April- Wintour then went to Flanders to seek Spanish support. In Flanders he located Guy Fawkes (1570–1606), a dedicated Catholic who had been a soldier in the Southern Netherlands, commanded by William Stanley. Wintour told Fawkes that "some good friends of his wished his company in England," and that certain gentlemen "were uppon a resolution to doe some what in Ingland if the peace with Spain healped us nott."

1604, April-- Fawkes and Wintour returned to England and told Catesby that Spanish support was unlikely.

May 24- Percy obtained lease of John Whynniard's house. Thomas Percy, Catesby's friend and John Wright's brother--in--law, was introduced to the plot several weeks after Catesby's return. Percy was working for his relative the Earl of Northumberland as agent for his northern estates.

1604, May 20-- The initial five conspirators met for the first time, most likely at the Duck and Drake Inn off the Strand in London, the temporary residence of Thomas Wintour. Robert Catesby, Thomas Wintour, and John Wright attended as well as Guy Fawkes and Thomas Percy, Father John Gerard (a friend of Catesby's), not yet involved in the plot, was celebrating Mass in another room, and the five men subsequently received the Eucharist which sealed their oath. The plotters then left London, returning to their homes.

1604, June 9-- The Earl of Northumberland appointed Percy to the Honourable Corps of Gentlemen at Arms, a troup of bodyguards to the king. Percy then moved to London, to a place near the Prince's Chambers owned by Henry Ferrers. Guy Fawkes, under the pseudonym "John Johnson," supervised the building. He introduced himself as Percy's servant.

1604- Costable of Castile arrived in England to confirm the Anglo-Spansh peace treaty.

Because the building was occupied by debating lawmakers, the plotters rented Catesby's Lambeth house across the Thames River from the city. They used the building to store gunpowder and supplies. These materials could be easily rowed across to the other building under cover of darkness.

1604, July 7-- The Royal consent was given to a new Recusancy Act and Parliament was adjourned. The next meeting of Parliament was scheduled for February 1605.

1604, October – The plotters returned to London. They recruited Robert Keyes, who was described as a "desperate man." Keyes would supervise Catesby's Lambeth house. Soon thereafter Catesby's servant Thomas Bates learned of the plot and was recruited.

December-- The announcement was made that Parliament would be delayed until October 3, 1605. This was due to concern about the plague. It is said that the plotters dug a tunnel beneath Parliament during the period caused by the delay.

December 6-- the Scottish commissioners had finished their work, and the conspirators were busy tunneling from their rented house to the House of Lords. They ceased their efforts when, during tunneling, they heard a noise from above. The noise turned out to be the then-tenant's widow, who was clearing out the undercroft directly beneath the House of Lords – the room where the plotters eventually stored the gunpowder.

25 March-- When the plotters reunited they were three more in number: Robert Wintour, John Grant, and Christopher Wright. The undercroft room was leased to the plotters. Ambrose Rookwood joined the plot.

June-- Second week-- Robert Catesby met in London with the principal Jesuit in England, Father Henry Garnet. They discussed the morality of a plot which might involve the destruction of the innocent, together with the guilty. Garnet answered that such actions could often be excused.

July-- Garnet met with Catesby, discouraging him from involvement in the plot in Essex. Garnet showed him a letter from the pope forbidding rebellion.

Soon after the Jesuit Oswald Tesimond told Garnet he had heard Catesby's confession and had learned of the plot. [

1605, 24 July-- Garnet and Catesby had a third meeting at the house of Anne Vaux in Enfield Chase. Garnet, who had received Tesimond's account which had been given to him under the seal of the confessional by Catesby, determined that he could not reveal the information but was determined to seek advice from Rome. Canon law therefore would not allow him to repeat it.

Garnet tried again to discourage Catesby. Garnet wrote Claudio Acquaviva, his superior, conveying his concerns about rebellion in England. He also told Acquaviva that "there is a risk that some private endeavour may commit treason or use force against the King," and encouraged the Pope to issue a public brief against the use of force.

July 20-- Fawkes stated that 20 barrels of gunpowder, followed by 16 more, were brought to the undercroft.

28 July—A plague threat delayed parliament until Tuesday, November 5. Fawkes left the country for a short time.

Late August—Sir Everard Digby joined the plot and Fawkes was back in the country, and he and Wintour noticed that the stored gunpowder had decayed. More gunpowder was brought in, with firewood used to hide it.

1605, Late -- The last three plotters were recruited.

Late September (Michaelmas) -- Ambrose Rookwood was convinced to rent Clopton House.

October 9-- Catesby added Francis Tresham to the conspiracy

October 14--. Catesby and Tresham met at the home of Tresham's brother-in-law and cousin, Lord Stourton. Tresham claimed that he had asked Catesby if the plot would damn their souls. Catesby replied that it would not, and that the plot was necessary to help Catholics.

October-- Details of the plot were finalized in meetings at London and Daventry taverns. Fawkes would light the fuse, then escape across the river Thames. At the same time the plotters would orchestrate a revolt in the Midlands and capture Princess Elizabeth who later they would make Queen. Fawkes would go to Europe where he would inform European Catholics of the plot.

October 24—Robert Cecil wrote Sir Thomas Lake indicating he may have some knowledge of the plot.

October 26, Saturday-- Lord Monteagle, (Tresham's brother-in-law) was sent a letter when at his house in Hoxton. Having broken the seal, he gave the letter to a servant who read it out.

Confused by the letter, Monteagle promptly traveled to Whitehall and gave it to Robert Cecil Lord Salisbury, Salisbury told the Earl of Worcester and Henry Howard 1st Earl of Northampton. The King was not informed as he was hunting in Cambridgeshire. Monteagle's servant Thomas Ward, who was related to the Wright brothers, informed Catesby of the letter. Catesby suspected Tresham. Catesby and Wintour confronted Tresham but Tresham convinced them of his innocence. Tresham encouraged Catesby to give up the plot.

October 30- Fawkes tells Catesby that the powder has not been discovered.

November 1, Friday-- The letter was shown to the King. James thought that it hinted at "some stratagem of fire and powder" -- perhaps an explosion

November 2, Saturday -- The King met with the Privy Council at the Palace of Whitehall. They planned to search the Houses of Parliament on Monday. The search would be led by the Lord Chamberlain, Thomas Howard, 1st Earl of Suffolk.

Sunday November 3-- Percy, Catesby and Wintour met. A ship had been arranged for their escape at anchor on the Thames.

November 4—Having moved to Coughton Court, Digby was busy with a "hunting party" at Dunchurch on Dunsmore Heath. They were to kidnap the Princess Elizabeth. Percy visited the Earl of Northumberland (who was not a plotter) to ask him what the government had discovered. On returning to London, Percy told Wintour, John Wright, and Robert Keyes that they had nothing to worry about. In the evening, Catesby with John Wright and Bates went off to the midlands. Fawkes met with Keyes who gave him a pocket watch, a gift from Percy, so as to time the fuse. Rookwood picked up several engraved swords.

November 5, 1605-- Fawkes was discovered in the undercroft under the House of Lords just after midnight. Fawkes was taken to the King.

November 6, 1605-- Plotters were still in London when the news of the discovery came out. They fled northwest, Christopher Wright and Thomas Percy first and Rookwood later. They were met by John Wright and Bates. Thomas Wintour, who had stayed in London for a while, then traveled to Huddington Court. They traveled on to meet with Digby at Dunchurch. Warrants were issued in London for the arrest of the plotters.

November 6-- Lord Chief Justice Sir John Popham started investigations. Further names were discovered. Torture was authorized by the King. The plotters raided Warwick Castle where they obtained horses and supplies. Father Garnet, staying at Coughton Court, was informed of events by a letter from Catesby carried by Bates. Garnet replied asking Catesby to end the revolt.

November 7-- Guy Fawkes confessed and revealed the plot.

November 8- The plotters went to Holbeche House, home of Stephen Littleton. Gunpowder drying by the fire caught fire and burned Catesby, Rookwood and Grant. Thomas Wintour and Littleton, on the way to join Catesby, were told that Catesby was dead. Littleton turned back, Wintour traveled on to join Catesby. The Sheriff of Worcester, Richard Walsh, and 200 men laid siege to Holbeche House. All the plotters there were killed except Grant, Morgan, Rookwood and Wintour who were arrested.

Image: The Shoot out at Holbeche House. The end of the rising in the Midlands by Ernest Crofts, 1892, The Art Journal

1606

January 9—Robert Winter captured. The last plotter at large.

Janyary 19—Hindlip House searched for Jesuits

January 26—Jesuits captured at Hindlip

January –Trial of the plotters.

January 30—Capture of Father Garnet and Father Oldcorne at Hindlip.

January 30-31—Execution of the plotters

March 38—Trial of Father Garnet

May 3—Execution of Father Garnet

1829- Catholic Relief Act, Catholic Emancipation in England

Appendix III, Places Relating to the Rebellion in the Midlands

Ashby St. Ledgers

Home of Catesby's mother. The house was the focus for the hunting party which was expected to become the rising in the Midlands. On a foul dark night the weary fugitives met in a sheltered field on the estate. Catesby sent for Robert Winter who met him in the fields. They then departed for the 6 mile ride to the inn at Dunchurch.

Dunchurch

At the Inn at Dunchurch, on the edge of Dunsmore Heath, south of Rugby, the band was to launch the rising. They arrived there at about 8:00 P.M. Tired and wet, the conspirators did not stay long but set out at night with a force of not more than fifty horse. The A.A. Gazetteer (1965) describes the "Guy Fawkes House," formerly the Old Lion Inn. Upon word of the success of the plot, the conspirators were to set out to seize the Princess Elizabeth from nearby Combe Abbey. This was not to be.

Warwick

The band reached Warwick in the early hours of November 6, Wednesday. A critical error was made when Catesby led the band to break into Warwick Castle to obtain fresh horses. This raised an alarm and the Sheriff of Warwickshire, Sir Richard Walsh, was on their trail.

Norbrook

The Conspirators reached Grant's home at Norbrook where they met Rookwood and where Grant provided them with a cache of weapons. From Norbrook, Catesby notified Father Garnet who was at Coughton Court with Lady Digby. Arriving at three A.M., the band was about 17 miles south of Norbrook at sunrise.

Clopton

Clopton was rented from Lord Carew by Ambrose Rookwood for a base in the Midlands. Lord Carew was a good friend of Cecil. He kept the horses provided for the rising here.

Coughton Court

After Mass in a secret room above the gatehouse, Lady Digby received Bates who carried a letter from Catesby to Father Garnet summoning him to join the band. Father Garnet, fearing the consequences, refused and stayed with Lady Digby who had broken down with the news. Father Tesimond, however, rode out with Bates to join the band. Lady Digby, recovering from the shock, sent James Garvy with fresh horses for the conspirators.

Huddington

(5 Miles S.E of Droitwich, Worcester) Through the November rain the band reached Huddington between noon and two P.M. on November 6. Huddington was Robert Winter's house. Winter would not be convinced to draw John Talbot of Grafton Manor to the North to join the plot. The band had lost many men to desertion. These deserters were captured, leading the Sheriff onto the fresh trail. At Huddington, Thomas Winter, Bates and Father Tesimond joined the now very desperate band. From Huddington Catesby tried, through Tesimond, to enlist the support of Thomas Abingdon at nearby Hindlip Manor. Abingdon politely refused. At 3 A.M. Catesby roused his band, now less than forty in number. They all heard Mass and took communion from Father Nicholas Hart and departed before sunrise. It was Thursday the 7th of November.

Hewell Grange

It was 12 miles from Huddington to Hewell Grange, Lord Windsor's home. He was the brother of John Talbot. The band reached Hewell at noon. Their mission at Hewell was not to obtain assistance but to plunder the house for weapons and gunpowder. They knew Lord Windsor would be away to London for Parliament. Even the local villagers would not join the band.

Hagley Hall

On their way from Hewell bound for Holbeach House, the band took the road which became the A 491. On their journey they passed below Hagley Hall, home of Humphrey Littleton. Hagley later was the refuge of the Winters before their capture.

Holbeach House

Home of Stephen Littleton, Holbeach House was twenty two miles from Hagley, just across the Staffordshire border and two miles above Kingswinford. The band reached Holbeach House at 10 P.M. It was here that Sir Richard Walsh, High Sheriff of Worcestershire, caught up with them and where the dramatic showdown would occur which would bring the plot to a close.

Apendix IV Architecture

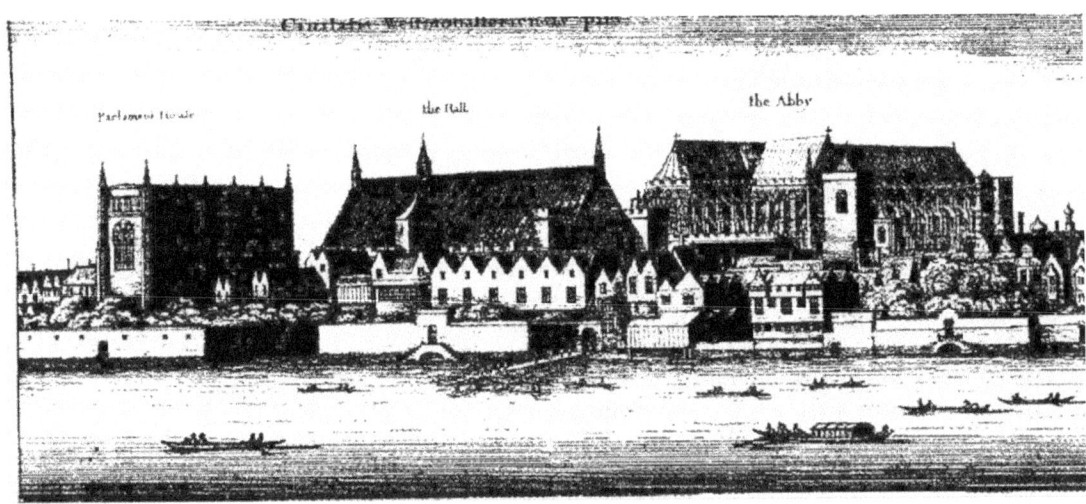

Parliament House and part of Westminster. By: Wenceslaus Hollar, 1641

Westminister at about the time of the plot

East Side of the House of Lords from a print of 1807-Sidney, Philip, <u>A History of the Gunpowder Plot</u>, 1905.

The Gunpowder Plot Cellars, J. Capon, 1799

-Sidney, Philip, A History of the Gunpowder Plot, 1905.

Westminster Hall and Palace Yard, Etching by Hallar

-Sidney, Philip, A History of the Gunpowder Plot, 1905.

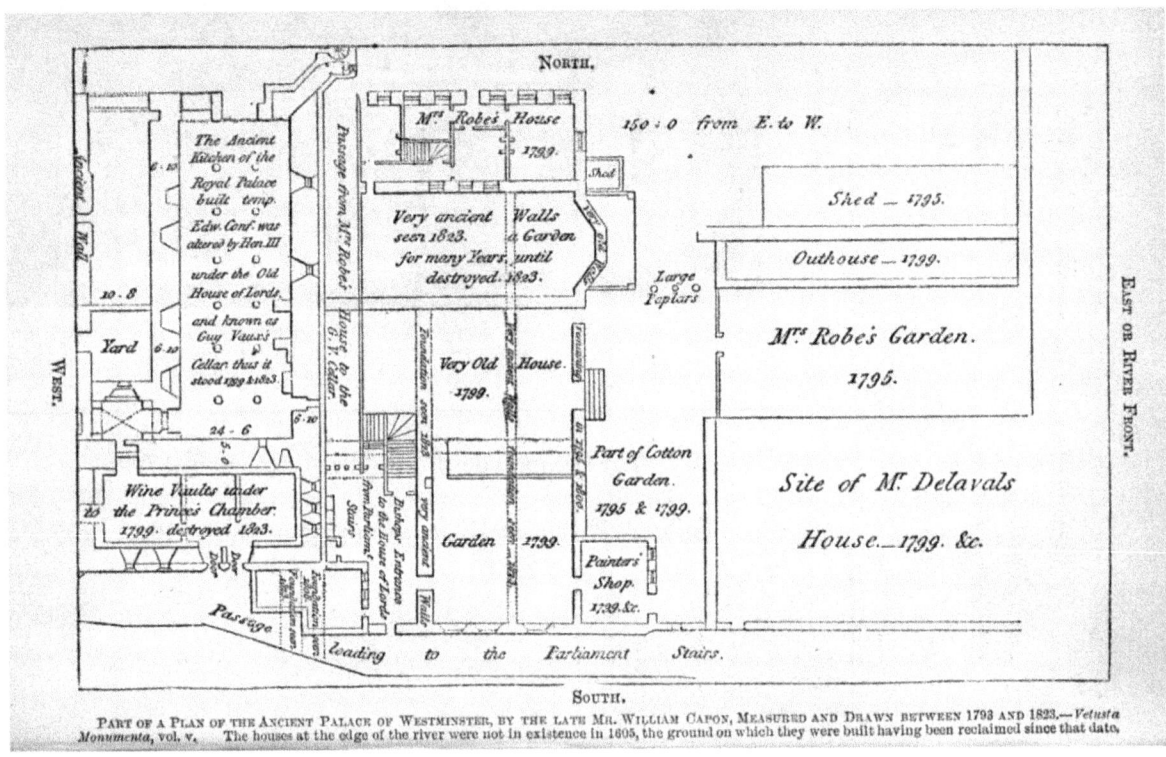

William Capon's map of Parliament clearly labels the undercroft used by "Guy Vaux" to store the gunpowder.

Meeting Place of the Conspirators, Newton Hall, English Illustrated Magazine, Vol. 17, 1897, p.141.

Apendix V, Two important accounts from outside of the Political Establishment

These two sources provide important insider views of the Gunpowder Plot as it unfolded. They are, however, outside of the realm of the received view which shaped the development of the celebrations so are therefore outside of the scope of this work.

Morris, John, Ed. The Condition of Catholics under James I, Father Gerard's Narrative of the Gunpowder Plot 1871.

Edward, Francis, The Gunpowder Plot; The Narrative of Oswald Tesimond, Alias Greenway, 1973.

Apendix VI, Early Analytical Sources

Although analysis of the records of the plot lies outside the scope of this work it may be hepful to note a few important early sources.

Sidney, Philip, A History of the Gunpowder Plot, 1905.

Lingard, Dr., A True Account of the Gunpowder Plot, 1851.

Spink, Henry Hawkes, The Gunpowder Plot and Lord Mounteagle's Letter, 1902.

Gardiner, Samuel, Rawson, What Gunpowder Plot Was, 1897.

Gerard, John, What Was the Gunpowder Plot?, 1897.

Lathbury, Thomas, Guy Fawkes: or, A complete History of the Gunpowder Treason, 1839.

Apendix VII Guy Fawkes did not say: "A dangerous disease requires a desperate remedy."

While this may seem a minor point I have found a large number of miss-atributions, so it is worth documenting this here.

The only quote from primary documents that comes any where near this is the one attributed to Robert Catesby by Thomas Winters in his confession of November 23, 1605:

"At the second summons I presently came up, and found him with Master Iohn Wright at Lambeth, where he spake with me, how necessary it was not to forsake our Countrey (for he knew I had then a resolution to go over) but to deliver her from the servitude in which she remain'd, or at least to assist her with our uttermost endevours. I answered, That I had often hazarded my life upon far lighter termes, and now would not refuse any good occasion, wherein I might do service to the Catholick Cause; but for my self I knew no mean probable to succeed. He said that he had bethought him of a way at one instant to deliver us from all our Bonds, and without any forreign help to replant again the Catholick Religion; and withal told me in a word, It was to blow up the Parliament-House with Gunpowder; for, said he, in that place have they done us all the mischiefe, and perchance GOD hath designed that place for their punishment. I wondred at the strangeness of the conceipt, and told him, That true it was, this strake at the Root, and would breed a confusion fit to beget new alterations; But if it should not take effect (as most of this nature miscarried) the Scandal would be so great which Catholique Religion might hereby sustain, as not only our Enemies, but our Friends also would with good reason condemn us. He told me, The nature of the disease required so sharp a remedy, and asked me if I would give my consent. I told him, yes, in this or what else soever, if he resolved upon it, I would venture my life. But I proposed many difficulties, As want of an House, and of one to carry the Myne, noise in the working, and such like. His answer was, Let us give an attempt, and where it faileth pass no farther".

-The King's Book

Prior to the Gunpowder Plot there is a quote by Hippocrates which is quite close and might have been available to a gentleman like Catesby. "Extreme remedies are very appropriate for extreme diseases."

–Hippocrates, The Aphorisms, c. 460 BC – c. 370 BC.

Appendix VIII Harrison Ainsworth's Confusing Psuedo History

Ainsworth's Historical Fiction Guy Fawkes was published in serial form in Bentley's Miscellany, between January and November 1840. It came out as a three-volume set in July 1841, illustrated by George Cruikshank. While convincing, Ainsworth seriously distorted the historical record. Viviana Radcliffe was entirely invented as were the supernatural aspects of the life of John Dee, who actually existed. To this day tourists are directed to places mentioned in the novel by this manufactured history. The Ainsworth book, while fiction, was an important work reflecting the increasingly romanticized received view which projected Fawkes and the plotters as freedom fighters.

Guy Fawkes in Ordsall Cave

Appendix VIV The Official End of Celebration

The following Royal warrant has been issued abolishing, in accordance with the wishes of Parliament, the religious State services which marked the anniversaries of Gunpowder Plot, the execution of Charles I., and the Restoration of Charles II.

"Victoria R. Whereas, by our Royal warrant of the 21st day of June 1837, in the first year of our reign, we commanded that certain forms of prayer and service made for the 5th of November, the 30th of January, and the 29th of May, should be forthwith printed and published, and annexed to the Book of Common Prayer and Liturgy of the United Church of England and Ireland, to be used yearly on the said days, in all cathedrals and collegiate churches and chapels, in all chapels of colleges and halls within our Universities of Oxford, Cambridge, and Dublin, and of our Colleges of Eton and Winchester, and in all parish churches and chapels within those parts of our United Kingdom called England and Ireland.

"And whereas in the last session of Parliament addresses were presented to us by both Houses of Parliament, praying us to take into our consideration our Proclamation in relation to the said forms of prayer and service made for the 5th day of November, the 30th day of January, and the 29th day of May, with a view to their discontinuance.

"And whereas we have taken into our consideration the subject of the said addresses, and after due deliberation we have resolved that the use of the said forms of prayer and service shall be discontinued.

"Now, therefore, our will and pleasure is that so much of our said Royal Warrant of the 21st day of June, 1837, in the first year of our reign, as is hereinbefore recited, be revoked, and that the use of the said forms of prayer and service made for the 5th of November, the 30th of January, and the 29th of May, be henceforth discontinued in all cathedral and collegiate churches and chapels, in all chapels of colleges and halls within our Universities of Oxford, Cambridge, and Dublin, and of our Colleges of Eton and Winchester, and in all parish-churches and chapels within the parts of our United Kingdom called England and Ireland, and that the said form of prayer and service be not henceforth printed and published with, or annexed to, the Book of Common Prayer and Liturgy of the United Church of England and Ireland.

"Given at our Court at St. James's the 17th of January 1859, in the 22d year of our reign.

"By her Majesty's command, S. H. WALPOLE."

- The Annual Register, Or, A View of the History and Politics of the Year ..., Volume 101, J.G. & F. Rivington, 1860, P.87.

Appendix X Discovery of the Plot results in Oath of Allegiance

The Gunpowder Prepares the Colonists at Jamestown 1607

The oath below was administered to the 1607 Jamestown Island settlers, it clearly demonstrates the fear of the Papacy, not as a religion, but rather as a political force and threat to national security. Only two years afte the plot the political and social awareness which it shaped had been installed in America.

"I......M......doe trulie and sincerely acknowledge. professe testifie and declare in my Conscience before God & the world, That our Soveraigne Lord King James ys lawfull and rightful King of Great Britaine and of the Colony of Virginia, and of all other his Majesties Dominions and Countries. And that ye pope neither of himselfe, nor by any Authoretie of the Church or See of Rome, or by any other meanes (with any other) hath any power or authoritie to depose the King or to dispose any of his Majesties Dominions, or to authorise any forreine prince, to invade or anoy him in his Countries, or to discharge any of his subjectes of ther Allegeance and obedience to his Majesty or to give licence or leave to any of them to beare armes, raise, tumult, or to offer any violence, or hurt to his Majesties royall person, state, Goverment, or to any of his Majesties subjectes within his Majesties Dominions. Also I doe sweare from my hart, that notwithstanding any declaration or sentence of Excomunication, or deprivation made or granted, or to be made or granted by ye pope or his successors, or by any authoritie derived, or pretended to bee derived from him, or his Sea against against the king his heires or successors, or by any absolution of the said subjects from ther obedience: I will beare faith and true Allegeance to his Majestie his heires and successors and him and them will defend to the uttermost of my power, against all Conspiracies and attempts whatsoever which shall be made against his or ther persons, ther Crowne and dignitie, by reason or Color of any such sentence or declaration, or otherwise, ans will doe my best Endeavors to disclose and make knowne unto his Majestie, his heires and successors, all treason and trayterous Conspiracies, which I shall heare or knowe of to bee against him or any of them, And I doe further sweare, That I doe from my hart abhorr, Detest and abjure as impious and hereticall, this damnable doctrine and position That Princes which be excomunicated or deprived by the pope, may be deposed or murthered of ther subjects or any whatsoever. And I doe believe, and in conscience am resolved, That neither the pope nor any other person whatsoever hath power to absolve me of this Oath or anie parte thereof, which I acknowledge by good and full Authoritie is to be lawfullie ministred unto mee, and doe renounce all pardones and dispensations to ye contrarie, And theise things I doe plainely and sincerely acknowledge and swere according to theise expresse words by me spoken. And according to ye plaine and common sense and understanding of the same words without any equivocation or mentall evation or secret reservation whatsoever, And I doe make this Recognition and acknowledgment hartilie willinglie and trulie upon the true faith of a Christian So helpe me God."

-Records of the Virginia Company, Vol III, 1933, pp 4-5. Library of Congress; Edited by Susan Myra Kingsbury, PhD.

Appendix XI The Celebration of the Deliverance in the American Colonies

A detailed examination of the celebration of the Great Deliverance in the American Colonies will be taken up in a later volume. As Colonists settled in North America they brought the celebration with them. Perhaps the earliest record comes from the Plymouth Colony where a celebration resulted in a house fire.

Fifth of November Roystering in Plymouth 1624

But after he was gone, Mr. Weston in lue of thanks to the Gov[erno]r and his freinds hear, gave them this quib (behind their baks) for all their pains. That though they were but yonge justices, yet they wear good beggers. Thus they parted at this time, and shortly after the Gov[erno]r tooke his leave and went to the Massachusets by land, being very thankfull for his kind entertainemente. The ship stayed hear, and fitted her selfe to goe for Virginia, having some passengers ther to deliver; and with her returned sundrie of those from hence which came over on their perticuler, some out of discontente and dislike of the cuntrie; others by reason of a fire that broke out, and burnt the houses they lived in, and all their provisions [106 2] so as they were necessitated therunto.* This fire was occasioned by some of the sea-men that were roystering in a house wher it first begane, making a great fire in very could weather, which broke out of the chimney into the thatch, and burnte downe -3-or-4-houses, and consumed all the goods and provisions in them. The house in which it begane was right against their store-house, which they had much adoe to save, in which were their commone store and all their provisions; the which if it had been lost, the plantation had been overthrowne. But through Gods mercie it was saved by the great dilligence of the people, and care of the Gov[erno]r and some aboute him. Some would have had the goods throwne out; but if they had, ther would much have been stolne by the rude company that belonged to these 2 - ships, which were all most all ashore. But a trusty company was plased within, as well as those that with wet-cloath and other means kept of the fire without, that if necessitie required they might have them out with all speed. For they suspected some malicious dealling, if not plaine treacherie, and whether it was only suspition or no, God knows; but this is certaine, that when the tumultewas greatest, there was a voice heard (but from whom it was not knowne) that bid them looke well aboute them, for all were not freinds that were near them. And shortly after, when the ve[he]mencie of the fire was over, smoke was seen to arise within a shed that was joynd to the end of the store-house, which was watled up with bowes, in the withered leaves wherof the fire was kindled, which some,- runing to quench, found a longe fire brand of an ell longe, lying under the wale on the inside, which could not possibly come their by casualtie, but must be laid ther by some hand, in the judgmente of all that saw it. But God kept them from this deanger, what ever was intended.

• "This was on the fifth of November, 1624[1623]." Morton, *Memoriall,* Among those who met with losses by this fire, and went back to England at this time, was Timothy Hatherley, who came in the *Anne*. His connection with the Plymouth Plantation receives full notice in Bradford's pages. Smith placed the loss at £500, but overstates in saying that seven houses were destroyed.

-Bradford, William, History of Plymouth Plantation, 1620-1647, Vol. 1., 1669.

Later celebrations in the colonies became known as "Pope's Day."

Back Cover Image

A.B.C.D.E., Novembris Monstrum, or, Rome brought to Bed in England, 1641.

www.ingramcontent.com/pod-product-compliance
Lightning Source LLC
Chambersburg PA
CBHW081012040426
42444CB00014B/3179